PENOLOGY FROM PANAMA TO CAPE HORN

TEMPLE UNIVERSITY PUBLICATIONS

ARTHUR MURPHY

By

John Pike Emery

PENOLOGY FROM PANAMA TO CAPE HORN

By

Negley K. Teeters

Penology

From Panama to Cape Horn

By

NEGLEY K. TEETERS

Philadelphia

UNIVERSITY OF PENNSYLVANIA PRESS

For TEMPLE UNIVERSITY PUBLICATIONS

1946

Manufactured in the United States of America

London

Geoffrey Cumberlege

Oxford University Press

To

HERBERT ADOLPHUS MILLER

Teacher, Counselor, and Friend

Preface

In writing this book dealing with penology in South America the writer has been constantly aware of several responsibilities. Perhaps the most important is that he realizes that this book represents the first of its kind. In a previous work by the author, published in 1944 and entitled *World Penal Systems,* it was pointed out that there has long been a dearth of material on Latin America penology written in English. Few other sections of the globe have been thus slighted. It was possible to gather only meagre details on prisons and penal philosophy of the several countries to the south and it was obvious that these were incomplete and, to some extent, inaccurate.

Subsequently, in the summer of 1944, the writer was awarded a grant from the Cultural Relations Division of the Department of State to make a survey of some of the countries in question. But, even with this financial assistance which made possible a sojourn of four months over a wide territory, it proved extremely difficult to see everything that should be seen, to talk with everyone officially connected with penology, and to interpret adequately the many things worth seeing and ideas worth expounding.

Difficulties were many. Perhaps it is no more than fair that they be enumerated so the reader may know the limitations of the material contained in this work.

First, the time spent was so short. Four months were devoted to eight countries: Panama, Colombia, Ecuador, Peru, Bolivia, Chile, Argentina and Brazil. Obviously this was not enough. The time spent in each country ranged from one to three weeks. At the outset it was decided not to visit Venezuela and Paraguay. Uruguay later was added to the list of countries not visited. It is necessary for the traveler to spend at least a year in order to accomplish an adequate task in evaluating such a complicated sphere of social action.

The second handicap was that of language. The writer knew no Spanish or Portuguese. However, many South Americans are conversant enough with English to express themselves satisfactorily. With the aid of some interpreters, including representatives of the Cultural Relations Division of the Department of State and of the Coördinator's Office, this difficulty was minimized. But technical details cannot be understood without a thorough knowledge of a language.

The third handicap, always present when one visits a foreign country, is the differences in culture. The economic, social, and political philosophies are different from ours and they differ country by country. It is a mistake to view all South America as one homogeneous area. The writer has tried in this book to keep the basic differences in mind. Nevertheless he may be accused by some of misinterpreting or misunderstanding fundamental concepts which are reflected in penal codes, prison practices, or in other phases of the subject. The attempt has been made to assume the role of a penologist, who insists that essential human needs are alike the world over. Such a penologist must condemn, wherever he sees them, neglect, official inertia, apathy on the part of society and its representatives, as well as cruelty. The author attempts to be fair but at the same time critical. He would want South Americans to assume the same attitudes in evaluating the penal practices of the United States.

South America is vast and travel complicated. Many prisons and penal colonies are almost inaccessible. For example, to visit any of the argicultural colonies of Colombia or Ecuador, located as they are in the jungle *Oriente,* would take a week or more. Aside from the difficulty of travel, there is a health hazard to consider. The traveler from the States, innoculated as he must be before he leaves for a sojourn in Latin America, is constantly aware of the dangers that may arise from the dubious drinking water, the food, the milk, or from insects and other like hazards. He is warned by public health officials in the States, by his friends and other travelers not to indulge in unbottled drinking water or uncooked vegetables. He is even admonished to peel personally all fruit he may wish to eat. And this gratuitous advice applies to hotel dining-rooms in practically all countries, capital cities included.

The author is indebted to the officials of the Cultural Relations Division of the Department of State for the financial grant which made the trip possible and for the coöperation of the several attachés in the various countries. He also wishes to thank Srta. M. Arce of the Spanish Language Section of the United Nations, formerly instructor at the University of Pennsylvania, for reading the proof and checking the Spanish terms. However, the author assumes all responsibility for any mistakes that may persist.

N.K.T.

Temple University, Philadelphia
July 15, 1946

Contents

Chapter		***Page***
PREFACE		vii
I	LATIN AMERICAN PENAL PRACTICE	1
II	PANAMA	50
III	COLOMBIA	66
IV	ECUADOR	102
V	PERU	123
VI	BOLIVIA	151
VII	CHILE	162
VIII	ARGENTINA	191
IX	BRAZIL	214
X	INTER-AMERICAN COÖPERATION	249
	INDEX OF SUBJECTS	259
	INDEX OF PERSONS	267

Illustrations

Facing page

MAP OF SOUTH AMERICA 1
Drawing by John H. Geiszel

COIBA PENAL COLONY, PANAMA 54

UNITED STATES PENITENTIARY, GAMBOA, CANAL ZONE 54

MANUAL TRAINING: FAGUA REFORMATORY, NEAR BOGOTA, COLOMBIA 94

NATIONAL PENITENTIARY, BOGOTA, COLOMBIA 110
Courtesy of Dr. Jorge Pinzón Ferro

NATIONAL PENITENTIARY, QUITO, ECUADOR 110
Courtesy of Dr. Pedro Nuñez

RECREATION: NATIONAL PENITENTIARY, LA PAZ, BOLIVIA 156
Courtesy of Dr. Manuel López-Rey

TYPICAL SOUTH AMERICAN JAIL: WEAVING PONCHOS, CUZCO, PERU 156
Courtesy of Lyda Richman Tidwell

NATIONAL PENITENTIARY, SANTIAGO, CHILE 172

LOCATION OF PENAL INSTITUTIONS, ARGENTINA 198

ILHA GRANDE PRISON COLONY, NEAR RIO DE JANEIRO, BRAZIL 234

MODEL FOR NEW PENITENTIARY, FEDERAL DISTRICT OF RIO DE JANEIRO (BANGU), BRAZIL 240

U.S. PENITENTIARY, GAMBOA, CANAL ZONE
PANAMA CITY, PANAMA
COIBA, (PANAMA) PENAL COLONY
BOGOTÁ, COLOMBIA
COLOMBIAN ORIENTE
CALI, COLOMBIA
QUITO, ECUADOR
GUAYAQUIL ECUADOR
ECUADOREAN ORIENTE
RECIFE, BRAZIL
ITAMARACÁ PENAL COLONY BRAZIL
LIMA PERU
EL FRONTÓN PENAL COLONY PERU
CUZCO, PERU
LA PAZ BOLIVIA
AREQUIPA, PERU
BELLO HORIZONTE BRAZIL NEVEZ PENAL COLONY
ARICA, CHILE
NITEROI BRAZIL
SÃO PAULO, BRAZIL
RIO DE JANEIRO BRAZIL
PORTO ALEGRE, BRAZIL
SANTIAGO, CHILE
VALPARAISO, CHILE
MONTEVIDEO, URUGUAY
JUAN FERNÁNDEZ ISLANDS
BUENOS AIRES, ARGENTINA
TALCA, CHILE
SANTA MARÍA PENAL COLONY CHILE
CHILLÁN, CHILE
MAGALLANES, CHILE

I

Latin American Penal Practice

INTRODUCTORY STATEMENT

MANY years ago there was a popular song entitled the *South American Way*, the words of which were intended to convey the impression that life in that part of the Western Hemisphere is distinctly different from ours.

That it is different there can be no doubt. Yet, in many respects, the people belonging to the educated classes in every island or country included in that vast expanse of territory that we label Latin America, are very similar to the people of our own country. Not only do they know and respect their own culture but they are quite familiar with most of the basic elements of ours. In this fundamental respect they have the advantage over us since we are quite unfamiliar with much of the history, economy and social attitudes which are their heritage. For example, few people in the United States speak or read Spanish or Portuguese and hence know little of the exquisite literature of the Latins.

In Latin America, in every country in Central and South America, in every island of the Caribbean, English is almost commonplace, not only among the upper classes but, to a surprising degree, among domestic servants and shop-keepers. Nor is it unusual for the visitor from the States to be accosted on the streets of one of the capitals by a ragged stranger and asked, in English, for a pittance. Many of the shops have placards in their windows notifying the shopper that "English Is Spoken Here." Then, too, most of the movies are made in our country and, of course, English is spoken, although Spanish or Portuguese (in Brazil) may accompany the sequence.

It is not the purpose of this book to expatiate on the importance of fostering cultural interrelations between Latin America and the United States. This has been done, and is still being impressed upon us all by magazine writers, radio speakers and by goodwill advocates. Anything added here would be merely redundant. It might be stated, however, that the sooner we get busy in the task of understanding our southern neighbors the sooner mutual suspicion, distrust and even envy will be eliminated.

Nor can we censure the people of our own country for not studying the cultures of those countries whose penal systems are described here. There are valid reasons why we are so ignorant of Latin America. Truthfully, we have never been obliged to know very much about any cultures other than our own. Spanish and Portuguese have been offered in a rather desultory fashion in our schools and colleges, just as have French and German, but only as a hurdle to be negotiated for graduation. Even those who have majored in foreign languages have rarely entered any type of work where a knowledge of their major language is of use to them. It must be left to others to evaluate the importance of the knowledge of Spanish and Portuguese or of Latin American culture to our own well-being. However, it should be stated here that in the field of penology, our own students know very little of the history of penal treatment or of the modern practices of dealing with criminals in the countries or islands to the south of us. Very few penologists have traveled in that part of the world and almost nothing appears in the literature, in English, that would help us in evaluating the state of penal treatment in those countries.

It is rather important to digress for a moment in order to make a few statements regarding the dilemmas confronting citizens of the United States who travel in Latin America. It is confusing, for instance, to realize, perhaps for the first time, that we possess no clear-cut and unique name for ourselves that sets us apart from others. We say we are Americans. But can we restrict that word, so full of emotional meaning, solely to ourselves? Are not all nationals of all countries on this hemisphere Americans? The term American belongs to us all.

Then, to add to our confusion, we realize that we have no language of our own. In this we are like Latin Americans. They speak Spanish or Portuguese, but millions of people—the Indians—know neither of these languages. They speak the native dialects of Quechua or Aymará. To the Latin American, we are *Norteamericanos.* To us, they are Colombians, Peruvians, Chileans, *etc.* So I find it more accurate to refer to us as citizens of the United States, or Norteamericanos, or just plain *gringos.* Gringos, however, is the term applied to all foreigners and, contrary to popular belief, carries no stigma. Even the term *yanqui* has lost its venom.

But what shall we call our Latin American friends? The average national of any of the islands or countries graciously accepts the term *Latin American.* But discuss it with any intellectual and you are likely to be told that the term is inadequate since it can be applied precisely to only a small percentage of the people. Nor is the term Hispano-American desirable; nor Ibero-American, a term sometimes seen in print. The distinguished revolutionary dreamer of Peru, Haya de la Torre, likes the term Indo-American. He insists, as do many, that since so large a proportion of the Latin Americans are of Indian extraction, millions of them full-blooded, it is absurd to speak of Latin, or Spanish, or Portuguese. But there are many who are of pure Spanish or Portuguese extraction and, for that matter, pure Negro, in some countries. Is it, then, not equally absurd to use any term suggesting Indian? Regardless of this dilemma, it is obvious that for many years to come we shall continue to speak of those from this area as Latin Americans, not because there is any accuracy in the term but because habit has fixed it in our discourse.

In writing a book on the status of penology in any specific country or countries it would seem that the author should point out the necessity of understanding the status of prison discipline throughout the entire world. It is presumptuous for us in the United States, for example, to insist that we hold a monopoly of all that is good and effective in penal philosophy or treatment. True, many ideas and techniques that hold promise for rehabilitation and readjustment of criminals are in operation here and there throughout our country. Many of these can be recommended to other countries, including those to the South. But a fair and objective appraisal of what is actually being done in South America, as elsewhere throughout the world, would suggest that even we have something to learn. Some of it might well be adopted even if only for experimental purposes.

It is fitting that a statement by Dr. Hermann Mannheim, well-known German criminologist, at present associated with the London School of Economics, be incorporated at this point since it sums up the problem of the interplay of ideas between countries. He writes:

> There are obvious limits to what nations can learn from one another in this field. Many methods which seem to work admirably in some countries might completely fail in others where the essential material and ideological prerequisites are non-existent. . . . However, where such a repudiation of foreign methods is regarded as indispensable, it should be based upon the most complete knowledge of actual conditions abroad.
>
> It is, therefore, the foremost duty of the penologist to supply that knowledge. It should at least not be his fault if too little use is made of new ideas that have proved their worth in some parts of the globe. . . . There are very few civilized countries that have nothing to contribute to the general remaking of the various national penal systems which will probably be a common feature of the postwar period. Almost every country has been a pioneer in developing at least one particular idea worthy of special consideration by an international forum.[1]

It is the purpose of this chapter to describe the general picture of penal philosophy and prison administration, together with the treatment of both adult criminals and juvenile delinquents in the countries of Latin America as I found them in 1944. I have already pointed out in the *Preface* the difficulties involved when a person from one country visits others where languages are spoken with which he is unfamiliar. I also pointed out the many

[1] Quoted in Negley K. Teeters. *World Penal Systems* (Philadelphia: Pennsylvania Prison Society, 1944), p. 1.

possibilities that arise where misinterpretations of facts and concepts are not only accepted but absorbed unwittingly. These are the prices one must pay for not thoroughly understanding the language and culture of those countries. Yet if we were to wait until we were ideally prepared for such an investigation little if anything would be accomplished.

Some of the prison administrators and other persons in Latin America, who possess a high sense of social understanding and who would be of great assistance to modern penology were they to come to the United States for observation and study, know no English. Many excellently trained scholars in our own country would unquestionably make a definite contribution to Latin America but they know no Spanish or Portuguese. We must proceed within the framework of these limitations and frankly accept them.

HISTORY OF PENOLOGY IN SOUTH AMERICA

As stated in the *Preface,* my travels were limited to only one country in Central America, Panama, and did not include the South American countries of Venezuela, Paraguay and Uruguay. I shall discuss Panama's penology in the next chapter, and then follow in order the countries of Colombia, Ecuador, Peru, Bolivia, Chile, Argentina and Brazil.

The history of penal reform in South America is somewhat obscured. I must confess that I was unable to gain much light on the movements that fermented there, prior to the last few years and well within the memory of men still living. What little I did learn will be incorporated in the general description of each country.

We owe great thanks to our own Enoch C. Wines, that nineteenth-century stalwart, who not only was mainly responsible for the inauguration of the First International Penal and Penitentiary Congress held in London in 1872, but who described the penal systems of practically every country in the world, including some in South America. His work, *State of Prisons,* was published in 1880, the year following his death.

He tells us that he collected his information largely from official communications and governmental reports addressed personally to him. Another source of information was the consular officers, furnished through the courtesy of our Department of State. While Dr. Wines was personally familiar with many prison systems of Europe, he had not visited South America. Moreover, he described the penal systems of only four countries: Colombia, Peru, Argentina and Brazil. His sources of information regarding these countries were undoubtedly official publications.

But when it is remembered that communications between countries were very primitive in 1879, it is amazing that he was able to gather as much information as he did. The writer of this book certainly can appreciate the laborious efforts of Dr. Wines in compiling his monumental work and cannot refrain from revering his memory sixty-five years later.

Prior to that remarkable period in the first quarter of the nineteenth century when the several countries of South America threw off the yoke of the Spanish crown, these colonies were ruled by Spanish law, consisting of the Laws of the Indies and the Royal Decrees which had jurisdiction over all civil and penal matters. Justice was administered from the beginning by the Supreme Court of the Indies which functioned throughout all of South America. This was later followed by the *Audiencia,* a sort of court of *oyer and terminer,* in addition to local magistrates' courts.

Punishments were fines, imprisonment, whippings and death. Corporal punishments of the most brutal kinds were inflicted, including the mutilation of organs and other parts of the body. Other penalties involved confiscation of goods and exile. Death was usually by hanging. Imprisonment for debt was universal and commonplace.

The jails, or *cárceles,* were usually of two types: one for the rich and socially élite and the other for the masses. Some of these early Spanish *cárceles* are still in existence and a few of them are used. For instance, I visited the municipal jail in the city of São Paulo, in Brazil, parts of which go back to the seventeenth-century Portuguese colonization period.

Penal codes were slow in changing even after the period of Independence, since the Spanish influence remained only slightly diminished. But as time went on all of the countries gradually projected codes that were more or less in keeping with the social conditions existing in the New World. Nevertheless, the Spanish flavor tended to remain, and even the new codes followed the Classical tradition of the Old World, manifesting primarily the influences of Italy and France as well as of Spain and Portugal.

The history of the penal codes falls into three periods: first, the original Spanish codes (and Portuguese in Brazil) maintained for some time following the era of Independence; second, the earlier revisions, *e.g.*, in Bolivia and Peru in 1836–37, Chile, in 1874; third, recent revisions which involve in some cases entirely new projects or radical modifications.

The penal codes under which the countries I visited now operate are: Argentina, the Code of 1922, replacing the one of 1887; Brazil, the Code of 1942; Bolivia, a new project drawn up in 1943 to supplant the one in operation since 1836; Chile, extensive modifications of the Code of 1874, effective in 1928; Colombia, that of 1936 replacing the one of 1890; Ecuador, that of 1938 supplanting certain re-editions of the Code of 1870; Panama, that of 1922 with certain important Decrees in 1942; Peru, that of 1924 replacing the earlier one of 1862. Uruguay also revised its 1889 code in 1934. A word about the nature and content of penal codes will be introduced later in this chapter.

While the European influence manifests itself in the penal codes of South American countries, prison construction and penal philosophy followed the patterns so familiar in the United States during the nineteenth century. For example, all of the National Penitentiaries in the capital cities throughout the entire continent show the definite and unmistakable concepts of John Haviland, the architect of the Eastern State Penitentiary at Philadelphia. The central rotunda with emanating cellblocks is present in all, and practically all cells are of outside construction.

Regardless of the fact that these penitentiaries are, in most countries, called *Panópticos* after the fantastic extravaganza brain-child of the doughty Jeremy Bentham, they are really not so designed. There is not a true Panopticon in all South America similar, for instance, to the one built in Richmond, Virginia, in 1800 by Benjamin Henry Latrobe and Thomas Jefferson, or at Stateville, Illinois in more recent years. Starting with Santiago's prison, in Chile, built in 1843, we find the Philadelphia influence extending through to the year 1896 when the prison at La Paz, in Bolivia, was erected. They are all modifications of the architecturally "divine system" of the Philadelphia reformers.

However, there is strong reason to believe that the architectural *motif* came from Europe directly—at least in most cases—where it had previously been transported from Philadelphia. There is also evidence that the Auburn plan of penal construction, with its inside cellblock of many tiers, dominated many prisons, especially throughout Brazil. Some of that country's older penitentiaries are said to have been copied from the Pentonville prison in London, the Santé and the Fresnes-les-Rungis, in Paris, and even from the House of Correction at Bruchsal in the grand duchy of Baden. In only one country, Peru, is it possible to trace any early direct contact with the United States. That country's veteran penologist, Pas Soldán, did visit Philadelphia in 1853 and upon his return to Lima, drew up plans for his country's first modern prison.

So far as early penal philosophy and administration are concerned, there is evidence that both the Auburn silent system and the Pennsylvania solitary system were in use during the early nineteenth century. We gather from Enoch Wines that in 1879 the progressive stages system, formulated by Sir Joshua Jebb and carried into execution by Sir Walter Crofton in the Irish prisons, was in operation. In fact, many present-day administrators speak of their systems as embracing the progressive stages philosophy.

But there are many vestiges of the old separate system still remaining. Initial solitude is the rule in many countries, notably in Peru, Brazil and Argentina. But all prisons are in essence based on the modern concept of association just as is the case in our own country. It must be remembered that this congregate or association system was in operation in the early colonial jails in this country as well as in Britain long before the days of the penitentiary. It was this congregate feature of imprisonment that so horrified the Quakers of Philadelphia as well as John Howard because of the alleged contamination of one prisoner by another.

CLASSIFICATIONS OF CRIMES AND PUNISHMENTS

In the majority of the South American countries as well as in Panama there is a bi-partite classification of violations of the penal code. This consists generally of dividing them into felonies and misdemeanors, as with us. The former, representing the more serious offenses, which call for greater penalties and whose disposition falls to the judicial authorities, are called *delitos;* the latter, being less serious, calling for less severe penalties, and whose disposition falls to the police authorities, are known as *contravenciones.* In one country, Chile, there is a tri-partite division, following the Franco-German system. This includes crimes, simple crimes, and misdemeanors (*los crímenes, los simples delitos y las faltas*).

Punishments vary in number and grade, depending on the country's penal code. They are usually classified as serious (*principales*) and disciplinary (*accesorias*). The death penalty is relatively unknown, although it is invoked on occasion in Bolivia and Chile. Brazil also has the death penalty, but thus far no one has been executed. The usual delays, court reverses and executive clemency are prevalent just as in our own states.

Life imprisonment exists in some countries but commutation is easily attained so that few prisoners actually serve out such a severe sentence. Many countries sentence their criminals to no more than ten years and many prison officials take the position that ten years is enough punishment for anyone, regardless of the offense. However, in Colombia, occasionally criminals are committed to prison for a hundred years, but on several charges, since they are considered too dangerous to be at large in society.

CRIME NOT THE MOST SERIOUS PROBLEM

Anyone who is familiar with South America or has read any of the numerous excellent books describing the cultures of the various countries of that continent would probably agree that there are many more serious and pressing problems there than crime. Seldom does one hear crime mentioned in the capitals of these countries. It is there, nevertheless, as is pointed out below, but it is dwarfed into insignificance against the backdrop of a problem of frustrating proportions that every intelligent person accepts but would rather not discuss, especially with foreigners.

This is the Indian problem. Throughout Colombia, Ecuador, Peru and Bolivia especially, by far the greatest proportion of the population is of Indian extraction, and most of these live in misery. They are little more than beasts of burden. Their poverty is indescribable and their stolidity, apathy and ignorance almost inconceivable to the stranger who views them for the first time. Few of them are able to read or write and most of them live in a state of complete degradation, the like of which we in this country cannot possibly conceive. They have been described as an "extra-social class." Certainly I would not be truthful if I did not place their plight as first in the long series of major social problems confronting all of South America. Estimates place the number of full-blooded Indians in South America at thirty millions and if half-breeds and others possessing a large portion of

Indian blood are included in the count, sixty to eighty millions.

What the future holds for the Indian as well as for the economic prosperity of these countries no one can predict with certainty. The task of lifting the natives even to the level where they can read and write, vote, and be trained in the trades is one calling for imagination and social vision,—attributes that thus far only a small portion of the upper ruling class possesses. Yet South American countries will aways remain far behind in the procession of nations so long as their own leaders fail to find a forthright solution to this vital problem.

It is pertinent to set down at this point a statement made by the late Philip Ainsworth Means, an eminent student of ethnography and archeology, who knew the heroic past of these despised people. He wrote:

> He who has dwelt among these people, amid all the smoke, and grime and stink of their hovels, and has known the whole story of their muted, tortuous lives can never fail, so be it his soul contain one glimmer of sensibility and altruism, to understand at last that the hidden fires of artistic and political fervor still burn within the breasts of this oppressed, this miserable, this despised race. Mocked at for dullards, gulled for varlets fit only for the ox's toil, defended—when defended at all—only by the plausible, soap-tongued politician of demogogic proclivities and, usually of Negro or Oriental, rather than of Indian blood, the indigenes of the Andean region are indeed in a tragic plight. Not until a true understanding of their genius, of their requirements, and of their practical worth is won, will they come into their own, and in the ingredients of that understanding the materials provided by archeology will constitute the major part.[2]

This, then, is South America's number one problem.

And there are still other problems more serious than crime. Enter into a conversation with an intelligent resident of any country from Colombia to Chile or from Peru to Brazil and he will refer to one or more problems that cause great concern. For example, transportation is almost primitive in some countries, since there are few railroads, while air travel, though well de-

[2] *Ancient Civilizations of the Andes* (New York: Scribners, 1931), pp. 538–39.

veloped, must defer expansion for some time to come; sanitation and health are problems of the first magnitude in some countries; compulsory education, which is theoretically present in most countries but impossible to realize in some for obvious reasons, notably, lack of schools, teachers, and the abject poverty of the natives. Housing for the masses is deplorable, although some heroic work has been done in this field. Francis Violich has recently brought this problem into sharp focus in his stimulating work *Cities of Latin America.*[3] In fact, the entire realm of economics together with the equally explosive field of government give the leaders of all Latin America many a sleepless night.

In the United States we frankly admit that delinquency and adult crime are a serious menace and we allocate millions of dollars to cope with them. But in South America there is nothing comparable to our professional crime, our racketeering, our large-scale robberies, the insecurity of our persons and property, and our recently recognized white-collar crime. Regarding the latter, however, many persons in South America complain that there is widespread graft in high places; but because of the peculiar nature of government in those countries, few discuss it openly. In Lima, Peru, for instance, when I was asked to prepare a paper to read before the college of lawyers, the section which dealt with our own crime in big business circles was not read nor did it appear in the newspaper account of the speech, although the reporter had the manuscript. Commenting on this later I was bluntly told that such remarks could not be presented in a public gathering. It is possible, of course, that this was merely groundless apprehension but it can easily be interpreted as symptomatic.[4]

Crime in all of the countries consists primarily of murder, on the one hand, and petty stealing on the other. Now widespread

[3] New York: Reinhold Publishing Corporation, 1944.

[4] I wrote my paper in English and supervised the translation into Spanish. The Spanish script was read after I made a few perfunctory remarks in English. My speech in its entirety appeared in the *Revista de Ciencias Penales*, a Santiago, Chile publication, October–December, 1944, pp. 338–44.

murder in our own country elicits justifiable alarm and great publicity simply because we have been taught that murder is the most heinous of all offenses. It certainly is in so far as the individual who is murdered is concerned, to say nothing of its effects on the victim's family. Then, too, no one in the United States is immune from the fear of murder. But in South America things are quite different. Rarely is a member of the socially élite murdered. This crime is essentially restricted to the large Indian population and, since it is practiced only within that population, hardly counts.

Criminal statistics in most countries are quite inadequate hence it is difficult to obtain many accurate data on the extent of murder. However, there are a few bits of evidence that reflect the high rate of homicides. In Peru, a country that is preponderantly pure Indian, or *mestizo*,[5] for the year 1941, the latest available, of the 2,969 persons in jails and prisons, 1,482 were there for crimes "against life, the body or health" (*contra la vida, el cuerpo y la salud*). There is no way of determining, however, just what proportion of this number was convicted of homicide. But the figure does represent violent crime and includes almost fifty per cent of all prisoners.

Murder, to quote one writer, is almost casual in Colombia; if the exact figures were really known, the number of killings would seem staggering.[6] Much of the violent behavior in these countries having so large a percentage of uneducated and primitive Indians is due to insane jealousy and habitual brawling induced largely by the universal drinking of *chicha*. This beverage is distilled from corn and is a dangerously potent drink as well as cheap and easily obtainable. It is quite possible, however, that its widespread use is merely a means of escaping the grinding

[5] The term *mestizo* designates anyone with Indian blood mixed with white, although many of this group are held in high esteem. The term *cholo* is applied to the Indians and diluted breeds of the servant class. It carries a degree of opprobrium that is totally lacking in the term *mestizo*. I shall, however, use the word *mestizo* when referring to those possessing Indian strain.

[6] Kathleen Romoli, *Colombia, Gateway to South America* (Garden City, N.Y.: Doubleday, Doran, 1941), p. 36.

poverty and drudgery that is the lot of the South American masses, especially in the countries along the Pacific Coast.

But in spite of this high homicide rate among the Indians, life among the white ruling class is highly secure since few from this group are ever attacked by criminals. White people may walk the streets of Bogotá, Quito or Lima without fear of attack. I remember walking through the dimly lit, narrow streets of Cuzco, in Peru, after dark. I passed many Indians lurking close to the walled streets and momentarily became apprehensive until I remembered that these simple folk would never think of attacking a member of the favored race.

In the countries having a smaller percentage of Indians or *mestizo,* the homicide rate is much lower than in those countries on the West Coast, but still it is quite high. Take Argentina, for example. For the year 1941, of the total number in prison, 2,867, only 226, or less than ten per cent, were convicted of homicide. Ten per cent compared to fifty per cent in Peru. Of course, we in the United States would be justifiably panic-stricken if our homicide rate reached five per cent. As it is, it probably never exceeds two per cent of all crimes committed and yet we are stigmatized for our murders.

But it is petty stealing that concerns the good people of Latin America, throughout its length and breadth. This is their serious crime problem. The class of petty criminals who steals is called *los rateros* and represents a nuisance, if not a real menace. They are a curious lot as judged by a *gringo.* They are poverty-stricken, of course, and possess little if any education. They do not steal articles of great value but restrict their activities almost entirely to pilfering small articles of little real value. Such items as windshield wipers, hub-caps, valve caps, doorbells, apartment house mailboxes—in short, any article that is standing around or that can be pried loose from more substantial objects of greater value.

It is because of *los rateros* that the homes in the residential districts are surrounded by high walls or strong iron fences with big gates of heavy planking or iron securely padlocked. It is not an unusual sight to see the owner of a home drive up in his car, alight, and unlock his gate upon entering, in the daytime. Of course, this veiled mode of living is distinctly Spanish, but part of the reason for its persistence is the fear of thieves.

One prominent citizen of Lima remarked, when I mentioned that my fountain pen had disappeared and that I thought a *ratero* had stolen it: "No, a *ratero* wouldn't steal your fountain pen, but he would steal your pencil." There are limits of value beyond which these petty thieves will not trespass.

Because of the presence of thousands of these thieves, in the capital cities especially, car watchers are in great demand, but even they represent the nearest to a racket found in South America. These gentry are everywhere and almost "shake down" anyone who parks a car and refuses to hire them as watchers. On numerous occasions I told friends that these car watchers were as much a menace to the joy of living as *los rateros*. A good efficient police system would break up this petty racket in a very short time.

But it is not certain that an alert police system could eliminate the vast amount of petty stealing that abounds. It is so prevalent that automobile owners keep their windshield wipers in the compartments of their cars and apply them only when it rains. The jails available would not begin to hold all the petty thieves that swarm the streets of Bogotá, Quito, Lima or Santiago. The root of this problem can be quickly seen in the abject poverty and misery of the masses. Certainly it will not be eliminated or even curbed until the economic conditions that breed such wholesale poverty in these countries are improved.

Before passing on to the discussion of the biological emphasis on criminal causation, a word regarding the possible reasons for crime being relatively less serious in South America than in our own country or in most parts of Europe. The feudalistic nature of the economy of most of the countries, with its many repressions on the one hand and its paternalistic gestures on the other, has played its part in keeping the *indigenes* docile and amenable to discipline.

Nor can we overlook the stark reality that a complete lack of education of the masses makes it difficult, if not impossible, for the development of a will to commit crime. Witness our own country where much of the crime is committed by persons who have acquired just enough of a kind of education to recognize and be embittered by the inequalities in our social system; or the ease with which some in high places, even when better educated, commit crimes with impunity. In this sense, crime is a backwash of universal education. Moral conditioning and training in good citizenship must, of necessity, go hand in hand in order to correct possible distortions.

The illiterate and undernourished South American native does not possess the little insight necessary to make and reconcile the invidious comparisons between his status in life and the relatively high standards of living of the favored classes. When he does acquire learning enough to understand what has been done to him and his kind for so many generations, it will be quite necessary for educators to provide him also with a sense of perspective. This analysis does not condemn universal education, but it does point to the old adage that a little learning is a dangerous thing, and also suggests that education without moral discipline can certainly lead to crime among the masses as well as among persons in higher walks of life. This latter observation is best illustrated by the commission of what we call white-collar crimes.

EMPHASIS ON THE BIOLOGICAL CAUSES OF CRIME

A student of the crime problem who is at all familiar with the literature of continental Europe or Latin America dealing with the etiology of crime will immediately mention the almost complete emphasis on biology or its related disciplines. Our own criminologists who have traveled in Europe, aside from Great Britain, comment on this fact. Dr. Nathaniel Cantor, for example, and Dr. Elio Monachesi, have both pointed out this slavish adherence to the biological approach.[7] I anticipated this same enthusiasm in Latin America and I found it.

We in the United States have from the early beginnings of our own investigations into the causes of crime maintained that the socio-economic conditions have been most responsible for delinquency and criminal behavior. There was a short period in the early nineteenth century when phrenology had some standing even in the scientific circles of the day, but in the main it has been poverty, the depraved home, unemployment, lack of wholesome recreation, poor education, and a host of other such unfavorable environmental conditions which we blame for the high crime and delinquency rate. This country, for instance, never embraced the Lombrosian theory of the born criminal or the atavistic type which proved so popular on the European continent and in Latin America.

In justice to Lombroso, who certainly deserves great credit for focusing the spotlight of science on the criminal, it should be stated that he himself, in his later years, allocated no more than forty per cent of the criminal population to the category of the "born criminal." And certainly Enrico Ferri, a member of the Italian School and conceded by many to be even greater than Lombroso in his penetrating analysis of the causes of criminal behavior, placed considerable emphasis on the social factors of crime. It was Ferri who, on the one hand, showed the reciprocal relationship between the socio-economic pressures and the individual's structure and, on the other, conceived his notion of "substitution for punishments" (*sostitutivi penali*) or preventives of crime, as Parmelee so aptly puts it, such as free trade, freedom to emigrate, taxes upon the rich, public works, drastic regulation of the manufacture and sale of alcohol, freedom of marriage and divorce, and the like.[8]

While the concept of the "born" or atavistic criminal made

[7] Nathaniel Cantor, "Recent Tendencies in Criminological Research in Germany," *American Sociological Review*, I (June, 1936), 407–18; Elio Monachesi, "Trends in Criminological Research in Italy," *ibid.*, 396–406.

[8] Maurice Parmelee, *Criminology*, New York: Macmillan, 1918, p. 96. Parmelee quotes from Ferri, *Criminal Sociology*, Boston: Little, Brown, 1917, Part II, Chap. 5.

little impression in our own country, there has been considerable biological research into crime causation, especially in more recent years. Each phase of it has held the spotlight for a few years and then faded away when confronted by critics who pointed out its particularistic oversimplification. First, we were impressed with the studies by Dugdale, Goddard, Davenport and a host of lesser lights who attempted to show a high correlation between feeblemindedness and crime, their apologists usually being more enthusiastic than they; second, we had the early endocrinologists such as Berman, Schlapp and Smith, and others, whose opening blasts insisted that the "glands of destiny" were the cause of all our ills and our personalities; third, the studies of identical twins which were paraded by the students of crimino-biology as obvious proof that heredity is paramount in explaining antisocial behavior. The apparent impatience with which these studies have been all but repudiated in our country is largely due to the glibness with which their authors or their apologists have flaunted their claims.

It may well be argued that we have shown too great a degree of impatience with the biological findings dealing with behavior, but at the moment it is to the sociological and economic factors that we tend to turn in explanation of aberrent behavior, especially that which ends in the police court. Within the last few years, however, the more careful work in endocrinology by Hoskins, in twinning by Newman, and body-type by Sheldon of Harvard is being given the attention it deserves. Not so well received was the monumental research by Professor Earnest Hooton on race and crime. What will come of all this biological research so far as our understanding of crime causation is concerned, time alone will tell.

But throughout Latin America, the biological emphasis is paramount. This is easily understood since the continental European influence is more penetrating than any that has heretofore permeated those countries from the United States. Seldom is an authority from the States quoted in their *revistas.* It is not to be assumed, however, that the "Lombrosian man" still dominates the field of investigation, since few criminologists actually take much stock in that straw man annihilated so thoroughly by Charles Goring in 1912.

But the Lombrosian afterglow is there with all its radiance. It is the Constitutional School, so ably championed by the outstanding Italian, Nicola Pende, and his equally able colleagues and followers, which draws the attention of the Latin American students of crime. This school of criminology contends that it is the morphological and psychological properties of the individual that we must examine in order to understand his reactions to his environment. It is these components, biological in nature, which determine the capacity of the individual to adapt and react to the stimuli which make up his environment. His behavior, therefore, is motivated primarily by his heredity and only incidentally by the disturbing actions of the social situation.

A note about some of Pende's colleagues and followers is to the point since it is largely from them that Latin American criminologists draw their greatest inspiration and sustenance. First we have Salvatore Ottolenghi and his student, Benigno Di Tullio, who are both convinced that the "real" criminal is a biological phenomenon. The former's lectures at Rome, in connection with which he used prisoners for demonstration purposes, emphasized biological principles exclusively. He even reverts to Lombrosian hypotheses by pointing out the significance of scars and tattoo marks on the criminals. According to Ottolenghi, these marks have great value in giving knowledge of the individual's morality, sensibility and attitudes. In one of his studies of forty-five "real" criminals he found without the slightest doubt that forty of them had degenerate heredity.

Others of this school, probably not so well known in either of the Americas, but whose work shows the definite trend in biological research, are: Jacob Aisencitat who, in the main, studied neglected children and insists that the majority of this type show abnormalities of a biological nature; Rudolf Michel, whose study of 249 felons shows that 177 were offspring of parents who suffered from nervous and mental diseases; Filippo Saporito, following the master, Lombroso, finds criminality and mental illness among soldiers due to defective heredity. Then there are Arturo Morselli, and his colleague Rosolino Colella, who are both interested in the relationship between tuberculosis and criminal behavior.

One could continue with a discussion of other similar studies of this distinguished group of men—of their work with persons suffering from traumatic cerebral conditions, emotional disorders, glandular disturbances, and correlated criminal tendencies—but enough has been adduced to show the trend of the Italian Constitutional School. Practically nothing has been done in Italy with environmental causes of crime.[9]

However, the Spanish criminologists are not ignored in Latin America. The contributions of Bernaldo de Quiros, Dorado Montero, Eugenio Calón and certainly the stimulating works of Quintiliano Saldaña in the fields of criminal law and criminal anthropology are deeply respected and frequently quoted. Some of Spain's outstanding criminologists and professors of criminal law are now in Latin America where they are making their presence felt in the universities and in government posts.

In the classification or diagnostic clinics that exist in the penitentiaries of all countries, by far the greatest emphasis is placed on the biological aspects of the individual's nature. For example, sitting in some clinics are anthropologists. Nowhere in the entire United States have I ever seen or heard of an anthropologist being a member of such a prison clinic. A discussion of the prison clinics of South America will appear in more detail in later pages.

Also in the journals, or *revistas*, published in these countries, which are excellent, most of the articles dealing with the causes of crime reflect the criminal's physical nature. Seldom did I hear

[9] The above material is a short digest from Elio D. Monachesi, *loc. cit.*, 396–406.

in all my travels anything regarding the poverty of the criminal classes which involves wretched housing, tragic undernourishment, the lack of educational opportunities for the masses, the effects of alcoholism, the low moral tone of most of the homes of the poor, the illegitimacy that abounds, or any of the other effects of the widespread lack of economic opportunities.

In the following chapters, dealing with individual countries, this statement will be qualified to some extent. It would be unfair to give the impression that the governments, as well as many intelligent and socially minded citizens, are not alarmed concerning the widespread poverty among the masses with its many distressing concomitants. The point to be made here is that few of the students of criminology give more than passing thought to them as the reasons for crime. Immediately upon their reception in the prisons, inmates are subjected to a battery of tests dealing with their inner nature without so much as a fleeting glance at their miserable economic or social background. All are, it would seem, potentially abnormal physiologically. In a few instances I suggested that the clinics examine as meticulously all the guards in the prison to see if the born criminal or his successor was not also lurking inside their physical natures.

It is dangerous to speculate on the reason for this persistent devotion to the biological, but it may well be projected that it represents a rationalization. From the early days of colonization the white ruling classes have been in the minority. They have been obliged to hold the native Indian masses and the imported Negro slaves—who were brought in large numbers to Brazil primarily—in subjection while they exploited the vast resources by means of a feudal economy. It is easy to understand why the whites have developed a racial theory which places them in a most favorable position at the expense of those of color.

The Lombrosian theory was accepted with enthusiasm. The ignorant masses, never realizing their potential strength, were first cowed into submission, then later manipulated by a subtle benevolent despotism, which still is prevalent in many of the countries, so that few ever protested their degraded status. Misery was, and still is, their lot.

The social thinking of the white ruling classes has become blinded by fear of the effects of education, social melioration and the inevitable enfranchisement of the masses. The biological approach has become the *alibi celebre*. These degraded people are criminal, according to this approach, not because of their low social and economic status, but rather because of their poor heredity. It is as easily explained as that.

Of course this thesis cannot be maintained forever. In all fairness to many intelligent people throughout this vast area, a new dispensation for the masses is being advocated. But it may take a century at least before universal education is established. Today only persons who can read and write may vote, so most of the Indians are automatically disfranchised. If elemental education is furnished this outcast group and, added to it, vocational and agricultural training, the Indians will gradually approach a dignity that is their rightful heritage. Then they may vote and thus have a share in the government and, in the meantime, their standards of living will gradually be raised at least to the level of the members of the lower white classes.

While we in the United States have little to offer the students of criminology in the field of bio-criminal investigation, since, in recent years, we have become committed to the overall concept of "multiple causation," which includes economic, social and biological maladjustment, we have made a substantial contribution in the field of psychiatry. This is definitely appreciated by the many eminent members of this craft scattered throughout the entirety of Latin America. Child guidance clinics must become a part of the regular machinery of delinquency research, embracing both psychiatric and social case work concepts. Schools of social work, the first one opened in 1925, have now become well established and will undoubtedly make a larger contribution in the future. I shall discuss their rise and development below.

Many medical men in Latin America are familiar with our literature in psychiatry. Perhaps the most widely read of our publications in this field is the *Journal of Clinical Psychopathology and Psychotherapy*. Just as we are turning to the psychiatric approach, aided by social case work, it is possible that the students of biological causes who have thus far been shackled to the Neo-Lombrosians, may also see the light and follow it.

THE PENAL CODES OF SOUTH AMERICA

In turning to the penal codes of South America it is not out of place to quote from a poem which caustically criticizes our own criminal procedure.

LET'S CALL THE CODE[10]

That facile thing they've fashioned to their mode
Smug sophistries that smother and befool
That numb and stupefy, that clumsy thing
That measures mountains with a three-foot rule
And plumbs the ocean with a pudding string
The little, brittle code. Here is the root
Far out of sight and buried safe and deep
And the victim is the bitter fruit.
On every limb and leaf, death, ruin, creep.

Thus it is in all countries, in the United States as well as in South America.

Discussion of the penal codes, in the various South American countries, is perhaps the favorite form of intellectual gymnastics and academic casuistry. The *revistas* are replete with articles dealing with the penal codes. The codes, revised in most of the countries within recent years and modified from time to time,

[10] From "The Night Court" by Ruth Comfort Mitchell. *Home Book of Verse*, edited by Burton Egbert Stevenson, New York: Henry Holt & Co., 1942, p. 3056. *By special permission from the author.*

reflect the thinking of the savants. These codes have been referred to as "bright and shiny," which is a polite way of saying they are seldom, if ever, used, in so far as practice in the prisons is concerned. Hence, they have little meaning because they are not implemented by a modern court procedure or by a progressive penal philosophy.

This fundamental weakness, all too prevalent in our own country as well, was pointed out by the eminent Spanish criminologist, Dr. Luis Jiménez de Asúa, who until recently held a teaching post at the University of La Plata in Argentina. In a lecture at the National University of Cuba, de Asúa said:

> In every penal reform it is necessary to consider three essential aspects, as follows: first, the penal code; second, the judges who are to apply it; and third, the penitentiary system where sentences are to be executed. In order for a penal code to function it is not enough to have a perfect code in so far as the technicalities are concerned. It is just as necessary to have the judges well trained and possessing a knowledge of how to apply this perfect code and, in addition, a modern and reformative penitentiary system.[11]

The prisons and jails in most of the countries can be abominable, the interminable and archaic court procedure can be a mockery of justice, the penal administrators and their guards can be nonentities, but so long as the penal code can be discussed and debated by the brilliant professors of penal law, that is all that matters. There are few persons interested in penal reform in most of the countries and only rarely does one find anyone who really knows what actually transpires behind prison walls, yet dozens of scholars in each country are thrilled to expatiate on the meticulous details of their penal codes and on what modifications may be expected in the near future.

There are few, if any, courses in the universities in criminology and penology similar to the hundreds that we have in the United States. In the law colleges there are courses called criminology,

[11] Statement supplied the writer by the Panamanian penologist, Sr. Guillermo Zurita.

but they are invariably taught by lawyers with little knowledge of sociology, psychology, social work, penology, or any of the other fields that have contributed to the advance of the subject as we understand it. I was taken to a law college by a distinguished professor of law and shown the type of work his students did in his course in criminology. It amounted to pouring over court cases and writing up the facts that came out at the trials.

In short, the study of penal law in Latin America is a fetish. There may be no harm in this since it is a stimulating discipline. But the energy that goes into it is practically wasted when it might well be used to do something about penal treatment and prison administration.

Court procedure in all countries is technical and endless. Because of this weakness it is not unusual to find hundreds of suspected criminals detained in unspeakably dirty municipal jails for a year or two, or even as long as five, before their cases are disposed of. When I spoke to my friends of this notorious injustice they merely shrugged their shoulders and admitted no solution seems possible. It would seem to a *gringo* that some of the dynamic energy dissipated on matters of abstract justice and on the niceties of penal law could well be spent in alleviating this situation.

PRISON ADMINISTRATION

In discussing the prisons and evaluating penal administration I come to the most difficult phase of this analysis. This is because I found all types of prisons and prison officials. But this same situation would be found at any time in a survey of the prisons in the United States. Miss Margery Fry, the noted British student of penal affairs, admitted her confusion in evaluating our penology when she visited the prisons of the United States a few years ago. Good, bad and indifferent, from "the primitive to the sophisticated, from poverty to wealth, from the toughest to the most sensitive, the extremes are so unbelievably distanced, the means so hard to ascertain."[12] It is likewise with the prisons of Latin America.

Architecturally most of them are patterned on our old Eastern State Penitentiary at Philadelphia with cellblocks radiating from a common center. However, there are many interesting modifications of this basic idea. In many of the more modern structures one may find the Federal "telephone-pole" type of architecture and, strangely enough, a few inside cellblocks of the Auburn variety in these newer prisons. The National Penitentiaries and the dates of their construction are as follows: Brazil, at Rio de Janeiro, 1837; Chile, at Santiago, in 1843; Peru, in Lima, in 1862; Ecuador, at Quito, in 1874; Colombia, at Bogotá, in 1876; Argentina, in Buenos Aires, in 1877; and Bolivia, at La Paz, in 1896. All of these prisons, except the one at Rio de Janeiro, are still in operation. The Rio prison has been gradually razed to make room for a new modern institution.

New prisons, erected on modern principles are found at La Picota, a suburb of Bogotá, and at Palmíra, near Cali, both in Colombia; in several places in Argentina, notably the penal colony of Santa Rosa in La Pampa; and in Brazil, especially in Rio de Janeiro, Bello Horizonte, and Itamaracá. Argentina, through the efforts of Dr. Juan José O'Connor, began in 1934 to develop a system of jails and penal colonies. While he did not live to see his reforms completed, his country has not forgotten his amazing vision and energy and has practically completed his program of prison construction.

Brazil, also, has gone far in developing an excellent program of prison construction, starting with the penitentiary at São Paulo in 1922. Many new modern plants have been erected during the past fifteen years. Chile started a building program several years ago with the construction, in 1926, of new penal establishments in Chillán and Talca, but they have not been finished. In fact, there is little likelihood that anything new will develop in that country unless more officials in high places begin to take an active

[12] *The Spectator* (London), August 6, 1943, pp. 122–23.

interest in prison reform as well as in prison construction.

Peru has long delayed its prison construction until its ambitious road building program was finished. This has just recently been completed and in November 1944 the Congress appropriated forty million *soles*—some six million of our dollars—for new buildings. The plans were on the drafting-boards when the new Democratic Front government of Dr. José Bustamante came to power in the June 1945 elections. It is hoped that the present government will carry out this ambitious project so that Peru may at last make up for lost time in prison construction and administration. This program will be described later in the chapter on Peru.

There is practically nothing in the offing in prison construction in Ecuador and Bolivia. There is some talk in the latter country of developing a prison system along modern lines but it is doubtful that much will be accomplished in the near future. It has been only recently, since 1942, that Bolivia has become concerned with revamping its antiquated penal code.

The directors of the South American prisons vary as to background and political astuteness just as in our own country. In some countries the Directors-General of the prison systems as well as the wardens are merely political appointees, but an occasional one of these shows a satisfactory knowledge of penal matters and is attempting to accomplish a conscientious and honest job of running his institutions. There are also several wardens in some countries who have been appointed because of proved ability and past achievements in penology. They might be referred to as career men. This is especially true in Brazil, where I found two or three men of outstanding ability and prison experience. These men possess a high degree of penal insight and certainly compare favorably with some of the most capable officials we have in our own prisons.

The guards or keepers in the various prisons range all the way from the most capable to the lowest types of humanity, varying with the status of the political régime dominating the countries.

Where the compensation is reasonable—seldom does one find attractive pay in any public office in South America—the guards are likely to be highgrade. Stories circulate concerning brutality on the part of the guards in one or two prisons but similar behavior regarding our own prison guards is not unknown. There is much "pushing around" of convicts by the personnel, plenty of badgering, and even some rough treatment, but none of this was practiced or remotely apparent on the days I visited the institutions. My visits were carefully scheduled, usually a day or two notice being given so that establishments could be put in presentable shape. What I saw worthy of criticism, therefore, comes only from experience gained from many years of prison visiting.

Military pomp is quite noticeable in the prisons of some countries, especially in Chile and Argentina. Heel-clicking guards snap to attention at the approach of the warden and his entourage. The blowing of a mouth whistle announces his progress from shop to shop and in some prisons the inmates stand respectfully at attention until given the signal to resume work. In one prison in Chile the inmates were all lined up previous to the entrance of our party into the corridor. They were a motley group, of course, and the incident bordered on the ridiculous. In another institution an obsequious guard, who was standing rigidly at attention, was asked by the warden to run an errand for him. He literally ran, awkwardly clutching his sword and almost stumbling as he dispatched himself to do the warden's bidding. Pomp and servility, but little dignity.

Yet I was treated kindly by all officials. I believe I was shown everything, and usually without asking specifically to examine such prison mysteries as punishment cells, toilets, kitchens or condemned cells. For such gracious coöperation and courtesy I am duly grateful.

Provisions for inmate labor also vary. In most of the countries the contract labor system dominates the prisons, although in most of the countries the contractor has no jurisdiction over the inmate or his production, as was the case in the old-time prisons of the United States. The system might well be called by our own term, "piece-price." The prison usually employs an agent who sells the products to jobbers or retailers or contractors—any means of quickly disposing of the commodities. They may also solicit business from retailers or others. Private disposal of prison-made goods—those produced by the contract, or "piece-price" method—is usually referred to as *particulares.*

But in all countries there prevails what we in the United States understand as "state-use" production. This is usually referred to in South America as the *fiscal* system. Most of the directors I talked with expressed a strong desire to see this system supplant the present contract method. They all feel that production for governmental use, which our "state-use" system entails, is the superior method of disposing of their products.

The machinery in the prison shops in some countries is excellent and quite modern. Much of it was manufactured in Germany and includes equipment for shoemaking, weaving, printing and tool-making. But in one or two countries the equipment is worn-out and even obsolete, judged by modern standards.

Wages paid to prisoners are usually quite small; in this most countries follow our own short-sighted and patently unfair practices. Only in one or two prisons did I find a wage policy squaring with recommendations long enunciated by progressive penologists. In the Bogotá, Colombia, prison I saw inmates operating machinery who drew forty to fifty pesos ($25 to $30) per month plus cost of maintenance. Colombia's enlightened prison labor policy will be discussed in a later chapter. Some prisoners in the prison at Rio de Janeiro may also make as much money as free laborers.

Financial restitution for crime is characteristic of South America although the practice is not universal. The prisoner's wages are divided into three or four parts, depending on whether indemnity is required by law. A certain percentage is usually applied to the support of the inmate's family, a part withheld for release, and a portion made available to him for small purchases at the prison commissary.

One special activity found in the prisons of some countries is the development of hobbies. In Argentina and Brazil, especially, may be seen large classes in oil painting, wood carving, sculpturing and ceramics. The penitentiaries of Buenos Aires and São Paulo, Brazil, are remarkably well advanced in these fields. We have nothing like this in the United States. Then, too, there are the usual tinkering groups of prisoners in those institutions where productive labor cannot absorb all capable workers. These men make a wide variety of knick-knacks such as toys, inkwells, whips, cigarette boxes and the like designed from bone, wood, metal, cloth and from anything else available. In the prisons of the countries having a large Indian population many are engaged in weaving *ponchos* and blankets. These are usually sold by the wives and children of the prisoners in the streets and market places of the cities where the prisons are located. Most of these fabrics are beautifully woven in an amazing variety of colors.

Some of the prisons have bands and small impromptu orchestras. The band in the São Paulo penitentiary is worthy of comment since it is well-equipped, large and snappy, comparing favorably with our best university aggregations.

The prison schools vary from country to country. Some are quite pitiful, whereas others are diversified, well-equipped and staffed by trained teachers. Illiteracy is a universal problem so that the school must start with this extensive group unable to read or write. Every prison attempts to teach the bare fundamentals of an education. There is some higher academic instruction in a few prisons and in one or two institutions correspondence courses are offered for those who can profit from them. On the whole, however, there is nothing worthy of more than mere mention.

THE PRISON CLINICS

Most of the South American penitentiaries have classification or diagnostic clinics although a few of the countries scarcely understand their implications, if even their real meaning, to the problem of adjustment of the prisoners. These clinics vary, naturally, as to personnel, equipment and function. Psychiatrists, psychologists, and even anthropologists delve into the heredity and measure the bodies of the inmates, probe for glandular disorders and measure for intelligence, all, apparently, to endeavor to locate the hidden *criminal nato*, that is, the born criminal. But social workers are conspicuously absent except in the National Penitentiary at Santiago, Chile, where the director of the clinic is convinced of the importance of the socio-economic causes of criminal behavior.

The diagnostic clinics have been set up in the prisons by law and the personnel is usually well-trained and, in most countries, most conscientious. There can be no doubt, however, that they are dominated by a particularistic approach to criminal causation. Every criminal is such because of his atypical physical mechanism or some malfunctioning unearthed by their probings. It apparently never occurs to these excellently trained specialists that they would uncover the same biological defects in the average random sampling of the non-criminal population if the same tests were given. The common social history of the inmate, familiar in all our prison clinics, is seldom assembled, no analysis made of the community or neighborhood from which he came, no previous employment record checked, nor is a study made of his family relationships.

But aside from the serious lack of a social investigation and this almost fetish-like faith in the biological, another criticism can be made of these South American prison clinics. Nothing is done with their findings; they are merely filed away and become dusty with disuse. In very few, if any, instances are their results acted upon by the prison administrations. In one clinic, after the capable staff members showed me their excellent equipment and explained what they did with respect to every incoming inmate, I asked to what use their results were put by the prison officials. The director smiled and sadly replied that nothing, absolutely nothing, was done with them. They were merely filed away. In another clinic I discussed this at some length with its director. He told me that on occasions the warden, who, incidentally, often sits in on the clinic's investigations, asks for specific information regarding an inmate but never acts on its recommendations. He further added that he was meticulous in maintaining the clinic on a high professional plane and kept careful records so that at some future time, when the clinic might have some standing, his successors could say that his pioneer work was carried on with scientific precision.

There are undoubtedly several reasons why this situation exists just as there are reasons why our own prison clinics are so neglected by wardens and superintendents. In South America many of the prison directors are untrained men and, like so many of our own wardens, have more faith in repression and traditional work training than in more individualized programs of treatment. Another reason is that the prisons are operated from above by the politicians and while the government may give lip service to scientific treatment by establishing the clinic, it cares little for methods of reformation as developed by clinical specialists. But perhaps the main reason is that the bulk of the prisoners come from the lower social and economic classes and their lot is supposed to be hard while serving a prison term. Thus, while the administration of the prison may tolerate the diagnostic clinic it will not sanction the use of its findings.

Of course much of this same criticism can be applied to many of the wardens of our own prisons. In some states there are wardens who talk glibly of classification procedure, yet there are few staff members actually doing classification or diagnostic work in any realistic manner. There is also the same lag existing between diagnosis and treatment.

However, the results of the diagnostic clinics in South American prisons are of some value to the members who frequently contribute articles to the various *revistas.* The compilation of statistical charts within the prisons is almost a form of "indoor sports" in some countries, where efficiency and paper work have become a burden. But even the charts can have little meaning since they are of so little use in the actual planning of the inmate's program while in prison.

One of the biggest tasks confronting South American penologists is the implementation of the prison program with the clinic's findings. Also, the recognition that their approach is one-sided and well-nigh meaningless in working out an individual program for the inmate.

PRISON VISITING

Provision for members of the inmate's family to visit him range all the way from the traditional screened galleries, so familiar in our own prisons, to informal family visiting within the enclosure of the institution. The prison at Bogotá, Colombia, possesses the sanest and most wholesome system throughout South America. Here the members of the families may come each Sunday afternoon and sit in a beautiful *patio,* resplendent with flowers and hanging-baskets filled with exotic plants. Soft classical music plays constantly from the radio or recording machines. Many of the wives bring lunches and choice foods for their men. The same informality and liberality also exist in the overcrowded jails of all countries where the physical conditions are just the opposite from those of the Bogotá prison.

Colombia and, to a degree, Brazil, have met the serious sex problem of prisons in a courageous and realistic manner. In the former country, inmates may leave the prison once every two weeks, under guard, for a "conjugal" visit. They may meet their wives at a designated and approved rooming-house, or visit a licensed house of prostitution. The length of the visit is two hours.

In Brazil, small rooms in the prisons, specifically set aside for the purpose, are used by the inmates to receive their wives. However, no prostitutes are permitted in the Brazilian prisons. While in these two countries the prison administrators accept sexual visiting as an integral and necessary part of the prison program, some countries frown on it as severely as we do in the United States.

The practice of providing for prisoners' families in penal colonies, so popular in Soviet Russia, flourishes to a degree in some of the state prisons in Brazil. This is particularly true where agricultural colonies are a part of the state's prison system. However, many Brazilian penologists are quite lukewarm on the matter. In the chapter dealing with penology in Brazil a few further remarks will be made on this subject.

CONDITIONAL RELEASE—LATIN AMERICAN PAROLE

Parole, as we know it in the United States, is practically nonexistent in all of Latin America. Every country, however, has statutes dealing with conditional release, known generally as *libertad condicional* but sometimes referred to as *libertad bajo palabra.* In Brazil it is known as *livramento condicional.* Supervision is practically unknown, that is, the meaning of trained supervision and its importance to crime prevention as well as adjustment to a free society upon release from prison, is not recognized. The only devices that pass for a check on released prisoners is the absurd practice of reporting to the police or the prison periodically, or to the *Patronato.* A word about the *Patronato* is of interest since it is distinctly a Continental institution and is especially strong in Latin Europe.

The organization is quasi-public in nature and in some countries a subsidy is given to assist it in carrying on its work. In Spain and Italy the *Patronato* is, or was before the war, quite an established concern. It quite obviously owes its origin to the many early volunteer prison societies developed in the various Latin countries. As early as 1500 there was an organization of twenty-four "gentlemen of Salamanca" dedicated to ameliorating the abuses of the jails, and in 1572 another such society was formed in Seville. Later, in 1779, the Royal Association of Charity was founded. This organization was headed by the Count of Miranda and its statutes were approved by royal edict. In 1787 a society of women was organized in Spain which dedicated itself to jail visiting.

In Italy the same type of prison visiting was developed quite early. In 1519 Julius de Medicis, afterward Pope Clement VII, founded the *Archconfraternità de S. Girolano,* an association of prison visitors. And in 1655 the public was appealed to for support of prison visiting by Scanaroli of Modena, an archbishop, in his work entitled *De Visitatione Carceratorum.*

In the course of time subsidies were granted these private agencies and they became known as the *Patronato.* The personnel, however, continued to be untrained and to a large degree purely voluntary. But with official sanction and public subsidy many of them, in Italy especially, were clothed with a responsibility far beyond their abilities to fulfil. This is their status today in most Latin American countries.

There can be no serious criticism of private volunteer agencies to supplement the official services of prisons or for supervision after release. But it is important that their staffs be trained if they represent the only agencies dealing with these problems or even if they merely supplement official organizations.

The *Patronato* in Latin America is little better than a private agency without trained personnel. Its supervision at best can be nothing but desultory and sporadic. The governing board is usually composed of distinguished officials, such as professors of law, physicians or governmental employees, all of whom are busy with the exacting duties of their own professions. The board meets and discusses cases of released prisoners. The ex-prisoner reports at periodic intervals and is questioned by any person to whom he may be assigned. But there can be no real supervision as we understand it. I talked with many persons in the various countries and they were in agreement that the *Patronato* carries little weight so far as the adult discharged prisoner is concerned.

While it is true that in many jurisdictions in our own country there is little real supervision connected with what is called parole, no one understanding the necessity of trained personnel for such services will condone shoddy practice. In Latin America the *Patronato* means superficial treatment for the released prisoner, and it is acceptable to all but a few who understand its weaknesses. In this country parole without all its fundamental elements is repudiated by everybody who understands the meaning of such a service for released prisoners.

Conditional release in Latin America, as stated above, is determined by statute in the various countries, that is, by the penal codes in operation. Conditions for such release will be discussed in the later chapters dealing with individual countries.

THE STATUS OF PROBATION IN LATIN AMERICA

While every country has on its statute books some form of "probation" known usually as *condena condicional,* but also referred to on occasion as *libertad vigilada,* it certainly is not what is understood as probation in our own country. It merely follows the Franco-Belgian form of the suspension of the execution of the sentence by the judge.

According to Professor N. S. Timasheff, who has given us an excellent report on probation throughout the world,[13] "probation" exists in some rudimentary form in at least nine of the Latin American countries. It was first considered in Brazil as early as 1893, but adopted first in Chile in 1906. Due to the Continental influences found in all these countries, it is not at all surprising that they have failed to grasp the significance of supervised liberty as we know it. Space forbids the review of the conditions

[13] *One Hundred Years of Probation,* in two parts (New York: Fordham University Press, 1943). Probation in Latin America is discussed in Part II.

affecting the suspended sentence in the various countries but the reader may learn for himself what these are by referring to Timasheff's work.

However rudimentary, or "masked," probation may be, there is in most countries a lively interest in real probation. Many penologists expressed the conviction that this phase of a rational penal program is extremely important and that it should be adopted in their countries without delay. It is questionable, however, if probation will gain much popularity, because, even in the United States, its use is determined by the liberality of the judges. Judges in South America follow the familiar pattern of conservatism found all too frequently in our own country. Probation can never succeed until judges are willing to give it a fair trial, and it is extremely doubtful that this will be realized for many years in Latin America.

JAILS ARE DEPLORABLE

In writing about Latin American jails (*cárceles*) it is difficult to choose words that will adequately describe the unwholesome conditions that prevail in by far the majority of them. Anyone familiar with the deplorable conditions of filth, idleness, apathy and despair that abound in our jails may find it difficult to imagine that it is possible to reach further down to new lows in these phases of jail life; but it is.

Yet in appraising the jails in South American countries, especially in those along the West Coast, it should be stated that the bulk of the population is Indian, a subject race, and it is from this disinherited and miserable group that the jail population is largely drawn. It might be argued, fatuously it is true, that to provide wholesome housing, food, medical attention, and the like, would be to give to these people more than they are accustomed to when at home. This argument, of course, has the same old familiar ring of all times in all countries and cannot be tolerated by the progressive penologist. There are minimum standards of decency below which no jail should be permitted to sink, regardless of the type of population it houses.

Few South American jails are equipped with cells. Congregate housing is the rule with dirty overcrowded dormitories practically universal. In many of these charnel houses—for many are literally that—no beds are provided, the inmates sleeping on the bare ground or on pallets made of boxes or slats. Pegs filled with inmates' dirty clothes stud the walls. Toilets are filthy and bathing facilities, where provided at all, are far from sanitary or adequate. Cooking of food is done in a very primitive manner and meals are eaten in the open air without tables or chairs.

What passes for food is furnished gratis by the jail management, but it is quite unwholesome and unpalatable, judged by our standards. And this must be so since in practically all city jails it seems necessary for the institution fare to be supplemented by hot soups, vegetables and meat brought from the homes of the inmates. It is a familiar sight in practically every city to see ragged urchins or wornout dirty women milling around outside the jail gate waiting to give their fathers and husbands some food from home.

In very few jails is there to be found any work or organized occupation for the inmates. Many, however, engage in carving of various media, weave *ponchos* or other knitted goods, make toys, hats and other objects, which are disposed of by the inmates at the jails to chance visitors or through members of their families in the city's streets. Some resourceful jail wardens have provided work benches and tools for the inmates and some have enlisted the interest of private individuals and organizations in the plight of their idle men. There is nowhere any official work policy; nor is there in any country the equivalent of a municipal work farm such as we have in our own country on a limited scale.

But aside from these deplorable conditions, the real tragedy of Latin American jails is that those awaiting trial must languish in these miserable surroundings for a year or two, and sometimes even as many as five years, before their cases are disposed of by the courts. Interminable delays due to an outmoded colonial jurisprudence are the reason for this abuse, and no one seems to know when or how this state of affairs can be eliminated.

Most of the South American countries maintain, especially in the large cities, a special treatment in their jails for those suspected of crime, who come from higher social classes than the peasants. The quarters for this group are known as *pensionados* and are "rented" to those willing and able to pay. These *pensionados* are set apart from the rabble and in some jails are quite comfortable, though not luxurious. They usually consist of an apartment of living-room and bedroom. Individuals who can purchase this special type of quarter may also have their food brought into the jail by members of their families or engage it from those who make it a business to supply them. Rarely do they partake of the regular jail diet. The inmates of these special quarters are usually far superior economically and socially to the average inhabitants of a South American jail.

There is also bail in South America, but many of those from the higher social classes are not wealthy enough to negotiate a bond, nor do they have affluent friends. Few people in South America have money. Gaining a livelihood among the socially or intellectually élite is precarious.

Because of the nature of the climate in South American countries where it is rarely severe—although cold weather is certainly prevalent during the winter season—there is no heat in the jails (nor in private homes for that matter) and, in the rainy season, the jail yards are constantly filled with mud puddles. I visited a couple of jails during a severe rain storm and the condition of the jail yards was miserable. The inmates huddled together in those portions of the jail that were protected against the elements, and the yards were teeming rivulets of water. Most of the inmates were Indians and they could do nothing more than pull their ragged *ponchos* closer around them and wait for the rain to cease and the sun to come out and dry off the compound.

There are a few enterprising jail wardens but they are practically helpless to improve the terrible conditions that prevail. And in the remaining jails, administered by men of little imagination and possessing nothing but sheer inertia, the plight of the inmates is utterly degrading.

CHILDREN'S INSTITUTIONS

Perhaps the most significant feature of the treatment of children in South America is that dependent and neglected minors are treated together with delinquents. All are unfortunate and need supervision so no distinction between the classes is made. This is in direct contrast to the philosophy in practice in the United States, except in those few jurisdictions where the delinquent child is regarded as neglected by parents and community. There are many so-called delinquent children assigned to institutions for the dependent throughout our own country, especially where the term delinquent is considered a little too harsh, but the overall policy certainly makes a clearcut distinction between delinquency and the neglected or dependent.

In many South American countries there may be found children of fourteen and fifteen in the minor sections of adult penitentiaries but, as a rule, all children falling into the dependent, neglected and delinquent classes are treated alike. It should be noted, however, that thousands of dependent and neglected homeless children roam the streets of the capitals and other large towns. It is not an unusual sight to see young children, as well as adults, sleeping on church steps, in doorways and hallways, wrapped in their shoddy woolen *ponchos*. This is especially true of the countries with a large Indian population.

Another significant feature of the institutional care of children is the practical monopoly of the Catholic Church in dealing with this phase of the problem, especially in some countries. Various religious orders operate and administer the reformatories and *asilos* (asylums) for both children and women. A judgment of the quality of their work would simply be: that within the framework of the philosophy of the Church, a relatively good job is done.

However, the institutions are highly regimented and the nuns or brothers who are in charge are kind but exceedingly firm. Prayers and strict observance of the requirements of the Church are the most conspicuous feature of these establishments. In practically every children's institution, from the most benighted to the most progressive, whether operated by religious orders or by laymen, the dormitory abounds. Practically no child ever experiences privacy and of course never has his own individual room. Everywhere I went in South America I pointed out the advantages of individual rooms for children and criticized the dormitory system. In only a few places did I find anyone who would agree with me. But I did find some social workers and—of all persons—a contractor who built a children's institution, who confessed that economy was the compelling reason for the dormitories.

There is little understanding of the uniqueness of the individual in these institutions and little interest in developing the personality of the child. In many institutions the children are merely parked temporarily until they are "farmed out" to some family that wants a "mother's helper" or a good strong boy to do the chores around the home. During the interim they are afforded a superficial education and a course of training in household arts.

Release and after-care from children's institutions are in the hands of the *Patronato,* the private agency which was discussed earlier. This organization is, in reality, a philosophy. It is usually well-organized so far as children's cases are concerned and operates on a reasonably high level in one or two countries. But, in many countries, it is merely a desultory makeshift for a realistic child-placing agency. It often smacks of the "Lady Bountiful" type of charity which is understandable where there is such a wide cleavage between social classes as is found in all of Latin America. Farming-out of the children is the keynote of the *Patronato* system and, while those in control frown on exploitation, its program cannot help but be little more than a system of indenture.

While the Catholic Church accepts the responsibility of caring for delinquent women and dependent children, the trend seems to be away from such Church control. In later chapters dealing with individual countries the methods employed in dealing with women and children will be discussed.

There are many children's institutions operated by the State and administered by laymen. Some are outstanding and compare favorably with the best to be found in our own country. This is particularly true of the *Ciudad del Niño* of Santiago, Chile, the *Colonias-Hogares* of Argentina and some institutions in São Paulo in Brazil. The Santiago institution is patterned after Father Flanagan's "Boys' Town" in Nebraska, and was a special concern of the late President Ríos and his wife. It has been widely publicized as an outstanding achievement in the treatment of dependent and neglected youth. Social workers possessing the insight we might expect to find in our own members of that craft are making an excellent contribution in this institution. The school was opened in 1943 and embraces the cottage plan but features the dormitory system. The régime is progressive and regimentation is almost non-existent.

TREATMENT OF FEMALE CRIMINALS

Only a few words need be devoted to the treatment of women in Latin America, since only in a few instances is constructive penology applied to them. Women who run afoul of the law are quite likely to be both shamed and woefully neglected. Here and there are female reformatories run entirely by religious orders. But, in the main, they are found in a wing of a penitentiary, supervised in many instances by men. Their quarters in such places are barren and often quite dirty. Seldom is a program suited to their individual needs provided. Most of the women have been convicted of homicide and many are apathetic and not a few depraved. Their ages vary from sixteen to seventy. Those quartered in prisons usually have individual cells, although there is considerable doubling up.

The church-operated institutions for women are considerably more wholesome so far as physical comforts are concerned, although they are all run on the dormitory basis. The nuns are kindly persons but the programs are highly regimented. Misdemeanants and felons are often separated, but in some establishments they mingle with each other. In one or two *asilos* those women having very small babies are permitted to keep them although every attempt is made to discourage the practice. The nuns in charge prefer to farm the child out in a more normal environment.

In none of the female establishments can one find anyone who understands any of the aspects of modern penology as applied to women unless it is an occasional male director of a penitentiary under whose care women offenders are placed. In the Church reformatories the women possess an exaggerated sense of guilt, such an attitude being encouraged by those in charge. The tone is highly moral so that expiation for the wrongs against society is the dominating philosophy.

What South America needs in its treatment of women are separate cottage-type reformatories operated exclusively by women trained in penology. It will be many years before this ideal is realized, especially so long as the Catholic Church looks upon this field as its unique preserve.

THE STATUS OF SOCIAL WORK

Just as the psychiatric approach is now playing a more important part in the understanding of delinquent and criminal behavior, as well as a more important role in treatment, than formerly, so may the social case work technique become more acceptable in the not too distant future.

Social work needs no apologists in our own country, since it has become a definite part of the field of diagnosis and treatment of many human ailments, especially in the area of social disorganization. In more recent years social group work has also become established as a technique in individual adjustment so that more and more settlement houses, recreation centers, homes for the aged, orphanages and other such institutions are demanding trained personnel rather than just kindly disposed untrained persons or socially élite butterflies who possess a penchant for "doing good."

But before assaying the status of social work in South America it should be pointed out that also in the United States there are certain areas of social maladjustment where the social worker cannot or will not tread. Part of this neglect is obviously due to official resistance to such aid proffered by the social workers, but much of it demonstrates failure of the members of this profession to accept responsibility in certain fields other than those which lie in such traditional areas as family relief, child placement, and the like. For example, social workers are slow to offer their services in dealing with beggars and homeless men who roam our metropolitan areas, whose only haven is the outmoded and wholly inadequate city mission with its religious appeal. Nor has the social worker done much in the fields of prostitution, chronic alcoholism and drug addiction.

While it may be too much to expect social work to venture into these fields of maladjustment, certainly its neglect of adult criminal treatment cannot be excused. There is plenty of evidence to show that those trained in case work technique can be of real service in the prison and in the community in assisting the prisoner and the ex-prisoner to make an adjustment; in the former case to authoritarian regimentation, in the latter to social stigma or indifference. The Pennsylvania Prison Society in Philadelphia has amply demonstrated that these areas are most fruitful for trained social workers to lend their services. What is envisaged is not merely the jotting down of social histories of the inmates, as is the situation in most of our prisons at the moment, but more vital case work purposively related to the emotional needs of the prisoner or parolee. The technique is well established in our own country; the will to function in this area is almost completely absent. And the social work field deserves censure for this neglect.

It is with the foregoing in mind that the status of social work in South America is here analyzed. Being familiar with the work of the Pennsylvania Prison Society, mentioned above, and convinced of the importance of social work in the prison as well as in the realm of adequate parole planning, I felt it incumbent to stress its importance to all prison administrators and directors of diagnostic clinics in the various countries.

Social work is only in its pioneering stage throughout all of Latin America, yet there are actually two women social workers in the clinic of the National Penitentiary of Chile in Santiago. To the best of my knowledge this is the only prison in the entire Americas where this condition exists.[14] It is, therefore, all the more remarkable when we realize that social work is a very recent development in Chile.

The first school of social work in all of Latin America was begun in Chile in 1925, only twenty years ago. Since that time, however, practically every country has taken steps to set up some sort of training for those who are interested in this field. In some cases it was inaugurated to meet existing demands in the fields of public health, child welfare and other traditional areas; in others it was provided by those who recognized its potential importance for the future in solving or controlling social problems.

In discussing the status of social work in the various countries I was informed that European influences were much more dominant than those from the United States; that the philosophy permeating the training was primarily Belgian; and that most of the

[14] Since the war and due to the shortage of men some prisons in the United States have "tolerated" women social workers, but they are not accepted wholeheartedly.

directors were graduated from the Brussels schools. I was also aware that the Catholic Church maintained several training schools. It was obvious, too, that none of the schools demanded very high academic standards for entrance. I noticed also that few, if any, young men were entering this important field.

Since returning I located a survey of the schools of social work made in 1940 by Mrs. Elisabeth Shirley Enochs of our own Children's Bureau, the results of a tour of Latin American countries during that year. Much of what follows are facts gleaned from this excellent report in which Mrs. Enochs displays a tolerant, sympathetic, yet objective, attitude.[15]

We learn that the schools are divided almost equally between those sponsored by Catholic groups and those founded through governmental initiative. All of these schools have patterned their curricula upon European philosophy and, in the Catholic schools, on the International Catholic Social Work Union of Brussels. In only a few cases is there any contact between these schools and those of the United States. In only one or two schools is the so-called bachelor's degree required for matriculation, the bulk of them admitting any person of 17 or 18 who had completed the equivalent of a secondary school education.[16] The degree known as the *bachillerato* has been rated in the United States as the equivalent of a junior college diploma. Thus, even if such a degree is necessary for admittance it cannot measure up to our own requirements since most of our recognized schools of social work are graduate in character.

The curricula in some countries call for two years of work while in other countries three years are demanded. Some schools offer night classes only while others operate throughout the daytime with field work constituting a definite part of the requirements for a certificate. Library material is woefully inadequate

[15] "Training for Social Work in Latin America," Children's Bureau, November 19, 1940, *mimeographed.*

[16] In most Latin American countries, secondary education means completion of our sixth grade, usually at the age of 12; college runs for the next six years and university for another six years.

in most schools and, naturally, most of what there is on file comes from Europe. As Mrs. Enochs writes: "If the curriculum of the typical school of social work in Latin America differs greatly from that of the schools in the United States, the practice of social work differs even more and offers limited opportunity for progress." She points out that there is much emphasis on health work but relatively little on social service; that field work in many of the older types of hospitals, homes for foundlings, maternity homes, day nurseries, offers little to the student. She further describes a combination type of school known as *polivalente* which is quite popular in some countries. This type assumes training for both social workers and public health nurses.

Since contacts with European countries were broken down throughout the war period, there have recently been established more relationships with schools of social work in the United States. Requests for books, bibliographies, and scholarships show a practical and friendly interest in developing the long-neglected ties with our own schools. Thus, as time goes by, it is quite probable that social work will be placed on a different plane in those countries where a modern sense of social responsibility is taking root or is already flourishing. As Mrs. Enochs states: "In view of the serious economic conditions prevailing in so many of the republics of South America, it is obvious that the social worker will be called upon to play an increasingly important role. The value of assistance and coöperation from the United States is recognized."

LITTLE PHYSICAL CRUELTY IN PRISONS

A word should be included here regarding institutional punishment. It will be recalled that most of the criminals immured in South American prisons are not professionals nor widely experienced in the field of crime. The vast majority of them come from the servile classes. They are apathetic, colorless, and subdued. They do as they are told and seldom do they rebel. Consequently there is little necessity for punishment. There are dark or punishment cells in most of the prisons and some of these are very drab. It may be that too many recalcitrant prisoners are kept in these places much too long, but the same criticism can be made of this practice in some of our own so-called "best" prisons. Deprivation of privileges is another penalty in most of the prison disciplinary programs, but since there are few cherished privileges in most prisons, the obstreperous prisoner has little to lose.

The stories of brutality in the prisons of some countries of Latin America deal almost exclusively with political prisoners. It must be remembered that in countries where revolutions occur as frequently as they do in that part of the globe, those belonging to the opposition of the party in power are likely to be imprisoned and even badly handled. While any sort of brutality is to be deplored and the idea of incarcerating persons who disagree with the party in power repudiated, such practices cannot legitimately be discussed as a part of the penal program of a country.

There is undoubtedly some man-handling done in some of the prisons, although I did not see any untoward brutality. There is obviously some "pushing around" of inmates by guards and, in one or two prisons, inmates reported that they were mistreated, but on the whole physical punishment is not conspicuous. There is, however, much neglect of the physical needs of the prisoners in many countries, and certainly such a practice cannot be condoned any more than overt punishment.

Stripes are worn by prisoners in only one or two prisons. The initial period of solitary confinement in Peru's National Penitentiary at Lima calls for the black and white stripes. In the National Penitentiary in Buenos Aires the prisoners wear striped uniforms of yellow and blue which are quite hideous. And in the United States Penitentiary at Gamboa in the Canal Zone the inmates wear the conventional black and white stripes, which constitutes an unsavory influence in Panama.[17]

[17] It is unfortunate indeed that the management and philosophy of the Gamboa penitentiary cannot be squared with the best, or even the average, that we have

One significant feature which is worthy of the most favorable comment is that nowhere in Latin America did I see or hear of children being flogged. I cannot be altogether sure of this enlightened policy being scrupulously followed but I can state that I saw nothing to indicate that the absurd and medieval practice of flogging was recognized; nor upon inquiry did I learn of its existence. Here is certainly one field wherein we may well profit from their example.

The chapters which follow are devoted to specific practices in operation in the various countries I visited. It will be noted that, in general, they are much the same although there are some unique differences. It will be noted, too, that a few of the countries have enlightened policies in penal treatment whereas a few have a long way to go to measure up to the average found throughout the world.

---

to offer in this country. While its buildings are modern and its equipment new and immaculate, especially the chromium kitchen, I actually saw punishment cells with shackle bolts to which men undergoing punishment are chained, in which position they remain for as long as eight hours—the entire working day. Such treatment is to be deplored by any penologist from the United States. It would seem that those in charge of this system in the Canal Zone should become acquainted with some of the literature as well as practices in the United States proper. However, since these words were written, an enthusiastic article describing this penitentiary has appeared in the March–April (1946) issue of *Prison World*. It is a typical press-agent description, expatiating on the good features but overlooking the points described above. The writer is Rufus Hardy and he is referred to as a press representative of the Panama Canal. See Vol. 8, No. 2, pp. 4 f.

II

Panama

THE COUNTRY

PRIOR to 1903 when Panama asserted her independence, her prisoners were housed in the ancient Presidio of Chiríqui which was built into the old bastions of the southernmost corner of the sea wall in Panama City. The inscription over the door of this ancient fortress reads: *Entran bravos como leones y salen mansos como corderos:* "They enter vicious as lions and leave mild as lambs." What happened to the poor wretches who were thrown into this damp and gloomy prison that was responsible for this remarkable metamorphosis is not recorded.

Today one may well wonder if the convicts sent to Panama's island penal colony of Coiba (Quibo) off the coast in the Pacific Ocean return to society equally docile. Certainly the history of deportation of convicts to penal colonies shows few, if any, examples of real reform. And while one may find some good features in the Coiba colony, the bulk of the evidence accumulated throughout the ages proves conclusively that such places are brutal and hold within them the seeds of degradation and despair.

Before describing the Coiba penal colony or any of the other features of the country's penal system a word about the people of Panama is of interest. As stated above, Panama has been an independent republic since 1903. Prior to that year it was a province of the country of Colombia. Following the revolution the United States became a powerful influence, so that today a strange anomaly exists in that our control of the ten-mile Canal Zone across the isthmus presents a glaring contrast to the rest of the country.

There is much of the primitive even close to the Canal Zone but more especially is this true in the provinces away from the cities. The country's population, exclusive of the Canal Zone, is about a half a million, with 125,000 living in the capital city. They are hopelessly mixed so far as racial characteristics are concerned: whites of Spanish extraction, Indians, Negroes and Orientals, with perhaps the bulk of them crossbred with various strains. Many of the Indians, especially some of the Cunas in the reservation of San Blas as well as some of the Chocola in the province of Darien, are still unsubdued and hostile.

One coming from the States, where tropical vegetation is somewhat diluted, gains immediate respect for the real jungle that literally encroaches on the capital city. Torrential rains during the wet season are a daily feature, many of them starting suddenly and stopping abruptly after deluging the countryside as well as the people for an hour or more.

One of Panama's major problems is poverty. The peasants are ragged and dirty. But they seem to be happy and carefree, a state of being that is totally lacking in many of the countries to the south. Poverty and misery are relative. While it would not be fair to minimize the pathetic condition of *los pobres* of Panama, it certainly does not approach the degradation of the masses of the West Coast countries of South America.

Because of the nature of my mission I had the opportunity of meeting and talking with the Minister of Government as well as the members of the Supreme Court and the Attorney General. I was also afforded the privilege of speaking before a distinguished group of public officials, college professors and others interested in penology. This meeting was held at the National University. It should be recorded here that my remarks before this group stimulated more discussion than in any other such group before which I appeared on my entire trip.

THE COIBA PENAL COLONY

The Coiba penal colony in the Pacific has had a short but interesting history. Its area is about 600 square miles and lies southwest of Panama City, some one hundred fifty miles. However, it is only thirty miles off the mainland from the province of Veraguas. Convicted felons are transported by small boat from Panama City.

The colony was founded in 1919 during the administration of Dr. Balisario Porras. President Porras held progressive views on penology, at least for that time in that country. Under him the *Cárcel Modelo,* the capital's impressive jail, was opened in 1920. A well-known Spanish penologist, Señor Frustoso Carpena, was employed as the first director of the *cárcel,* and a native of the United States, Robert C. Lamastus, was made director of the Coiba colony. Lamastus was a pioneer and a good administrator but those who worked with him in those early days say he certainly was no penologist since he lacked an understanding of men. He did introduce thoroughbred cattle and hogs to the island and also developed agriculture wherever the jungle could be cleared.

I had the privilege of making a visit to Coiba accompanied by several members of Panama's official family. A small Q-boat, manned by soldiers rather than sailors, was put at our disposal by the United States Army. But the skipper, a sergeant with a little sea training, knew something of navigation and we arrived offshore after a cruise of twenty-eight hours. We were obliged to anchor some distance out. A hand-made launch, manned by convicts, consisting of a scooped-out tropical tree with an engine in it, came out from the colony to meet us. But even this craft could not reach shore because of the breakers which run high off the island. So we were next transferred to a rowboat which managed to all but beach us, but we were obliged to finish our trip to dry land by being carried on the backs of still other prisoners who came out to meet us.

The penal colony of Coiba is technically a part of the system of jails and prisons of Panama and nominally under the control of the Commissioner of Correction, a newlycreated office dating from 1942. There is a captain-director in charge, four other administrative officers and forty guards.

But it was from the genial "physician" that I received my information regarding Coiba. He is Señor Jesús María Sifontes, known to all comers as the "Dean." He arrived at Coiba in 1920, one year after it was opened, and has been there ever since. He ministers to all the physical ailments of both prisoners and guards although he is not a trained physician. He gave me some interesting statistics concerning escapes and other untoward events which make life exciting on this jungle island. In the 24 years, from 1920 to 1944, 74 convicts have died either from illness or violence. Ten were killed by guards; four by other prisoners while fighting. Two guards were wounded and one committed suicide. Nine convicts escaped and were never recaptured. Many escape plots, some of them most ingenious, have been frustrated.

The physician-dean tells the visitor these things in his very matter-of-fact manner. The long term of service he has himself experienced on this island has made him at least a realist.

On June 3, 1944, there were 220 prisoners scattered throughout the nine camps that comprise the colony. Five of these were citizens of the United States and most of the remainder were Negroes, many of whom were housed in the large colony closest to the administration unit.

The day begins for the prisoners at five-thirty in the morning. Work starts at six-thirty and continues until one-thirty, at least during the rainy season. Farming and animal husbandry are the principal occupations. The men make various articles during their spare time which they may send to the mainland for sale. These trinkets show excellent workmanship and are constructed from bone, leather and metal. Sandals are also made. The prisoners may write and send all the letters they wish provided they pay the postage. They are given stamps for one letter each week. They may receive as many letters as come to them but, of course, all mail is censored.

Coiba is a typical jungle island, cleared of tropical growth around the edges only. Scattered around the perimeter of the island are nine camps varying in size from only a few men to possibly seventy-five in the largest. Persons who know Coiba well claim that the camps are well conducted and that the men like to be sent to them. The work is not considered difficult and, aside from loneliness and homesickness, life is not too severe. However, I had an opportunity of talking to three prisoners located at the central camp and they all complained bitterly of the miserable conditions of their lives. They spoke of the prevalence of malaria. There can be no doubt of that as the island is malaria-ridden. They also stated that they were obliged to work in the torrential rains, but this was denied by the physician. While Señor Sifontes did not paint a rosy picture of life on Coiba island, he did give the impression that conditions were none too severe for those prisoners who were willing to work. He maintained that most of the complaints come from Negroes who originated in the islands of the Caribbean, not from natives of Panama proper.

As stated above, Coiba penal colony consists, for the most part, of tropical jungle. The visitor from the temperate United States is tempted to imagine such a place as romantic. Tropical fruit grows wild. Shortly after the arrival of our party on the island a prisoner shinnied up a palm tree and threw down cocoanuts for the guests. They were quickly split open by another prisoner on the ground with a *machete* and passed around. The cool delicious milk was a pleasant initiation to the colony. A typical Panamanian dinner was served with ample supplies of pineapple and mangoes heaped high on the tables.

No one dares stay outdoors after dark on account of the malarial mosquitoes with which the island is cursed. And the deadening monotony of the place is ever present even to the overnight visitor. It may be argued that persons inured to tropical climates are able to thrive even in a penal colony of this type. But aside from this questionable possibility it is simply poor penology for a country to persist in operating a prison colony so far from the seat of government. "Out of sight, out of mind" is the rule wherever this outmoded method of treating criminals

Coiba Penal Colony
PANAMA

United States Penitentiary
GAMBOA, CANAL ZONE

is maintained. Cruelty cannot be avoided. The guards are prisoners just as much as the criminals. Their authority is out of proportion to their ability as true penologists. There can be no mistaking the fact that penal colonies such as the one at Coiba breed cruelty. It is well recognized in Panama that there are guards on this island who are notorious for their cold and vicious attitudes toward their victims. Some of them are police officers who were sent to Coiba as a penalty for insubordination or other offenses contrary to the "good of the services." Physical brutality can be expected from such disgruntled persons.

I had the opportunity of going by horseback to the camp closest to the administrative compound situated two miles down the beach. Only a few old men comprise this camp. They tend cattle and live in thatched cottages, windowless and unfurnished. They cook their own meals and to all appearances seemed to be reasonably contented with their lot. Prisoners stationed in remote camps rarely, if ever, visit the central camp unless they are seriously ill. They stay right on, doing the work assigned to them until their time is up.

The citizens of Panama City circulate a crop of legends concerning Coiba penal colony, many of which are pure fiction. They tell the stranger that no one sent to this island as a prisoner ever returns. This is obviously untrue since there are plenty of individual records of men who have been discharged and are now living in their homes throughout the country. I saw men in the *cárcel* in Panama City who had been in the colony during their criminal career.

But the tales of brutality are doubtless true. The headstrong convict undoubtedly suffers considerable physical maltreatment as well as deprivation of some of the scanty privileges of his camp. There can be only one recommendation to the Panamanian officials so far as the Coiba colony is concerned and that is its total elimination. This can easily be done by sentencing the better type of long-term prisoners to agricultural colonies on the isthmus and by constructing a national prison for those requiring maximum custody. The new colony under construction at Divisa, described below, is one of several that could be developed without much expense.

THE COUNTRY'S NEW PENAL PROGRAM

Under an agreement between the United States Department of State and the Panamanian government a survey of the country's prisons as well as an analysis of penal procedure to be considered and perhaps adopted was made in 1942 by Mr. Howard Gill of Washington, D.C. Mr. Gill has long enjoyed an excellent reputation as a penologist and prison administrator. He was the first superintendent of the Norfolk Penal Colony in Massachusetts where he developed a unique experiment in community living for prisoners.

As a result of his study of Panama's prisons and penal practices a new decree, No. 467, brought into existence a series of prison reforms, some of which have since been realized. Two important departments were created. First, a Department of Correction designed to control and administer all prisons and jails, both within Panama City and in the various provinces, was provided for. The object of this measure was to wrest from the police the time-worn prerogative of controlling the penal establishments. Second, an Institute of Child Welfare, known as *El Instituto de Vigilancia y Protección del Niño,* which has for its purpose the protection and care of all minors whether delinquent, dependent or neglected, was established. Third, a Psychiatric Clinic, designed to develop diagnostic services for all incoming prisoners, was contemplated. Thus far, this service has not been organized.

The Department of Correction has the responsibility of allocating all classes of prisoners into the different penal establishments. It attempts to distinguish between the jail population and those sentenced to prison. Thus far its attempt to assume complete control of the *cárceles* and prisons has been only moderately successful. The quaint practice of permitting the police to control the jails and prisons is quite characteristic of several small countries of Latin America which suffer from unstable governments. The party in control is loath to surrender police protection since its constant feeling of insecurity makes such a bulwark seem necessary. In return for this support the police are tendered certain perquisites. Having control of all jails is one method by which they can levy and collect graft in many ingenious ways. They can also place under surveillance any possible enemies to the party in power. Such a system is malicious, dangerous and even medieval. An independent group of public officials should be charged with the responsibility of handling all persons arrested and convicted of crime. This recommendation made in the survey was and is basic in developing a progressive system of penology.

So far as could be ascertained as late as June 1944 the police still controlled the *cárceles* and the penal colony of Coiba. Nominal control was in the hands of the Commissioner of Correction, but he had little authority. Lip service was given to his directives, but in the last analysis the police ruled the penal establishments. Recent word from Panama states that while the police do not *control* the jails they do hinder the effectiveness of the Commissioner of Correction by "not always wishing to abide by the orders from the department."

One of the recommendations of Mr. Gill's survey was to send a Commission to the United States to make a study of our prisons, penal philosophy, treatment of children and child guidance clinics, and from their observations and recommendations to develop a truly progressive penal system for their country. This Commission was finally appointed and visited this country in the summer and fall of 1942. It consisted of Sr. José Ignacio Quiros, Secretary to the Minister of Government and Justice; Sr. Francisco Cornejo, later appointed first Commissioner of Correction; Sr. Manuel Faundes, assistant to the Commissioner of Correction; Dr. Camilo A. Justiniani, Director of the newly proposed Psychiatric Clinic; Señora Clara González de Behringer,

Commissioner of Child Welfare; and Sr. Guillermo Zurita, assistant to the Commissioner of Child Welfare.[1]

Definite strides have been taken in the realm of child welfare since the establishment of the *Instituto de Vigilancia y Protección del Niño* although many of the more ambitious phases of the program have thus far not been realized. As no juvenile courts exist in the country, a special procedure was adopted in 1942 whereby children under sixteen were withdrawn from the ordinary court jurisdiction and placed under the supervision of the Institute. Children thus assigned and needing institutional care—and most of these are dependent rather than delinquent—are sent to a reformatory. In the capital, the reformatory is on the outskirts of the city. Under the direction of the Commissioner of the Institute the entire establishment has been thoroughly renovated and good wholesome food and sleeping quarters provided, thus making for a kindly régime of understanding treatment. Social workers are employed by the Institute and each child is carefully investigated before custodial care or other such treatment is recommended by the Commissioner.

A new receiving home for children in the Relleno de Barraza district of Panama City is under construction and is practically completed. The purpose of this home is to serve as a place of detention for children of all the hinterland provinces as well as of the capital until their cases are disposed of by the Institute. Heretofore such dependent or neglected children have been held by the police in their home towns. After the new detention quarters, constructed on the cottage plan, are completed it is hoped that a real juvenile court will be established.

The large jail serving the city of Panama is referred to as the *Cárcel Modelo.* It is an imposing structure built in 1920 of stone and is surrounded by a wall. It is large enough to be taken for a prison or penitentiary, and indeed is constructed along such

[1] Several changes have been made in personnel since my visit. Sr. Zurita is at present Commissioner of Correction; Sr. Cornejo has resigned and Sra. González de Behringer is secretary to the Ministry of Social Work and Public Health.

lines rather than those of a county or city jail of the Latin type. Most of these throughout Latin America are distinctly of the Spanish architectural style, not unlike a convent with inside *patio*. While the *Cárcel Modelo* is technically under the control of the Commissioner of Correction, there can be no doubt that the police dominate the establishment. One section of the jail, originally designed for housing female offenders, is utilized by the police for living quarters.

The layout of this institution is reasonably satisfactory. It is of outside cell construction with central corridors. The cells are large and the window in each permits a maximum of sunlight and air to enter. Unfortunately, two, four or sometimes six inmates are crowded together in each cell. However, there are no dormitories, which is the usual situation in South American jails. As in most jails, both in the United States and Latin America, there is no work provided the inmates. The men simply remain in their cells although those serving short sentences are permitted to wander around in the open courtyard. Those awaiting trial are kept in their cells. It was in Panama's *Cárcel Modelo* that I became aware, for the first time, that many persons in Latin American countries must remain in custody for long periods of time before trial. This injustice was referred to in the preceding introductory chapter and will be alluded to in subsequent chapters. This is a serious matter in itself, but in this Panamanian jail there are actually persons who have been detained for months, who have been neither indicted nor charged officially with a crime. This, of course, is simply inexcusable.

Another criticism is in order. There is no excuse for filth in any jail and, while the *Cárcel Modelo* is reasonably clean in its interior, the outside courtyard or compound is filthy. Chickens were running around when I was there and even pigs made their appearance. Upon being apprized of this irregularity in prison housekeeping, the Secretary to the Minister of Justice made the promise that animals would be eliminated from the jail. Recent reports from Panama advise me that the chickens and pigs are still ranging through the jail. In spite of orders from the Minister, from the Commissioner of Correction and from the health and sanitation officials, the captain of the jail still maintains his privilege of using this public jail as a chicken coop and pigsty. His only excuse is that he cannot find any other place for his animals.

Since my visit to the *Cárcel Modelo* a new kitchen and dining room have been established. Accommodations for 250 prisoners have been provided for and reports state that eating arrangements are now quite sanitary. Refrigeration has also been installed.

A new reformatory for women has been under construction for some time at Los Santos. This institution will supplant the "famous and tragic" *Reformatorio de Mujeres* now functioning in Panama City. The new establishment will be known as the *Centro Femenino de Rehabilitación* and was scheduled to open in May 1945.

One of the new establishments recommended by Mr. Gill in his report on Panama's penal program is the agricultural colony at Divisa, in the interior. There was already located in the vicinity an agricultural school for boys, an excellent institution for training scientific farmers. This school is well-equipped and has been making a splendid contribution to the economic life of the country by sending young boys back to their home provinces trained in modern agricultural methods.

Adjacent to the grounds of this institution is a provincial police station and *cárcel*. These have been supplemented by a penal colony which is in the process of development. A new modern minimum-security prison has been erected and subsequently many of the good risk prisoners from the Coiba penal colony will be transferred to Divisa, otherwise known as Santa María. Thus, in time, perhaps, Divisa may become a large agricultural penal colony and totally supplant Coiba. At least, such a move would be highly desirable. The sooner the Coiba colony is abandoned, the better for the country of Panama.

The provincial jails of the country may be described as fair, poor, and abominable. But this is no more serious an indictment of Panama than it would be of our own county jails, many of which are as degrading to their inmates as the worst in Panama.

Those in the town of Las Tablas, in the province of Los Santos, and at David, in the province of Chiríqui, are new structures, having been built since the visit of Mr. Gill. A new jail in the city of Colón, on the Atlantic side of the isthmus, was recommended by the survey and has recently been completed. Conditions in the old jail were positively primitive and disgusting. If any *cárcel* in Panama needed eradication certainly that in Colón did. The new jail at Las Tablas is small but is reasonably well adapted for use as detention quarters for those awaiting trial and for short-term offenders. Unfortunately, the females are housed in a small portion of the jail—the usual practice in most small jails—and attended by the male police.

The jails in Santiago (Veraguas) and in Penonomé (Cocle) are fair. Those in the other provinces are little better than small detention quarters and, in general, not very presentable. Of course, the local police have charge of these establishments. While there may be some excuse for local police to assume charge of the detention quarters in the smaller towns, there is no justification for such control in the larger centers. Eventually all police control should be abolished and a separate staff of individuals under the control of the Commissioner of Correction be installed.

Panama's penal code dates from 1922 but a new project has been completed and is now awaiting adoption. Present offenses are divided into the traditional categories, crimes and misdemeanors (*delitos y contravenciones*). The former are under the jurisdiction of the judicial authorities whereas the latter are under the administrative departments of the government, that is, the police.

Punishments for serious offenses (*delitos*) include imprisonment, arrest, confinement, fines and the denial of certain rights or functions; for the less serious offenses, denial of certain rights or functions, supervision by the police, or confiscation of certain goods.

There is a distinction between *reclusión* and *prisión;* both apply to imprisonment, but the former envisages confinement in the Coiba penal colony while the latter means incarceration in a provincial jail. The sentence of *arrest* calls for incarceration in the *cárceles* or station houses of the district police.

Conditional release (parole) in Panama is an administrative function attached to the Department of Correction in accordance with the following procedure: delinquents sentenced to *reclusión* or *prisión,* who have completed three-fourths of the former, or two-thirds of the latter, and have observed good conduct and shown repentance and reformation, may be awarded conditional release for the remainder of their sentence. There is, however, no supervision of released persons. The right of conditional release is denied those who have been members of a criminal gang (*asociación de malhechores*), to those who have been committed for robbery, extortion, or larceny, to those who have been previously convicted, and to those who have been sentenced to more than three years.

These exceptions are so inclusive that it seems doubtful that such release is granted to many; that is, if these provisions are actually enforced by the authorities.

There is no real probation for adults in Panama. However, there is the traditional suspension of the execution of the sentence (Franco-Belgian), a characteristic of all Latin American countries which, of course, does not contemplate supervision. In Panama this is known as *condena condicional.* The stipulations of this suspension are: when the punishment to be imposed does not exceed four months in prison, arrest, or confinement, or more than fifty *balboas* fine, the court can suspend the execution of the sentence providing the condemned person has never before incurred punishment and it is demonstrated that he has always observed good conduct. If such is the case the authority is limited to giving him a warning in public and notifying him of the suspension of the sentence. He must then place a bond or obligate himself personally that in case he violates any other law within two years he will pay a fine.

The situation with children is somewhat different, so far as probation is concerned. The *Instituto de Vigilancia y Protección del Niño,* the work of which was described earlier, has been practicing a kind of probation with considerable success. This has been carried out without intervention of the courts. This disposition is referred to by the officials of the Institute as "social treatment" and is similar to the practice found in many of our own juvenile courts. The former Director of the Institute, Señora González de Behringer, holds a master of law degree from New York University and has long been familiar with the work of our juvenile courts and our Children's Bureau. The work which she inaugurated, however, has been seriously handicapped by lack of funds and the enormity of the delinquent problem. Whether the new director can overcome these handicaps remains to be seen.

CONCLUDING REMARKS

As was pointed out in the *Introduction,* the jail and penitentiary operated in the Canal Zone by the United States government represent an outmoded penal philosophy and, accordingly, need drastic renovation. There is no reason why this system should not approximate the enlightened administration of the Federal Bureau of Prisons. It seems somewhat futile to suggest to Panama that she adopt more progressive methods of dealing with her criminals when, just alongside in the Canal Zone, she may behold an example that is none too flattering to the United States. Yet, in spite of the stripes and shackles so conspicuous at Gamboa penitentiary, Panama has not resorted to either and for this she deserves credit. And her new jails, especially the one at David with its adaptation to tropical living, are far superior to the horrible inside cellblocks which form a part of the new jail in the Canal Zone conceived by our own officials. The cast-iron sheathing of which the cells are built is entirely out of place in such a tropical country and is indicative of inept planning.

But there is much room for improvement in Panama's penal system. Complete separation of the police from the jails and prisons with control vested in the Department of Correction is fundamental and should be realized as quickly as possible. A plan suggested by one who is familiar with the country's penal administration offers a possible solution whereby coöperation between the police and the Department of Correction could be developed. Since the police make up a large section of the army of the country and thus must be scattered throughout the isthmus with arms available, certain of the smaller *cárceles* could serve as police headquarters and still be divorced from the administration of the prisoners. The *Cárcel Modelo* and some of the larger *cárceles,* perhaps the one at David, which is on the outskirts of the city, and the one at Santa María, could be separated from the central police and administered exclusively by trained prison personnel. In other words, if complete separation cannot be adopted, some compromise plan should be worked out. Police control of the jails may be offered as the most serious criticism of Panama's penal system.

The gradual abandonment of the Coiba colony should be recommended. Back in 1919 President Porras envisaged this colony to serve as an experimental agricultural station for the improvement of livestock and was too progressive a person to think of such a place as a brutal penal colony. Coiba can be abandoned by the gradual absorption of its prisoners into agricultural colonies scattered throughout the interior provinces, together with the establishment of a maximum custody prison on the mainland for the small group needing such treatment. The agricultural colony at Divisa (Santa María) as the first of its kind in the country should set an example for the future development of colonies of this type. Elimination of the old *cárceles* and the construction of newer and more scientifically planned structures, such as the one at David, are also necessary.

With the new reformatory for women at Los Santos and more careful treatment of women detained for trial, the female offenders of Panama should realize a more promising future than has been their lot in the past.

The development of juvenile courts and the extension of probation and the social work technique for children should materially strengthen the work of those who are already handling the problem of juvenile dependency and delinquency in a gratifyingly adequate manner. A new reformatory for children should be provided as soon as possible to take its place along with the new house of detention already nearing completion in Panama City.

Creation of a psychiatric annex, already provided for in the Decree of 1942, should be the next major move in bringing Panama's penology into line with other countries described in this survey. This service should examine all convicted felons who are sentenced to prison. It is hoped, of course, that when it is established it will be integrated with social service as well as with psychological technique. In short, it should develop into a well-rounded diagnostic clinic.

III

Colombia

THE COUNTRY

PERHAPS the most impressive feature of the vast country of Colombia is the three snow-capped mountain ranges, or *cordilleras,* that traverse its length from north to south. While these majestic mountain chains inspire the visitor to Colombia, he cannot avoid the realization that they block both commerce and transportation to no mean degree. Life in Colombia is essentially found in the valleys between the *cordilleras* and on the upland plateaus, although the country's largest city and capital, Bogotá, has an altitude of 8,600 feet.

The country is essentially tropical, all of it lying well within the Torrid Zone. But despite this fact, most of the nine million of Colombia's people live in a climate that is temperate the year round because of the high altitude. It has been stated on good authority that only one per cent of the people live in the steaming tropical *Oriente,* that vast and tractless area that stretches off to the Amazon country to the east.

This colorful and intriguing country of some 450,000 square miles is twice the size of continental France or almost twice the size of our own Texas. Travel, aside from air, is difficult and sometimes quite impossible. The railroads are not well developed and the bus lines are handicapped by roads that at some portions of the year are mere quagmire.

The bulk of the population of Colombia is *mestizo,* that is, of Indian and white blood of various mixtures. There is only a small percentage of pure Indians and they are primarily concentrated in the *Oriente* and are totally uncivilized; a small percentage of Negroes, mostly along the coasts of the Pacific and Caribbean;

and about twenty per cent pure white, of old colonial Spanish extraction. These latter live in the cities, especially in Bogotá, Medellín and Cali.

Certainly one of the most fascinating experiences one can have in Colombia is to visit the capital city of Bogotá, perched high on top of a wide plateau, which prompted one imaginative writer to speak of it as the "Penthouse of the Andes." The weather of this charming and sophisticated city is perpetual spring, the average temperature ranging from fifty to seventy degrees, but with a long-drawn-out rainy season. Much of the year the pedestrian must leave his home prepared for a shower and *gringos*, especially, are rarely seen without their raincoats.

Many writers have described the charm of Bogotá. A potpourri of this mountain capital that attracts and even amazes the visitor would include: the incessant cries of the lottery ticket hawkers—the lottery is a national institution in most South American countries, the summer street cars always jammed to more than their capacity with dirty ragged urchins hanging precariously to the sides and backs without fear of the conductor, and these same street cars decorated in front with large floral wreaths placed there in loving memory of the recently departed; the printed posters pasted on sides of buildings announcing the deaths of relatives; the clanging of church bells, raucous and incessant at all hours of day and night; the narrow streets filled with swarms of people hurrying, standing, milling about; the smartly dressed women venturing out in late afternoon only; the barefoot Indians, some loafing with subdued demeanor, others rushing by with tremendous packs on their backs, all wearing *ruanos*—the Colombian *ponchos*—made of wool and slipped over their heads by means of a hole woven in the garment, all of sombre colors, never gay or gaudy as in Peru, for example; the open air soft drink and short-order emporia, flush with the narrow sidewalks and filled exclusively with men; the free news of daily world events chalked up on blackboards in the streets with hundreds of idlers blocking transportation without the slightest sense of being a nuisance; all of these phenomena, and many more, make up the restless and exciting life of Bogotá.

Bogotá was founded in 1538 by Don Gonzalo Jiménez de Quesada. Its full name, Santa Fe de Bogotá del Nuevo Reino de Granada de las Indias del Mar Océano, is quaintly reminiscent of the homesick Spanish explorers who, in the sixteenth century, tramped through the endless wastes of this hemisphere for love of country, devotion to religion and greed for gold.

I reached Bogotá on Corpus Christi Day, June 8. My reception on this most holy day affected me deeply. The streets were lined with people watching the long procession that annually marks this sacred celebration. The doleful music and solemn cadence of the marchers, the hundreds of little girls dressed in their symbolical bridal dresses, were evidence enough of the deeply religious fervor of the citizens of this Catholic city. In fact, of the twenty-two holidays listed for Colombia, by far the great majority are religious.

The poor of Bogotá live miserably. Men, women and children from the peasant Indian classes rarely ever have a pair of shoes. Most of them wander the streets barefoot although some do wear a cheap type of sandal, characteristic throughout South America and known as *alpargata*. Many of *los pobres* sell fruit, handmade toys, biscuits or rolls from broadmouthed baskets over which is ingeniously stretched a network of stout cord to prevent quick-fingered urchins from stealing their wares. Children work as long and as hard as adults. Many youngsters of eight and ten carry loads on their backs that would stun an adult laborer in the United States. Women carry their wares in their hands and their babies on their backs. While most of the men work, some do loaf; but the women, never.

Bogotá is sharp in contrasts. Aside from its large poverty-stricken population, it reflects the country's wealth, culture, energy and sophistication. Many of its homes, especially in the swanky suburban Chapinero, are elegant with their Spanish architecture and exotic plantings. It is a city of flowers; in fact, the whole country is a floral paradise. Orchids grow wild and even the cultivated varieties can be bought from the florist for sixty cents a corsage. Calla lilies and deep red carnations abound in the hotel lobbies, store windows and the homes of the affluent. Tropical fruits in abundance and variety, most of them unknown to the stranger from the States, are on the menu or merely set down by the waitress after the conventional dessert is served. For those who are prepared to pay, food is plentiful and diverse.

The city is full of private schools for the upper classes and the social climbers. Poor but proud white folks never send their children to the public schools. Compulsory education is present only in theory, not because it is not acceptable in principle, but because there are not enough school buildings and trained teachers available. Since thousands of children cannot gain admission they become "little merchants" and grind out a life of toil. The experience of a young bootblack who frequents the Supreme Court building illustrates this lack of educational facilities. He wanted some schooling badly and went to a night school. But after a few weeks he was barred because there were too many other ambitious children ahead of him. He was at the moment waiting his turn to be enrolled.

The great mass of the children of the poor roam the streets eking out a meagre existence by shining shoes, running errands (no white man or woman will carry a bundle on the streets), selling papers or lottery chances, or just plain stealing, and by catching a little sleep, day or night, curling up in their tattered *ruanos* in doorways, entrances to cathedrals, or just anywhere. Beggars are everywhere. Mothers with their babies—some actually rented for the occasion—walk the streets pulling at the heartstrings of strangers in order to collect a little money. This tragic sight is especially prevalent late at night when the theatre and cinema crowds are leaving for their comfortable homes.

Bogotá has long been called the Athens of America. It gained this sobriquet from von Humboldt in the middle of the last century and travelers still call it the intellectual capital of South

America. It is also commonly stated by *gringos* that the best Castilian is spoken here. On the other hand, some critical writers have branded these bouquets as mere generalizations, insisting that this culture is a mere façade developed to cover up the provincialism that of necessity the city originally acquired due to its almost complete isolation until the arrival of the airplane.

Nevertheless, Bogotá has its share of colleges and libraries, cultural societies and public forums. Its newspapers are exceptionally highgrade. And to top it off, Colombia is perhaps the purest democracy in the entire continent although both Chile and Uruguay will question this. This democratic flavor gives the Colombians prestige as well as a measure of pride and dignity.

An excellent illustration of this democratic attitude is the country's great University City. Created only within the past few years, and standing on the outskirts of Bogotá, it is a remarkable tribute to the educational vision of the people. Every building is modernistic in its design, all of them constructed of gleaming white stone. An unusual break with tradition is the democratic philosophy regarding the payment of fees. Tuition is based on one's ability to pay, that is, on the income of the father of the student. Those coming from homes where the income is less than one thousand pesos (about $600 in our currency) pay an annual tuition of thirty pesos, or about twenty dollars; with incomes of from one to two thousand pesos, forty pesos, and thus graduated to an income of twenty thousand pesos and over when the tuition amounts to four hundred pesos.

However, this system of payment fails to work satisfactorily since the wealthy classes rarely send their children to the University. Either they do not go to college at all or they go abroad for their education.

The names of Bolívar, Santander and Nariño are revered throughout Colombia. The country's history was bloody and grim. Heroic tales of its leaders and their ragged soldiers advancing from Venezuela by forced marches through fetid jungles and over the towering snowclad Andes to free the colony from Spanish rule are indeed a proud heritage. The city's plazas, theatres, nightclubs, streets, are named for the intrepid and ambitious warriors mentioned above. Aside from the story of Pizarro's conquest of the Peruvian Incan dynasty, nothing is so exciting as the epic of Colombia's struggle for independence.

On the outskirts of the city of Bogotá, nestled against the towering mountain peaks overlooking the city, is the Quinta de Bolívar, one-time residence of the Great Liberator, Simón Bolívar. Here he lived an idyllic interlude with his mistress, Manuela Sáenz, the legitimate wife of an English physician. The rambling house, modest in its simplicity, but surrounded by luxurious gardens, is maintained as a shrine exactly as it appeared when the master enjoyed the tropical beauty and the passionate affection of his paramour.

Near the Quinta of the Liberator ascends an amazing funicular railway to land the visitor eventually on the very top of one of the two peaks that dominate the city, Monserrate and Guadalupe. The funicula of Monserrate was built by a Swiss engineer, Karl W. Marthaler in 1929 and represents an interesting piece of engineering skill. The seventy-degree angle of this tramway led the writer of a guidebook to state that it takes a little nerve to ascend the escarpment. However, no one takes this warning seriously although some do walk up the tortuous path at the side of the funicular.

Perched on the crest of the mountain, at a perilous angle, is a church, *La Iglesia de Monserrate*, destroyed by earthquake in 1917, but since rebuilt. This modest little church is visited daily by hundreds of the faithful as well as by the curious. And even here, in the vicinity of the church, are many beggars and cripples, some of them selling candles, crucifixes, flowers and baked goods.

The view of Bogotá from this mountain shrine is one never to be forgotten. The mass of magenta roofs, with the sun shining on them, affords a bird's-eye view of majestic beauty. The environs of the city stretch far out on the plain below, and still farther away the endless *sabanas*, or grassy plains, give the impression of distinct isolation.

PENAL SYSTEM

One of the visitors to the first National Prison Congress, held at Cincinnati, Ohio, in 1870, was Señor Enrique Cortes of Colombia. Speaking of the condition of his country's prisons at that time, he said: "The iron rule of Spain left us as a legacy the most tyrannical ideas regarding the management of prisons. A criminal was an outlaw; and hunger, filth, nudity and insult were his lot. Philanthropists have been struggling for a long time past to change this order of things; and the movement, although slow, is gaining ground." [1]

The visitor from Colombia continued by stating that the death penalty had been abolished in his country and that the constitution had placed a limit on the length of time a criminal could remain in prison. He added that the prisons and the jails were overcrowded and "kept in a lamentable state." He said, however, in so far as possible, each inmate had a separate cell in the penitentiaries and that attempts were being made to develop labor in common.

In more recent years, the officials who have been identified with prison reform in Colombia have taken their labors seriously. It would perhaps be unfair to neglect those who preceded the present officials in charge of the prisons. But as these early reformers have passed out of the picture after making their contributions to penology, a discussion of the work of their successors is of special significance.

Since the year 1936, when Dr. Gabriel Turbay was Minister of Justice in Colombia, a realistic and progressive philosophy has permeated the penal program. It was stimulated primarily by Dr. Francisco Bruno, who, at the time, was Director-General

[1] Quoted by Enoch C. Wines, *State of Prisons*, Cambridge, 1880, p. 548.

of Prisons. Dr. Bruno, now a member of the Supreme Court, is Italian in origin and brought to his work much of the old-world tradition regarding criminals and prisons. He is a man of great charm and ability. It was Dr. Bruno who served as my sponsor during my stay in Colombia.

At present Dr. Bruno finds his exacting duties as judge do not permit him to give much thought to prison administration, but he was succeeded by another man of tireless energy and daring vision, Dr. Jorge Pinzón Ferro, the present Director-General of Prisons. Dr. Pinzón Ferro, previous to his appointment, had been warden of the National Penitentiary in Bogotá for eight years where he had inaugurated a number of interesting reforms which shall be discussed later.[2]

In addition to these two students of penology, Dr. Rafael Escallón, Attorney General of Colombia, is also keenly interested in the country's penal program. I left Colombia with an honest respect for the integrity, vision and energy of these three gentlemen who represent the high type of the country's public servants.

When Dr. Bruno began to give serious thought to the status of the country's penal program in 1936, he envisaged two objectives: first, the prevention of recidivism, and second, the improvement of social defenses against the criminal. He attempted to achieve these ends by a threefold program: first, the scientific treatment of the criminal; second, the segregation of the various types of delinquents; and third, the social readaptation of those released from prison.

The first of these objectives was realized by establishing in the prisons a classification program to be operated by a trained staff of psychologists, psychiatrists, directors of industries, recreation leaders, and school teachers; the second was to be attempted by a building program of new establishments together with the remodeling of the existing institutions; the third was contemplated by strengthening the laws dealing with conditional release

[2] The previous Directors-General of Prisons were: Dr. Tuzio Rubiana from 1933–36; Dr. Bruno from 1936–39; and Dr. Hernan Montoya from 1940–42.

(parole) and by creating social agencies to deal especially with children.

Dr. Bruno and his successor, Dr. Pinzón Ferro, have accomplished much that is worthy of praise. But the prison program is handicapped by lack of funds and undoubtedly also by some official inertia. For example, at the Fagua Reformatory for boys, near Bogotá, the new building program as well as the renovation so essential to an efficient school have been woefully neglected through the years. When I visited that institution I saw many half-finished buildings that looked exactly like the pictures of the same institution taken several years ago. This criticism, however, in no way reflects upon the type of work that is done in that reformatory today. A few words regarding the Fagua boys' school appear later in this discussion.

The adult penitentiaries and jails of Colombia are as follows:

The National Penitentiary (*Panóptico*) at Bogotá—for men only—capacity, 400

La Picota, on the outskirts of Bogotá, in process of construction, designed for the *Panóptico* prisoners after December 1944

Medellín—for men only; also a *cárcel* (jail)

Palmíra—near Cali, for men only; in process of construction in the summer of 1944; to be used for prisoners from the institutions at Manizales, Ibagué and Medellín

Ibagué—composed of three sections: detention quarters for those awaiting trial, one for men prisoners, and a section for women

Manizales—a penitentiary for men; also a *cárcel*

Pamplona—a penitentiary for men

Popayán—composed of several *cárceles,* one for women

Cartegena—*cárcel* only

Pasto—*cárcel* only

Barranquilla—*cárcel modelo;* also a district jail

Tunja—for women only
Cúcuta—for women only
Bogotá—two city *cárceles* (described below)
Cali—city *cárcel*
Acacías—agriculture colony
Araracuara—agriculture colony

THE COUNTRY'S PENAL CODE

The penal code under which the country's prison system operates dates from 1936. Prior to that year the code of 1890 was in operation. The new code classifies all infractions of the law into felonies, known as *delitos*, and misdemeanors, or *contravenciones*.

Punishments for adults over eighteen years of age consist of long-term imprisonment, short-term imprisonment, arrest, simple confinement, and fines. If an individual is arrested for a mere infraction of the law, the following disciplinary measures may be invoked at the discretion of the judge: (a) prohibiting him from residing in certain places; (b) a special publication of his sentence posted in a conspicuous place; (c) prohibiting him from participating in certain functions or denying him certain rights; (d) denying him pension or retirement privileges; (e) demanding of him a guarantee of good conduct; (f) banishment (*relegación*) to an agricultural colony; (g) suspending or revoking the rights of citizenship; (h) deporting him if he is an alien.

In a country where probation, as it is known in the United States, is not well developed, these measures may be accepted as its equivalent.

Probation, however, is provided for in the penal code, although it merely consists of the suspension of the execution of the sentence. In this Colombia copies the practice of all Latin American countries. Colombia adopted this measure in 1915 and formally incorporated it into the 1936 penal code. Its provisions are as follows: When a long-term sentence does not exceed three years or a short-term sentence does not exceed two years, the judge may invoke probation, known as *condena condicional,* for a test period (*período de prueba*) of from two to five years if the following requirements can be met: (a) that the probationer shall not commit another offense during the period; (b) that his previous conduct has been above reproach; (c) and that he can convince the judge he will take advantage of the privilege, not be dangerous to society, nor revert to crime.

There is no supervision as we understand it and from information available, few persons are awarded the privilege of *período de prueba.*

Conditional release, Colombia's equivalent of parole, is granted short-term prisoners when they have completed two-thirds of their sentence, providing they can convince the judge that their conduct in prison has been exemplary and that they will no longer be a liability to society.

After the Public Ministry and the disciplinary council in the prison have given their report as to the conduct of a prisoner while serving his sentence, the granting as well as the revocation of the release are in the hands of the judicial authorities.

One interesting modification of conditional release, as practiced in Colombia, was introduced a short time ago by Dr. Bruno. It is known as "preparatory release" and precedes the prisoner's conditional release privilege. Two or three years before this moment arrives he may be permitted to find employment outside the prison, but he must return to the institution at night. If this arrangement proves satisfactory he may, within a few months of his conditional release, both work and live in the community provided he reports once a week to the prison authorities. According to Dr. Bruno this preparatory period stimulates and encourages the prisoner to make his adjustment to society much more easily than if he were thrown on its mercy suddenly. In a country where there is no meaningful supervision for adults released from prison, this seems to be a most sensible plan.

THE COURT SYSTEM

The courts of Colombia are, in many respects, similar to those in all South American countries and, indeed, not too far removed from our own system. In their order, from the lowest to the highest, they are as follows:

Juez Permanente, police judge or magistrate's court; the judge holds office indefinitely until removed for cause.

Juez Municipal, appointed by the Municipal Council, for a term of one year.

Juez de Circuito, appointed by the *Tribunal Superior,* a higher court, for a term of two years.

Juez Superior, one in each of the large cities, also appointed by the *Tribunal Superior* for a term of one year. In Bogotá there are four of these courts.

Tribunal Superior, composed of eight judges appointed by the national Congress and the Supreme Court for a four-year term. There is one of these courts in each department, or state, of Colombia.

Corte Suprema de Justicia, the highest in the country, composed of fifteen judges appointed by the President of the Republic and Congress for a term of five years. The Court is divided into three *Casas* each composed of five justices. Cases come to the judges from the lower court individually, by lot. After studying the case assigned to him, the judge submits his findings to his colleagues within the *Casa* to which he belongs. This is known as the Project of Sentence. Acceptance or rejection of his verdict is decided by majority vote.

THE JAILS OF BOGOTÁ

When a person suspected of a crime is arrested in the city of Bogotá he is taken to the city lockup known as a *calabozo.* It is from the corruption of this Spanish word that we get our slang expression for a jail, calaboose. In many respects the building and the lockup are much like their counterpart in any large city in the United States.

One evening I visited one of these jails in the suburb of Chapinero accompanied by a local attorney, Sr. Vicente Olarte, who speaks English fluently. I was shown the prisoners by one of the guards and, at the time, there were several men, women, and a few children occupying the cells, all of which were bare of any furniture or cots. These persons had been arrested for all types of offenses but most of them were vagrants or sneak thieves with which the city abounds. One child had stolen a penknife. In the morning the individuals in this lockup appear before the *Juez Permanente* for disposition of their cases.

The next stage in the criminal prosecution consists of a trip from the *calabozo* to the *Cárcel de Sumariados,* an unspeakably filthy jail. Here the suspect remains until his case is decided before the *Juez Municipal,* who either discharges him because of lack of evidence or decides to hold him for further hearing or trial.

I visited this *Cárcel de Sumariados,* a rat trap of a building housing at the time about four hundred derelicts. The newspaper *El Tiempo* summed up what our party, consisting of Drs. Bruno and Pinzón Ferro and our interpreter, Señor Andreas Sampér, found in this antiquated jail: (1) Cells originally designed for one, occupied by four inmates; (2) *Patios* (enclosures) damp, filthy (*sucios*), smeared with mud or stained (*embarrados*), in which those detained were thrown like animals with wretched conditions relative to cleanliness, clothing and eating prevailing; (3) Wholesale idleness throughout the entire establishment with the accompanying train of viciousness on the part of the criminals; (4) Obvious injustices everywhere, including the presence of persons who had already languished there for over five years without receiving their court sentences.[3] This *cárcel* is often referred to by the citizens of Bogotá as *El Infierno.*

When the victim's case warrants a trial he is usually removed

[3] In the July 3rd, 1944 issue of *El Tiempo.*

to the *Cárcel distrito de Procesados,* or as it is better known, *Cárcel Modelo.* This is a relatively new structure composed of two separate units, one across the street from the other and connected by both a tunnel and a "Bridge of Sighs." In the basement of one building are housed those arrested for less serious offenses and awaiting trial. The entire unit across the street from this building and the larger of the two, is designed for those detained for the more serious crimes. Here, on the day of my visit, were found approximately four hundred men milling about, idle and sullen. It had rained hard that day, one of Colombia's torrential rains, and the jail yard was filled with mud puddles. This made it necessary for the men to restrict themselves to the rooms and semi-open balconies, so common in Spanish architecture.

Some of the inmates were playing cards but most of them just stood or sat, miserable and dejected. Most of them were Indians and wore dirty *ruanos* and dilapidated felt hats of an ancient model. A few were working, making novelties from cow horn. All the men sleep in dirty and crazy-looking dormitories as there are no cells in this jail.

Here, again, we found many inmates who had been in this jail for as long as two years, awaiting trial. The reason given for this horrible delay is that it is difficult to obtain evidence and investigations are interminable. The warden of the jail deplored this curious characteristic of South American criminal procedure but no one seems to know how it can be remedied. A gesture of official interest in these victims of a neglectful justice is the requirement that a list of those awaiting trial must be submitted to the courts every Saturday morning.

In the upper three floors of the unit set aside for the housing of the misdemeanants may be found those who come from the higher social classes but who, likewise, are detained for court hearing. Class consciousness is a major characteristic of Latin American countries so that it is expected even in a jail. This section is referred to as a *pensionado.* Those of the highest social status occupy apartments on the top floor of the building. They are composed of two or three rooms, one of which is fitted up as a bedroom and the other as a living-room. There are attractive bedspreads and center covers of different colors, book cases, and sanitary toilet facilities. The occupants of these quarters pay for this special privilege. Food is usually brought to them by their families. Another privilege is that of leaving the prison on occasion to visit their families. One of the occupants of this section was a university student who, because of his poverty, had been given a small space in the jail to sleep and study.

There is no Public Defender in Colombia but lawyers are required to take cases of the poor if called upon by the judge. This custom is called *De Oficio*.

THE PANOPTICO

The National Penitentiary of Colombia, located in the heart of the capital city, Bogotá, deserves a few words of special mention since it is not only the oldest and largest prison of the country, but the most picturesque. Its capacity is about four hundred prisoners.

While present plans call for the abandonment of the *Panóptico* as a place of imprisonment for convicted felons, it is still a going concern and probably will be for some time. Its future has been earmarked as a place of detention for those from Bogotá's courts who are awaiting trial. Thus, it will replace the filthy jails now being used for this purpose.

The *Panóptico* is a large structure covering the equivalent of four city blocks or six *hectáreas* (about fifteen acres). It is located on one of the main boulevards within walking distance of the center of the city and only two blocks from the giant bullring stadium. It stands almost majestically on a slight elevation above the street, its approach being in the nature of a profusely flowered esplanade. The façade is of cream-colored stone built in helter-skelter fashion so characteristic of much of South American construction, designed in ripples which present an interesting and architecturally unique feature. There are no windows or breaks of any kind in this front wall except for the iron gate in the center.

Upon entering the prison one's attention is immediately attracted to the floor which is fashioned in small green tiles with white cement between, which presents a pleasing sight. The design of the establishment is more like that of the Eastern Penitentiary at Philadelphia than of Jeremy Bentham's *Panopticon*. There is a large rotunda in the center from which radiate four large and commodious blocks. Three of these are used as cellblocks and the fourth serves as a chapel. The cells are all of outside construction with semicircular barred windows, but with no glass in them. Since the temperature of Bogotá throughout the year ranges between fifty and seventy degrees this lack of glass entails no serious hardship on the inmates. Naturally there is no heat provided in this prison but then, few, if any, of the homes in the city can boast heat except for small portable stoves or fireplaces.

Each cell is occupied by one man only and as there are no automatic locks, each must be locked by the guards individually. The cell floor is of wood laid over stone and the furnishings consist only of a cot and a shelf for the prisoner's toilet articles. Any books he may have are on the floor. There is an electric light but no wash basin or toilet. The prisoner's luggage and clothing are stored until he is released. The cell walls are bare since it is not permitted to have pictures of any kind. No pinup girls in this prison!

In the basement of the *Panóptico* is an inscription which, translated, reads: "The distinguished citizens, Dr. Eustorjio Salgar and Dr. Carlos Sáenz, promoted with courage and tenacity the construction of this Panóptico in the years 1874–1876." I endeavored to locate in the city's libraries or in government reports some data regarding the development of the reform movement which brought this prison into being, but was unable to unearth any information. No one seems to know anything about these two pioneers who "with courage and tenacity" succeeded in erecting this truly remarkable prison. For even today it is unusual since it is maintained on a high level of efficiency and cleanliness, a fact that calls for some mention since no other country in South America possessing such an old prison, except perhaps Argentina in the prison at Buenos Aires, has kept its national institution in such an excellent condition.

Inside the prison and between the cellblocks is a commodious *patio,* or garden, filled with exotic tropical plants and flowers. Even hanging baskets of colorful flowers are a part of this attractive section of the prison. There are benches placed around this garden and on Sunday afternoons the members of the prisoners' families may visit with their menfolk for two hours. Grass grows easily in Bogotá so that the garden is deeply carpeted with a velvety lawn.

I attended a Sunday visiting session and was deeply impressed. Wives and sweethearts of the men, as well as children, sat on the benches provided for visitors. They laughed and talked without any repressions whatsoever. Many had brought lunches and choice tidbits for their men. Soft classical music from the radio played throughout the afternoon. It was with a sense of gratification that I noted there is no screened visiting gallery in this prison, something that we must eliminate entirely from our prisons in time.

Beyond the prison proper, yet within the walls, is a slight hill fenced off from the main part of the institution. In 1930, Dr. Pinzón Ferro, who was warden of the prison at the time, reclaimed this waste area for gardening purposes. Loads of topsoil were carted in and the ground was terraced so efficiently that vegetables and cut flowers may now be grown in abundance. The vegetables are used at the prison and the flowers are sold in the markets of the city. Only prisoners coming from the rural areas are employed in these gardens and no other prisoner is permitted in this section. On the very top of this hilly slope is a huge statue of the Virgin Mary and nearby is a guardhouse in which an official is constantly stationed.

The prisoners wear a blue denim overall suit which seems to fit more tightly than those worn by many prisoners in our own country. There is little regimentation in this prison and the men seem, from their demeanor, to be reasonably contented. This may be attributed to the fact that they are well cared for and provided with employment which is profitable to them. Another remarkable feature of the prison is the complete absence of institutional odor. Cleanliness and orderliness are conspicuous everywhere.

The present director of the *Panóptico* is Dr. Jorge Castro Movilla, a bachelor, who occupies quarters within the prison. He, together with Dr. Bruno and Dr. Pinzón Ferro, showed me about the prison on my first visit. I made two additional trips there and feel that I saw everything. I was impressed with the amount of testing material with which their diagnostic laboratories are equipped. Biological and psychological devices of the latest design and a well-equipped medical laboratory are conspicuous. At the time of my visit, Dr. Pinzón Ferro and his staff were engaged in a study of the relationship between diet, exercise and sexual aberration. He has taken his cue from Pierre Janet's interesting work, *Psychological Medicine.*

The *Instituto de Antropología y Pedagogía Penitenciaria,* the official name for the diagnostic clinic, publishes an excellent journal known as the *Revista Colombiana de Biología Criminal.* It is dedicated, to quote the words of its editors, to the "study of criminal sciences: biology, anthropology, psychology, psychiatry, legal medicine, and endocrinology." The emphasis is always on the biological; the social and economic conditions are never mentioned. Trained personnel in the various fields mentioned above examine each prisoner upon entrance and elaborate individual records are maintained but for what reason it is difficult to determine. As was pointed out in the *Introduction,* the results of these meticulous studies in the diagnostic clinics of the penitentiaries are seldom translated into action in the prison program.

While the educational program merely attempts to cope with illiteracy, it is staffed by outside teachers only. No inmates are employed as is the practice in many of our own prison schools. There is also an outside band leader who comes to the prison one hour each day. There is a canteen which does a thriving business since all prisoners are paid something for their labor and hence have spending money. It was interesting to note that the cigarettes from the States are in much greater demand than local brands although they cost three times as much. Soft drinks are also sold as well as the local newspapers, which are not subject to censorship. This liberality reflects a much more progressive policy than that found in many of our own prisons.

There are no punishment cells in the *Panóptico*. Unruly prisoners or those who have violated the rules are disciplined only by being deprived of privileges and locked in their own cells with regular prison diet. The guards carry clubs only and none are stationed on the walls and, naturally, there are no machine guns or tear gas. There have been no escapes in the past five years.

There is adequate provision for recreation for the inmates. There is a cement outdoor basketball court and a large grass-covered space for football. I was told there are two full-time athletic directors although I saw no recreational activity on any of my visits. Radio music constantly emanates from the master receiver and is amplified throughout the entire institution. Programs consist largely of classical music. There are movies occasionally and a small crude theatre with homemade scenery is provided.

Many of the inmates are serving accumulated sentences of over one hundred years. While there is a system of conditional release, previously described, some men will never leave the institution since they are regarded as professional criminals or too dangerous to be at large.

Two remarkable features of this National Penitentiary which cause even a penologist from the United States to be impressed are the work program and the "solution" to the prison sex problem. Each deserves some attention.

Every man in this institution works full time and is paid for his labor. The minimum pay is the equivalent of ten cents per day. Those unskilled men who cannot work in the shops are employed at cleaning and scrubbing. The work day is theoretically eight hours. There is some idleness, although not so much as in many of our own prisons.

The factories and the number employed in each on the day of my visit to the prison are as follows: a machine shop in which 18 men were employed, where excellent castings, cogs, and the like, are produced and in which shop the workers make from a few dollars to fifty dollars per month; a furniture factory employing 31 inmates where clothes presses, cocktail cabinets, chairs and desks are manufactured from a hard native wood known as *chuhuacá;* a bookbinding shop with four men working where government books and pamphlets are bound; a shoe shop employing 46 men, all machinery of which was made in Germany and of the latest design (shoes are bought by the government and sold or given to schools for poor children); a sewing room with 12 men employed; a rug weaving shop employing 18 men in which rugs are woven in beautiful colors; a coffee sack shop employing 16 men where bags are made from the *fique* plant which grows in Colombia (the shreds are disentangled, wound onto bobbins and woven into coarse bags).

There is a small shop which makes davenports, a small print shop and a slipper factory. At least half the prison population are gainfully employed in these shops. I saw the work sheets for the preceding month and was impressed with the wages paid the men. One prisoner who had only one arm, but who was a skilled machinist, made $31 during that month.

Most of the goods are sold on the open market (*particulares*) by a prison agent who solicits business from contractors or managers of retail stores. The contractor has nothing to do with the productive process but merely specifies what he needs and buys when the product is finished and acceptable. Thus this system approaches our own piece-price method of production of prison goods.

There is, in addition, considerable state-use production. Government documents and forms are printed and the former bound, office furniture is made, shoes produced, etc. There is also a system of accident insurance for the workers. This alone reflects the enlightened status of the prison administration in Colombia.

The purposes of prison labor in Colombia, according to the officials, are to produce goods for sale, to keep the inmates productively employed, to teach trades to those who are unskilled but able to profit from such instruction, and to provide the men with money for their own use and to help support their families.

The second unusual feature of Colombian penal policy, certainly so far as the National *Panóptico* is concerned, is the handling of the sex problem. The present director of prisons, Dr. Pinzón Ferro, is convinced that it is highly important that each of the inmates should have an opportunity of pursuing a normal sex life, if that is at all possible. Accordingly, each "well-behaved" prisoner is permitted to leave the institution twice each month to make a sexual visit. If married he may see his wife in some rooming-house or in his own home, if he comes from the city of Bogotá. This rooming-house has previously been approved by the prison authorities. If the inmate is single he may visit a house of prostitution. In all cases, the man is accompanied by two uniformed armed guards. It is not an unusual sight to see a man, dressed in civilian clothes, walking along the city's streets with a woman, followed closely by two guards.

Intrigued by this unusual and realistic procedure, I asked permission of Dr. Pinzón Ferro to accompany an inmate on a sex visit. He gladly acquiesced so I went to the prison one afternoon, saw a candidate "frisked" before he left the prison, and went along, by taxi, to a house of prostitution. Two guards, of course, accompanied us. It was quite apparent that this prisoner, a bachelor of some forty years of age, who had already served five of his ten-year sentence, had frequented this same house on previous occasions. He was greeted affably by the prostitute of his choice and proceeded to make himself at home. The guards, both of whom wore wooden expressions throughout the entire visit, first searched the harlot's room and then gave a nod of permission for the man and the girl to enter. The door was closed and the couple remained in the room for two hours. The guards stood at attention throughout.

At the end of the interval, one of the officers knocked on the door of the room and in due time the couple emerged. After the prisoner paid for his visit, amounting to five pesos (about three dollars), we hailed a taxi and returned to the prison. Each prisoner, upon returning to the prison after such a visit, is given a prophylaxis.

On another occasion while walking on the streets of Bogotá I chanced upon an old man with a woman, whom I presumed to be his wife. He was buying a lottery ticket and two guards stood nearby. I asked these officers if this was a "sex" visit and they nodded that it was. Here was an old man, a prisoner, given the privilege of walking on the streets of the city with his wife, to window shop or to buy a lottery ticket.

The Catholic Church mildly frowns upon the practice of "sex visits" as a necessary evil. Dr. Pinzón Ferro is the authority for stating that within the past five years over 10,000 such sex visits have been arranged from the *Panóptico* prison alone. This is an average of five per day. I commented on the man hours it would take to operate such a system, "frisking," guarding, and administering prophylaxis, but this did not seem to concern the Director in the least.

There are four methods of coping with the prison sex problem. First, it can be totally ignored as is the case in the prisons of the United States; second, it can be met evasively and clandestinely as it is in several countries of South America and in some county jails in our own country; third, women may be permitted to visit the prison as in Mexican prisons and, to a degree, in Brazil's institutions; and fourth, by permitting the inmates to leave the prison to meet their wives, sweethearts, or prostitutes in some predetermined and approved places. Only Colombia has adopted this last method.

It is obvious that no realistic and honest penologist will accept the first two methods as solutions of this problem. To ignore it simply means the encouragement of homosexual tendencies which are the bane of all prisons in the United States. To grant it as a favor to a privileged few is not only evasive and cowardly but also discriminatory and conducive to graft. Prison administrators of South America are divided between the other two realistic solutions. It is perhaps easier to control and certainly much cheaper, if cost of man power is reckoned, to permit the women to come to the prison. If privacy can be safeguarded by providing visiting rooms in a section of the prison apart from the populations, as for instance, in the penitentiary at Rio de Janeiro, this would be the most sensible method. However, there can be no doubt that an occasional visit away from the prison is a good thing from a therapeutic point of view.

In the United States, the mores surrounding sex would not permit either of the two methods in operation in some Latin American countries such as Mexico, Colombia and Brazil. But it would be possible and quite feasible for carefully selected prisoners, chosen by the classification clinic, to be granted a furlough to go home to visit their families periodically. This would be in line with the present practice of permitting prisoners to work outside the walls. If such a selection could be made without graft or favoritism the sex problem inherent in prison life would be solved or at least some of its more revolting aspects controlled.

New Construction

The Department of Prisons of Colombia had two new prisons under construction during 1944. One, at La Picota, on the outskirts of Bogotá, was scheduled to receive the inmates from the *Panóptico* in December 1944. The old prison is to be used to house those awaiting trial in the city of Bogotá. If this plan is carried out, it will probably mean the abandonment of the old *Cárcel de Sumariados* which is conceded by many to be a disgrace to the city. The other new construction is at Palmíra, not far from Cali in the Department of Valle. I was able to visit La Picota but due to a misunderstanding as to time of appointment, I was not able to see the Palmíra prison when I was in nearby Cali.

La Picota was begun in 1936 but because of many delays it is only now ready for occupancy. Its architecture is similar to many in our own Federal System of prisons, not unlike the Terre Haute, Indiana, penitentiary; that is, it is self-enclosed and follows the "telephone pole" type of architecture. It is a strange coincidence that the site selected for this prison was formerly a farm known locally as La Picota which, in Spanish, means gibbet, or pillory. No one seems to know why it was thus named.

The prison buildings are constructed of brick, pinkish orange in color, which is pleasing to the eye as it is approached. The most conspicuous feature of this institution to the visitor is the profusion of flowers throughout its many *patios,* planted and carefully tended long before any prisoners have been sent there. Landscaping is judiciously planned by persons who obviously manifest a love for flowers. In addition to the wide variety of tropical foliage, the grass plots are likewise beautiful.

Four of the proposed eight cellblocks, with an ultimate capacity of 1,200, were finished at the time of my visit in June 1944. They each consist of three tiers, but unfortunately the cells are of inside construction; hence there are no windows in the cells, thus shutting off sunlight and fresh air except from the corridors. The old fear of communication between prisoners across the corridors prompted the architect and administrators to adopt this outmoded feature. Of course, this could have been obviated by furnishing each cell with a door designed to prevent such communication.

Another defect which will be remedied is the poor location of showers which are much too far from the blocks for convenience.

But aside from these criticisms, La Picota prison is modern in every respect and the country deserves congratulations for its construction.

The cells measure six by eight by nine but are completely bare of plumbing fixtures. Washrooms and toilets are provided at the ends of the cellblocks.

A word regarding the type of toilets in use in Colombian prisons is of interest. They are called *sanitarios* and are merely holes in the floor surrounded by sloped sides fashioned with cement. The hole is really the end of a pipe which drains off the feces. There is no toilet seat, so the user is obliged to squat. A valve overhead is used for flushing. In La Picota institution these *sanitarios* are attractively constructed, which is evidence of the deliberate practice of providing such an unusual type. It was explained to me that this method is not only the natural form of elimination but is actually more sanitary than our own conventional method of using seats. Then, too, most of the prisoners come from a social group in which modern bathing and toilet facilities are unknown.

There are facilities for recreation although at present no special ball fields are laid out as at the *Panóptico*. Special covered sheds with open sides, known as *cobertizos*, are provided for recreation and shelter during the frequent rains.

The dining-room (*comedor*) and the kitchen (*cocina*) are commodious though at the time of my visit they were not yet equipped. There will be no cafeteria since this method of service is entirely unknown in South America. I attempted to explain how a cafeteria works but few of my friends were able to visualize it.

The wing designed to house the medical and hospital services is spacious and particularly well provided with flower gardens scattered throughout, an indication of the vision of those who thought of the comforts of convalescents.

Two special wings, each consisting of 150 cells and containing its own dining-room and kitchen, are designed, one for so-called dangerous criminals and the other for insane prisoners. Dr. Pinzón

Ferro feels that such a provision was a mistake since he disparages the notion that there are dangerous criminals. As for mentally diseased criminals, he feels none should be placed in prison. Such advanced concepts are characteristic of Dr. Pinzón Ferro. He is constantly on the alert for new ideas in penology, being a confirmed pragmatist.

Ample factory space is also provided at La Picota. While there is plenty of ground surrounding the prison it is worthless for farming. This sounds much like our own practice of selecting sites for prisons. Manufacturing, therefore, will be the chief form of prison labor. The excellent machinery now in operation in the *Panóptico* will be dismantled and brought to the new prison when it is ready for occupancy.

Outside the prison but within the enclosure will eventually be erected an administration building. Immediately within, on one side of the entrance, will be the chapel while on the other side a theatre will be constructed. The entire cost of this modern and progressively designed prison will be equivalent to one and a half million dollars in our money.

The new prison being erected at Palmíra near Cali is similar in construction to that of La Picota. It is being built to relieve the pressure of overcrowding in the older prisons at Manizales, Ibagué and Medellín. Its architect is the well-known Cali engineer, Dr. Hernando Bueno Figuereo. I talked with Dr. Bueno when I visited Cali and found him to be an alert, dynamic and progressive person. We made arrangements to visit Palmíra but due to a misunderstanding in time of appointment we were unable to negotiate the visit. This was the only disappointment of such nature that I experienced during my entire trip through South America. On this same projected trip I was also to see the reformatory for boys at Buga which likewise is not far from Cali.

TREATMENT OF JUVENILE DELINQUENTS

There are no juvenile courts in Colombia as we known them in the United States. However, there are children's judges and there exists a Code for Minors. Fourteen is the age below which a child is not responsible for his acts and comes within the provisions of the special tribunal dealing with children. All neglected children, theoretically, are cared for by this code: depraved, homeless, dependent and delinquent. Few, however, of the first three categories are afforded much consideration since in the cities hundreds, if not thousands, of them run the streets at all hours, ragged, hungry and apparently homeless and neglected.

Children are usually picked up by the police and taken before the children's judge. In Bogotá, the detention home is a sad place judged by any decent standards. I visited it one morning and cannot give it a very high rating. It was both dirty and depressing. There were about a dozen girls, ranging in ages from twelve to fifteen, sitting on the stone *patio* doing nothing. They were apathetic, dirty and disheveled. There was a matron in charge who apparently did nothing but watch her miserable charges.

In the open air corridors separating the girls' apartment from that of the boys, chickens were pecking their way about. In the boys' section there were about thirty youngsters ranging in ages from ten to sixteen. They were "exercising" by running at a dog-trot around a circle with an overseer urging them on from time to time. One public official told me later that this is not exercise but punishment. He deplored the sterility of this house of detention for minors. These children were awaiting a hearing before the judge.

The practice is for the children to remain in this establishment only long enough for the police to make their investigations, which is usually about two days. Then the child has a hearing, after which he is sent to the reformatory for a ninety-day period of observation and study. At the end of this period the superintendent of the institution, or his representative, appears before the judge to attend the *Audiencia*. If possible and necessary, the child's parents also appear. The child's case is then disposed of on the basis of evidence and the superintendent's investigation. He is usually returned to the reformatory although he may be turned over to a social worker on probation. The reformatory sentence is indeterminate with two years as a minimum. The child under fourteen is given *libertad vigilada* (probation) and sent to his home or to some other family. The delinquent who reaches his twenty-fifth birthday while at the reformatory goes to the penitentiary to finish out his indeterminate sentence.

The boys' reformatory for the city of Bogotá is located at Fagua, about twenty miles from the city. The buildings are in process of construction but there have been many interminable delays. The place was originally a hacienda. There were some four hundred boys at Fagua on the day of my visit with Dr. Pinzón Ferro.

The plan calls for a set of buildings in the shape of a quadrangle with a recreation field in the center. It will ultimately house one thousand boys ranging from fourteen to twenty-five. The inmates wear blue denim overalls and, since the time of my visit was Saturday afternoon, none was working. The entire population was milling about in a compound used for recreational purposes. There were no organized sports nor were the boys playing.

They were a most curious group and, on the whole, healthy looking. They rushed up *en masse* to see the *gringo* and were quite uninhibited, which was a wholesome sign. The staff at the reformatory seemed responsible and understanding but it was apparent that they were laboring under severe handicaps due primarily to the lag in construction. Sleeping quarters as well as dining facilities left much to be desired. The window glass in all the shops as well as the church was broken and many of the windows were boarded up. The excuse for this condition was that the entire reformatory was in a state of construction.

The boys are occupied at trade training and farming. There is also an academic school. The initial investigation of each boy appeared to be thorough and adequate but, aside from gathering data for the appearance before the judge when the child's case is disposed of, it is doubtful that any further use is made of it.

The girls from Bogotá sentenced by the children's court have more attractive quarters. Some years ago, when Dr. Bruno was Director of Prisons, he renovated an old building within the city which had formerly been used for insane women. The place is known as *El Asserío* and on the day of my visit there were 335 girls, ranging from three to fifteen, being cared for by the nuns who have charge of the school.

El Asserío is an attractive place although it looks more like a convent than a school. It is clean with plenty of sunlight and fresh air, but there is an atmosphere of firm religious repression throughout. The girls sleep in dormitories, go to school together and eat together. There is no privacy, which, as I have pointed out elsewhere, rarely exists in any penal institution in South America.

The girls are taught the conventional skills: sewing, laundry, housework and cooking. In the school they recite in unison which is a marked feature of Catholic education. The incessant droning of forty or fifty children is a marvel to listen to. Each is oblivious of the others. Progressive methods of education are a long way from this school or others like it in all the countries where education is controlled by the Church. Religious observance is strictly adhered to and the chapel dominates this institution as well as others of its type. Most of the girls in *El Asserío* have been abandoned or are there for sexual offenses.

While I had it on the authority of Dr. Bruno that there is no *Patronato* in Colombia, that is, as it is understood throughout South America, there is a private organization known as *El Patronato Bogotano del Niño,* which assumes the function of caring for the children of those incarcerated in jails or prisons. I visited the home maintained by this group. It is called *El Hogar del Niños* and maintains a genuine homelike atmosphere. The personnel in charge are laymen, many of them trained social workers or students of the school of social work in Bogotá. The

Manual Training: Fagua Reformatory
NEAR BOGOTA, COLOMBIA

place is clean and actually cheerful, although in the classes there may be heard the same droning of reading lessons as is heard at *El Asserío.* I especially note the feature of cheerfulness since so few institutions or homes for abandoned children in South America are cheerful.

An investigation is made of the home of each child and if the parent who is not under duress seems inadequate to care for the child, he is taken to *El Hogar,* his maintenance being paid by the government. Colombia, or rather Bogotá, seems to be the only place in South America that segregates in a special home, children whose fathers or mothers are prisoners. The traditional program of education, recreation, dental and medical services is found in this institution also.

The advisability of segregating children of prisoners in specialized asylums or homes is questionable, however worthy the care provided the children may be. The stigma connected with such establishments may outweigh the advantages of a wholesome program. Italy for many years maintained homes for children of prisoners but such leading Italian prison administrators as Giustino de Sanctis and Commander Alessandro Doria opposed specialized institutions. De Sanctis, for example, denounced them at the Seventh International Penitentiary Congress held at Budapest in 1905. He contended that the names of such schools were used for publicity purposes to expedite the raising of funds for their support. Commander Doria insisted that children should be sent to regular schools so that they would escape the stigma of "asylums for the children of prisoners."

Social work training made its debut in Colombia in 1937. Due to the energy and vision of Señorita María A. Carulla of Bogotá who had studied social work in Barcelona, as well as in France and Belgium, a school was opened in the capital under Catholic auspices. It became identified with the *Colegio Mayor de Nuestra Señora del Rosario* and is administered by a technical committee composed of the rector of the church, the dean of the Faculty of Medicine, the president of the Consultative Committee on penitentiaries and penal matters and the director of the National Library.

The curriculum is three years in extent and is quite broad in its offerings. There is a constant demand for its graduates and the quality of training is held in high esteem. The municipality of Bogotá has entrusted to the school the organization and direction of three "Secretariados Sociales" which are small housing developments for workers. The school also operates kindergartens, makes family investigations for child-placing agencies and has charge of social service work in the children's hospital.

A VISIT TO CALI

In sharp contrast to Bogotá is the city of Cali, capital of the Department of Valle. It lies some three hundred miles from the capital just inside the westernmost *cordillera* of the Andean chain. Since it is not too far from the Pacific Coast, it serves as the airplane stop between Balboa and Guayaquil, Ecuador. Here passengers from both north and south leave the Pan American planes and transfer to Avianca ships flying up to Bogotá.

Avianca has a practical monopoly on air travel in Colombia although Pan American owns part of the stock with the government controlling the remainder. It represents the old German line Scadta which, in the years prior to 1939, had pioneered and developed air transportation in the country.

Cali, a city of some 125,000 people, serves as a collection point for the products from that area of Colombia which are to be shipped by sea from the port of Buenaventura. It is a wealthy and a delightful city situated in the heart of a prolific agricultural region. The sun shines here a good portion of the year for it lies in the tropics but at an altitude of 3,200 feet. The traveler from Bogotá, making the trip to Cali by air, senses the change of altitude by the ringing in his ears and the temporary deafness as he alights from the plane.

Cali can best be described by the Spanish word *bonita,* but the

Latin penchant for superlatives would never be satisfied with such a conservative description. Viewing the city of Cali from the window of the Hotel Alférez Real or from the mountain overlooking its well-kept streets the South American would surely be tempted to exclaim, *vista preciosa.* And in this the *gringo* could agree. Cali's lovely homes are distinctive. The city is bisected by the narrow but fleeting Cauca River whose banks have been landscaped and otherwise beautified in excellent taste by the city fathers. In fact, there are many signs that the municipality shows a definite interest in making Cali a show place for travelers. Rubbish boxes tucked against buildings in an ingenious but not too conspicuous fashion are liberally placed throughout the business district; small trees and shrubs are protected by tastefully designed rustic fences, and here and there may be found signs asking citizens to protect the small trees.

Mammoth tropical trees, notably the *ceibas,* attract the attention of the visitor. The public square, ablaze with flowering trees and exotic plants, boasts the statue of Don Joaquín de Cayzedo y Cuero, born in Cali in 1773. The inscription tells the sightseer that this man was the last Alférez Real (royal ensign) and a protagonist of the revolution. Cali is also proud of the fact that Colombia's most famous novelist, Jorge Isaacs, who wrote the classic novel *María,* lived in the Valley. His novel depicts the life of the Cauca valley, the center of which is Cali.

The western *cordillera* rises abruptly at the edge of the city and perched part way up the steep mountain may be seen many palatial residences. On the pinnacle of the crest is a crucifix of imposing dimensions.

The incessant jangling of the taxi drivers' horns is as conspicuous and as annoying as in Bogotá. At least fifty per cent of the "toots" are by actual count unnecessary. The Latin possesses a childlike pleasure in sounding his automobile horn on the slightest pretext, real or fancy. It was reported on excellent authority that an intrepid mayor, back in 1938, took the horns away from the taxis and public cars so that, for one wonderful month, Cali enjoyed calm and peace. But the chauffeurs could not tolerate this encroachment on their freedom so they not only went on strike but had enough influence to oust the mayor.

Cali censors her movies, or at least, suggests what movies are suitable for children. In the cinema advertisements each day appear notices such as *censura para mayores* (for grownups), or *para todos* (for all). Parents may then decide whether to permit their children to attend. However, there is no way of enforcing this censorship.

This beautiful city also has its *pobres* or poor people but they are not so conspicuous as in Bogotá. The stranger is not molested constantly by hawkers or beggars. Lottery tickets are sold, of course, and shoes are shined with orange peel for polishing, but there is a trifle more grace present among the vendors than in Bogotá.

A word about the lottery, found in all Latin American countries, should not be amiss here. It is a national institution. Charitable and other private and public institutions are financed wholly or in part by this means. Each department, or state, has its turn to initiate a lottery. To a native of the States it presents nothing more than confusion. The poor buy tickets as well as the rich. Drudges working for a few pesos a month buy them but, of course, seldom win. But there is always hope. There is no attempt by anyone to build up sales resistance to the lottery among the poor; in fact, those operating them do everything in their power to stimulate the desire for the tickets. Perhaps the most ironical sign I saw was a poster near the Cali city jail depicting a pair of hands and arms chained to a plank on which the following words were printed: *Rompa las cadenas de la miseria* "Break the chains of misery" and buy a lottery ticket of Valle.

While in Cali I visited the city's jail and the institution for delinquent girls and women. The former establishment was filled to capacity although it is a large building, portions of which were formerly occupied by an order of nuns. The warden of the jail, only recently appointed, was laboring under the handicaps always present in such an institution, overcrowding and idleness. He had immediately sensed a shortage of space within the walls and extensive renovations were underway when I was there. He was also attempting to furnish employment to all who wished it, although this consisted mainly of handicraft work. One inmate was putting the finishing touches on a handcart with which he hoped to peddle fruit upon release. It was visiting day and hundreds of women and children were milling about the yard. The jail was much cleaner than those of Bogotá, which speaks well of the management. A surprising feature was a school functioning in this lowliest type of all penal institutions, which is remarkable.

The female institution is publicly supported but administered by the religious order, *El Buen Pastor*. It is a new institution on the outskirts of the city and occupies a pleasant site on a slight rise of ground. The population was composed of sixty misdemeanants and thirty-five felons. There were some young girls of about sixteen mingling with the older inmates. One woman insisted on keeping her baby with her and, although this was the only baby in the population, the woman's whim was good-naturedly tolerated by the nuns, although those having small children are urged to provide for them elsewhere. The nuns are patient and gentle and as jailers are unquestionably performing a noble work for the good of unfortunate women as well as for society.

The newspaper account of my visit to this institution misinterpreted my attitude toward the supervision of female delinquents by religious orders. I was purported to have stated that I preferred this type of treatment to that of laymen as it is carried out in our own country. This is my opportunity to keep the record straight and I must reiterate what I stated in the *Introduction*, and what I really said in Cali: that while the nuns accomplish an excellent piece of therapeutic work within the framework of the Catholic Church, I feel that trained laymen would accomplish a much more satisfying service.[4]

CONCLUDING REMARKS

Shortly after Dr. Francisco Bruno assumed charge of the prisons of Colombia he diagnosed the apathy, if not the ignorance, of the citizens of that country regarding modern penal methods in these words: "The scientific treatment of the criminal is a universal movement which is not appreciated in the cafes, in political circles nor in the clubs."

This, of course, is equally true of all countries. Apathy and ignorance are universal when penal matters are under consideration; in the United States, Great Britain, Turkey, or Colombia. It was Dr. Bruno's task to start from a scientific beginning and gradually develop a system of prisons and penal administration in keeping with the findings of modern thought on penology. He has done an excellent piece of work. And the encouraging note in Colombia is that his ideas are being carried out successfully by an able administrator and man of vision, Dr. Pinzón Ferro. Both of these men are the equal of our best prison administrators. They are well read in world penology and they know what they want for their country.

Lack of financial means, however, is the drawback to a rapid development of the country's penal program. Colombia is not rich and there are so many demands made on the national

[4] The Cali *Realtor*, July 6, 1944, in quoting me, states: "En Estados Unidos no tenemos cárceles para mujeres regentadas por monjas, lo que en mi concepto, es una deficiencia, ya que los resultados obtenidos por estos métodos, basados en la más estricta como encomiable vocación de quienes dedican su vida a esos arduous e ingratos menesteres, son superiores a los que se obtienen valiéndose de los servicios de personas extrañas a las disciplinas que rigen las comunidades. Las monjas son sencillas, pacientes y suaves y como carceleras realizan una nobilísima labor." "In the United States we do not have jails for women managed by nuns which, in my opinion, is a mistake since the results obtained by this method, based on the strictest and most praiseworthy vocation by those who dedicate their lives to a thankless occupation, are superior to those obtained through the services of people unaccustomed to the discipline which the community demands. The nuns are simple, patient and gentle and as jail keepers perform the noblest kind of work."

treasury. But even so, it is my firm conviction that Colombia has the best system of penal administration of the five countries on the West Coast of South America. Yet she cannot be satisfied merely with this distinction. There remains much to be done. Better housing of her prisoners in the backward departmental prisons, an expansion and extension of her system of prison labor, a realistic training program for her guards and, above all, drastic reforms in her treatment of juveniles, are goals that must be met in the future. In addition, a complete renovation of her city jails is long overdue.

IV

Ecuador

THE COUNTRY

THE average traveler to Ecuador sees only the cities of Guayaquil and Quito, which are connected by air as well as by railroad. Few of the smaller towns have the advantages of air communication so most *gringos* leave the country without learning to know the real Ecuador.

Guayaquil, situated on the Guayas River, is the center of the commercial trade of the country and, while not on the ocean, serves as the country's seaport. For many years this enterprising city of 180,000 had an unsavory reputation due to its unsanitary conditions. In recent years, however, most of the hazards to health have been eliminated, although strangers are still warned to be circumspect in their eating and drinking.

The city is subject to earthquakes intermittently so that its buildings, colonial in design, are flimsy and monotonous in architecture, built of bamboo slats covered with mud. The upper stories seem to be all windows with wooden lattice-work for purposes of shade. One interesting feature of the city is its massive arcades of shops. These represent the hub of the city where *guayaquileños* love to promenade, to shop and to gossip.

There is a keen rivalry between the coast population and the mountain *quiteños*, especially in their attempts to gain control of the government. The citizens of Guayaquil are progressive in business matters whereas the patricians of Quito are conservative and leisurely. There is very little contact between the people of these rival cities and seldom do they intermarry.

The railroad from Guayaquil to Quito runs trains every other day and from the capital to the seaport town on alternate days. At every station *en route* Indian women and children swarm about the train selling fruit and trinkets. Perhaps the most majestic scenic wonder of this trip—and there are many—is the appearance, one by one, of the great volcanos of which Ecuadoreans boast: Chimborazo, Altar, Tunguaragua, and in the distance, famous Cotopaxi. One is amazed by the thought that the English physicist, Edward Whymper, scaled most of these forbidding peaks back in the 'eighties. The great Simón Bolívar is also supposed to have climbed Chimborazo which is 21,220 feet high.

Famous and colorful Indian towns, noted for their markets and fairs, are passed one by one, on the way to Quito; Yagauchi, Riobamba, and charming Ambato. Indians hop on and off the train; they love to ride. They are excluded from first-class accommodations, naturally, so they content themselves with the second-class coaches. They swarm the dirty cars which have seats lengthwise and the overflow, which always consists of more of these childlike travelers than the cars can accommodate, climb on top. Here they seem to enjoy themselves thoroughly and, for once, forget their dreary existence.

Quito is finally reached, the train usually running two to three hours behind schedule. The capital city has a population of about 150,000 and stands on the Andean tableland at an elevation of 9,600 feet. It was a thriving metropolis in the times of the Inca. Its history is inextricably associated with the potentate Huayna Capac and his ill-fated son, Atahualpa, who was murdered by Pizarro. While Cuzco in Peru was the seat of the Incan empire, Huayna Capac made Quito his royal capital. Here he married a princess who bore him his favorite son, Atahualpa. Any account of this fabulous Incan race cannot neglect Quito in Ecuador.

This mountain capital is old-world even today. It lives in the sixteenth century. But its charm is proverbial. The most conspicuous feature is its narrow streets, some of them traversed by Toonerville trolleys, swarming with Indians. The motorman takes the fare in Quito. The conductors, most of them mere boys, jump off at street corners, keeping an eagle eye on the passengers who board the trolley. They then blow a whistle, jump on, and the cars are on their way.

Quito has some tall buildings and a few smart shops but most of the places of business are mere holes in the wall along the older narrow streets. They are quite dark and are padlocked at night in crazy fashion. Several oversize locks are clamped on the doors to ward off some stray *ratero*, or sneak thief, who might conceivably carry a string of keys from which one or even two would work, but seldom three, it is hoped.

The main Plaza de Independencia is the hub of the city. Flanking it are the government buildings, the cathedral, the archbishop's residence, and the university, as well as nondescript shops, with the sidewalks overhung by the second storied residences, a characteristic of Spanish architecture.

Many of the city's streets are still paved with cobblestones. Beggars mill through these narrow thoroughfares with imploring looks and pathetic words softly mumbled, calling upon the saints with folded hands in supplication. Typical of their pleas for alms is: *Una limosnita por amor de Dios*, "a little alms for the love of God." The misery and even debauchery of the large masses of these tragic Indian peasants of Quito is depressing. It is not an unusual sight to see Indian girls of ten and twelve caring for their baby brothers and sisters, retrieving lice from their hair and eating them.

In all South America I did not see such heavy loads on the backs of human beings as in Quito. Two by eight planks of ten to fourteen feet, three, four, five of them at a time, being carried on the backs of men—and women—at a dogtrot up the hilly streets, in an altitude of 9,600 feet. It is no excuse to exclaim that these Indians are used to such work. True, they have to get accustomed to such drudgery in order to live. But there can be no prosperity in Ecuador until these human beasts of burden are emancipated from a condition little better than slavery.

The whites of Quito, most of them of Spanish extraction, as well as those of Indian strain who have risen to places of influence, if not wealth, are proud, cultured and brilliant. And their hospitality to strangers, especially if they carry credentials, is unlimited. But their provincialism is even more obvious than that of the residents of Bogotá in Colombia. Both cities have been isolated from most of the world until quite recently.

Convents, monasteries and churches seem to be everywhere. The Catholic Church literally owns half the city. The largest of the cathedrals, San Francisco, is reputed to be the most extensive in the Americas. But Ecuador does not like the Church and carries on a bitter below-the-surface war with it. There is religious freedom in the country, but Protestantism has thus far made little progress since the masses are fanatically devout Catholics. Many of the intellectuals are, however, free thinkers.

A morning spent in visiting the churches of Quito causes the perplexed stranger to wonder when the masses do any work since they all seem to be muttering prayers before the image of some special saint. The churches are marvelous in their interior splendor. Gold and silver laid on with lavish hands, carvings of the most exquisite intricacy, paintings that are world famous for their workmanship, represent the pride of these massive cathedrals. But one must be callous indeed not to think of the grinding poverty and the painful toil of the little people throughout the centuries in order to produce these garish displays of sacerdotal vanity.

There is a definite health hazard in Quito, especially for strangers. There is no wholesome drinking water available so that the visitor must resort to bottled water. The city is temperate to cold throughout the year in spite of the fact that it is called the Equator City; in reality it is about twenty-five miles from that imaginary line. The climate is similar to a wet spring in our own country. Flowers are grown in profusion throughout the year and tropical fruit is sold by hawkers for a pittance.

The good people of Quito fear the night air just as our grandmothers did. Rarely do they venture out after dark and when they do, they cover their noses with handkerchiefs. There is a prevalent superstition that miasma is caused by breathing the foul night air. Girls, especially, do not venture out at night. Aside from the fear of the night air, they are restrained by the old Spanish tradition that girls and women should be safe at home after dark. Aside from the regular theatrical performances, to which the *señoritas* may be properly escorted, Sunday evening movies are the events of the week. This performance starts at six o'clock and is called *Especial.* Everybody attends, but the girls must be chaperoned. There are a few emancipated females in Quito but they are those who have been abroad or have come under the influence of *Norteamericanos.*

There are no playgrounds in Quito, that is, municipally operated recreation centers. Nor has the Catholic Church ever accepted this challenge. In fact, few children of the masses know what play means. They start work almost as soon as they can walk. A project worthy of mention is that supported by the Brethren (*Servicio de los Brethren*) and administered when I was in Quito by the kindly understanding of Mr. Kurtis F. Naylor and his wife. They have actually initiated what might be called the first social settlement in Ecuador. Here the children may come and play under supervision. Abandoned children—and there are many of them—are cared for by these *Norteamericanos.* Mothers come to the settlement and beg those in charge to take their babies and rear them decently since they cannot possibly give them anything that approximates a minimum standard of decency. The work that the Naylors did was unique. Latest reports advise that the country has finally awakened to the importance of this project and is coöperating with the Brethren in expanding the service to the poverty-stricken people of Quito.

PENAL SYSTEM

Ecuador is an excellent example of a country that does not have a penal philosophy or a prison system worthy of the name, but which has fine hopes for the future. In this case, however, she is not alone in South America since several countries, notably Peru, Bolivia and Chile, have some plans which may or may not materialize.

Ecuador differs from Colombia, for example, in that she has little, if anything, that may be called a realistic system of restraint for her criminal population, whereas the country to the north has a policy as well as a reasonably good system of restraint and treatment.

In evaluating Ecuador's penal status, it must be noted that the country has been torn with internal political strife for decades. She is one of those countries that finds it difficult to maintain for long a stable government which can accomplish anything constructive. Even when I visited the country it was experiencing the aftermath of the revolution of May 1944, when the government of Dr. Carlos Arroyo del Río was overthrown by the admirers of Dr. José María Velasco Ibarra. The streets and buildings of Guayaquil were still smeared with crudely painted signs denouncing the overthrown government and calling for *libertad con Velasco.* Others read: *No hubo otro 15 de Noviembre* (Never again another November 15); and *Ni un día más cayó el tirano* (Not another day for the tyrant).

By the time I arrived in Quito the new Velasco government was installed, albeit with some doubt in its stability. The people were jittery and one could scarcely avoid noting considerable tenseness all over the city. I met no public officials except during the routine investigation to which a tourist must submit when he enters and leaves a country.

My stay in Quito was made both profitable and pleasant by Dr. Emilio Uzcátegui, prominent lawyer and social worker, and his many friends. Nowhere throughout the continent was I more graciously received or more hospitably treated than in Quito.

In colonial days while Ecuador was under the domination of Spain, the seat of the *Audiencia* was at Quito. This Tribunal was composed of a president, four lawyers and an attorney general, in addition to a reporter and a notary public. Its judgments were called mandates and were handed down after the attorney general was heard. The mayors of each city and town exercised jurisdiction in all civil and criminal matters, but appeal could be made from their judgments to the *Audiencia*.

The police in those early days were known as the *Institución de la Santa Hermandad*. Jails and prisons were primitive and discriminatory against the poor. Severe penalties, such as whippings, mutilation of organs and other parts of the body, were practiced, together with confiscation of property, exile and the gallows.

The first distinctly indigenous penal code of which Ecuador could boast was promulgated in 1872. It was taken almost literally from the Belgian code of 1870 which, in turn, was inspired by the French code of 1810. Since 1872 there have been many modifications, more in specific detail than in doctrine, such as isolated reforms and re-editions, the principal ones being those of 1889, 1906 and the most fundamental, that of 1938.

It was in 1906 that a significant reform of the code took place since it was in that year that liberalism was introduced to Ecuador and a progressive constitution adopted. The great break with the Church took place at that time and freedom of worship was introduced and guaranteed.

But it is the code of March 1938, introduced during the government of General Alberto Enríquez, that is really practiced in Ecuador today. While it is modern in some respects, since it follows the Positive School of thought to a degree, it still clings fairly close to the classical spirit of the older codes.

The political constitution of the country establishes two standards on which the penal system is supposed to rest. They are, first, the right to be considered innocent until proved guilty, and second, the guarantee of not being compelled to testify against members of one's family or relatives. This second guarantee is interesting since, according to Article 26 of the constitution, it extends to "wife or husband, offspring, ancestors or relatives to the fourth civil grade of consanguinity or to the second grade of affinity." A further provision of the same article forbids any suspect to be held in detention for more than twenty-four hours or be subjected to any form of torture.

The form of offenses follows the traditional pattern: misdemeanors, or *contravenciones*, which come under the jurisdiction of the Chief of Police, and felonies, or *delitos*, under the control of the judiciary, *Tribunales* or *Jurados de Imprenta*, depending on the type of the case. It is possible, in general, to appeal sentences all the way through to the Supreme Court.

Ecuador, through its penal code, provides for two types of imprisonment: penitentiaries, and correctional prisons, or *cárceles*. More serious offenders are sent to the National Penitentiary at Quito under the sentence of *reclusión*. This is divided into two categories, *reclusión mayor* and *reclusión menor*. The former calls for forced labor and cellular confinement with the ordinary sentence from four to eight years and the extraordinary sentence sixteen years; the latter category, that is, *menor*, calls for the ordinary term from three to six years, the extraordinary, twelve. Those subjected to the latter form of sentence may be called upon to do forced labor but this is usually carried on outside the prison in agricultural colonies. In such cases isolation is used only as a punishment for infractions against the administration of the institution and then only for eight days as a maximum. All misdemeanants are sent to the municipal *cárceles*, or correctional prisons.

THE PANOPTICO AT QUITO

On the lower slopes of *Pichincha*, the dormant volcano rising above the city of Quito, was built Ecuador's only penitentiary. It owes its origin to President Gabriel García Moreno who established it in 1874. Its architecture follows the traditional lines of the Eastern Penitentiary at Philadelphia in our own country, except that instead of seven cellblocks as in the Philadelphia institution, there are only five wings radiating from the rotunda or common center. It has been described as wheel-shaped, but that is hardly correct since there are no connecting blocks between the wings.

When I visited this institution, which for many years has been the scene of so much misery and grief, it was a dreary place to behold. Over the central gate, which breaks the monotony of the front wall, are the words: *Penitenciaría Nacional García Moreno —1874.* Of the five cellblocks, two are much longer than the others, making for an unsymmetrical plan. There is no way of knowing whether the original plan has been altered since its construction, but it is quite likely. One architectural defect has caused the authorities considerable trouble. The end of one cellblock is almost flush with the outer wall. Inmates who might succeed in getting to the top of the block can jump off into the hill immediately beyond the wall. Some have escaped in this manner but a few have been killed since the drop is excessively high. The cellblocks are all three tiers high. Within the enclosure are a couple of gloomy buildings utilized for prison production in which there is a little machinery, crude and antiquated.

One of the strangest features of this *Panóptico* is its swimming pool, a fairly large square of cement wedged in between the wings and filled with cold mountain water. Alongside the pool are stone tables used by the inmates for laundering purposes. While I saw no prisoners in swimming, as it was a fairly cold day, there were a few standing about in swimming trunks. I was told that this pool was constructed at the time of the erection of the prison as a punishment device. However, it is doubtful that this is true since it shows more modern lines than the vintage of 1874. No one seems to know why it was built. Apparently some previous government had not only the prisoners' welfare in mind, but also a diabolical idea of using the cold water of the pool for purposes of dousing an occasional recalcitrant prisoner. This, however, is pure conjecture, although it was mentioned as fact by some of Quito's citizens.

The cells on the first floor of the blocks are without cots and

National Penitentiary
BOGOTA, COLOMBIA

National Penitentiary
QUITO, ECUADOR

their iron doors are quite rusty. It is possible that the peculiar atmospheric conditions hasten the rusting of iron in Ecuador. Gloom, apathy and disrepair are the chief characteristics of this prison. Built only two years before the *Panóptico* in the neighboring country of Colombia, at Bogotá, it seems strange that it could not have been kept in equally good repair. In discussing the future of this prison with interested citizens of Quito, I stated that, while it was in a rundown condition, it could be renovated and otherwise modernized without too great expense. In view of the poverty of the country, new prison construction will undoubtedly be postponed for some time to come. The Quito *Panóptico* has another twenty-five or even fifty years' use but renovation is absolutely necessary.[1]

The cellblocks are all quite dark in spite of the outside cell construction. Tables for eating purposes are set up in a few of the blocks but the inmates stand while eating. There is a row of punishment cells in the basement, all of them dark and gloomy, entered by means of heavy, rusty iron doors. When I was there, only one inmate was in this punishment block.

The central rotunda is the only bright spot in the prison. It is decorated with hundreds of little flags of various colors. On top of this rotunda one may view the entire establishment throughout all its nooks and corners. The day I was there, only a month after the most recent revolution, there were some fifty police officers, most of them mere boys, sitting and lying around on the roof of the rotunda. Each had a gun in his hands. This force was a temporary expedient to supplement the thirty-two guards on regular duty. The government was taking no chances with a potential jailbreak. For there were still fifty-five political pris-

[1] In *El Comercio*, Quito, July 13, 1944 the article reporting my speech at the *Centro* states regarding the *Panóptico*, "Con respecto el Penal *García Moreno*, expresó: 'Tiene mucho interés, en cuanto a su formación arquitectónica, por su estilo similar al de las penitenciarías del Este de mi país, en Filadelfia; no estoy de acuerdo con las opiniones oficiales que me han hecho conocer de que este edificio debe ser destruído. Creo que su construcción debe ser renovada y pintadas nuevamente sus decoraciones interiores y exteriores, pudiendo, así, servir para unos 25 o 50 años más.

oners isolated in one of the cellblocks. These men, members of the ousted Arroyo government, could be seen exercising in the yard. They wore civilian clothes and were, I was told, reasonably well treated. They were housed in the "political" wing of the prison, a sort of permanent fixture. In this wing is the famous cell from which a former president, Eloy Alfaro, was dragged through the streets of Quito and, in an orgy never to be forgotten in all of Ecuador, lynched in the Plaza Ejido. This cell contains the death mask of the martyred ex-president and, through a peephole in the door, it is proudly shown to visitors.

The practice of imprisoning members of an overthrown government is not peculiar to Ecuador. It is a Latin American practice which is difficult for *Norteamericanos* to understand. In view of the fact that revolutions occur so frequently that the faction in power one year may be out the next, it would seem only good sense to provide decent segregation camps, perhaps in the country, for political prisoners. It is poor procedure to penalize a political leader for belonging to the opposition party. Yet the Velasco government has been especially brutal in its treatment of ex-president Dr. Arroyo del Río and his followers.

As stated above, the prison shops are quite primitive, being equipped with machinery of ancient design and poor repair. The products made are shoes, *alpargatas* (sandals worn by the poor), clothing, and handmade brushes with bone handles. Some carpentering and a little simple mechanical work are also carried on.

The inmates are paid for the pitiful prison work produced in the *Panóptico*, but in an amount proportionately less than the wages of free workmen. Since the amounts are quite small, even for skilled labor, the prisoners must receive a mere token in payment. Yet from this microscopic amount, one-third is retained for the prisoner's credit upon release; one-third pays for his maintenance in the institution; and the remaining third is claimed by the court to take care of his civil obligation incidental to his crime.

There is a women's department in this men's prison. The females are isolated in quarters of their own, but their needs are ministered to by the male guards only. The day I visited the prison there were fourteen sentenced and sixteen detained women. Their quarters are a trifle cleaner and sunnier than those of the men, but four or five occupy one cell. They were a pathetic group of females, most of them serving time for murder. It seemed incongruous to find those awaiting trial and sentence mingling with those already serving time, but this is the only detention place for women in Quito. The population of the prison was 395 convicts in addition to the fifty-five "politicos."

In 1936 a penal agricultural colony was established by Ecuador in the *Región Oriental* on the banks of the Pastaza River. This camp, for it is no more than a crude labor camp, can accommodate about fifty men who are "carefully selected." The majority of those selected are from rural areas and custody seems to be a minor problem. Since I did not meet anyone officially connected with the prisons, except the director of the *Panóptico,* who apparently had his hands full at the time with his political prisoners, I was unable to learn in just what manner the colony in the eastern jungle was administered. No one seemed to know more than merely that it existed. I understand that the officials are pleased with its results since, aside from the production of agricultural commodities—sugar cane, corn, bananas and yucca, in addition to the breeding of birds and hogs—there have been no escapes. One astute informant did state that the administration of both the penitentiary and the colony requires a complete renovation because of its archaic philosophy and extreme cruelty.

I was invited to speak before the *Centro Ecuatoriano–Norteamericano* as well as on the Radio Quito, and I was quite precise in questioning the advisability of penal colonies separated so far from the seat of administration. The temptation is great in Latin American countries to establish colonies in frontier areas to open up the land and place it under cultivation. While this represents good governmental policy, it is not recognized as good penology to use prisoners for this work unless the colonies can be properly administered and the rights of the prisoners maintained.

There is no classification procedure in Ecuador's prisons, although there is an excellent Institute of Criminology in Quito which is charged by the Ministry of Government to examine all prisoners sentenced to the National Penitentiary. This Institute was founded in 1938 by the noted engineer, Dr. Federico Páez, and is staffed by well-trained personnel consisting of a director, an anthropologist, a psychiatrist, a statistician, a chief of identification, a "medical lawyer" and a lawyer secretary. The first director of *El Instituto de Criminología* was Dr. Julio Endara, prominent psychiatrist of Quito who is well known in the United States in psychiatric circles. The present director, who is also a prominent psychiatrist, is Dr. José Justiniano Espinosa. The other members of the *Instituto* are: Drs. José Cruz Cueva, anthropologist; Alfonso Aviles Robalino, psychiatrist; Gonzalo Serrano Canadas, director of legal medicine; and Manuel J. Sastro, secretary lawyer.

The theoretical functions of this splendid organization and its ability to operate in a practical manner are wide apart, judging from the confusion of the country's penal philosophy as well as the backward state of its National Penitentiary. Examinations are given for every prisoner and this is attested to by the excellent files maintained by the staff of the *Instituto*. But implementing prison administration is another thing. It is this inability to coördinate theory and practice that marks the weakness of much of South American penology. But it is no more than fair to set down here the stated results of the Quito *Instituto*.

During its existence it has furthered the development of the following aims which have revitalized criminological and penal practices in that country:

1. Facilities were set up for the individual study of every offender prior to the imposition of sentence by the court.
2. Scientific methods were sponsored and instituted for the purposes of classification and treatment of prison inmates.

3. Agencies were set up for the registration and identification of delinquents.
4. Psychiatric control of delinquency in systematic and continuous form was instituted through coöperation of courts, prison, and justice officials.
5. General minimum standards were set up for penal and reformatory institutions.
6. Reports were made on individual cases which were submitted for commutation, remission of sentence, pardons, parole or granting of conditional liberty.
7. Researches into the study of crime and its determinant causes from the etiological, clinical and therapeutic aspects, were sponsored.
8. Standards were set for treatment, moral and intellectual education, and for work programs in prisons.
9. Suitable standards were built up for the building specifications of prisons and penal institutions.
10. Periodic reports were issued on penal matters.
11. Boards of visitors were set up to inspect institutions and qualifications for prison personnel were recommended.
12. Special courses, both theoretical and practical, were organized in Anthropology, Criminology, Psychology, Medical Law, and Special Education, to aid in the training of legal medical specialists.
13. Practical direction and supervision of the work of graduates in Penal Law and Forensic Psychiatry were provided as well as their placement in suitable positions.

One of the chief problems of this organization is that of tenure. No one on the staff has the slightest knowledge of when he may suddenly be replaced by another who may, at the moment, be more closely identified with the government in power. Politics plays a most important role in the country. However, there is no evidence that inferior men or untrained personnel are ever appointed.

In addition to the *Instituto*, there is in operation an Institute of Legal Medicine connected with the Central University. The general purpose of the Institute is to further the advancement and progress of the study of Legal Medicine and its related disciplines. Specifically, the Institute seeks to accomplish the following aims:

1. The dissemination of knowledge in the field of legal medicine.
2. The improvement of its teaching in the universities.
3. Scientific investigation and research to furnish the basis for the greater understanding and solution of medico-legal problems in Ecuador.
4. Technical cooperation with all agencies and officials engaged in the administration of justice.
5. Technical reform of the laws dealing with medico-legal problems.

Some specific activities are the rendering of expert opinions on particular cases referred to it by the courts, the establishment of specialized courses in various aspects of legal medicine, publication of scientific works in criminology, and the recommendation of desirable changes in the penal laws which would take into account the important findings of medicine and psychiatry.

CONDITIONAL RELEASE

Parole, as it is understood in the United States, does not exist in Ecuador. The penal code provides for conditional release in a perfunctory manner. Only those prisoners who are sentenced to correctional prison (not to the *Panóptico* with the sentence of *reclusión*) may be conditionally released after they have served three-fourths of their sentences provided they do not have more than three years to serve of their original sentence. Requirements for such a release consist of: residence in a determined place, some sort of work or career upon release, and the assurance that all civil obligations, including costs, have been satisfied.

Under the administration of Federico Páez in 1937, there was set up a system of aftercare for prisoners known as the *Patronato Post Carcelario y Post Asilados.* It is the theoretical responsibility of this organization to secure work for ex-prisoners, to provide educational opportunities, and to encourage crime preventive measures and practices. But up to date, this service, following the usual pattern in most of the South American countries, fails to function.

One unique phase of the Ecuadorean code calls for special vigilance. This simply means that the judge may prohibit the offender from appearing in certain places even after he has completed his sentence. Those originally sentenced to *reclusión mayor,* or strict imprisonment, can be subjected to the supervision of the police for from five to ten years and, if they commit further crimes and serve additional time, vigilance by the police for the remainder of their lives.

PROBATION

If probation, or anything faintly resembling it, exists in Ecuador, I could not find it. It does exist in the penal code now in operation, that is, *condena condicional* or suspension of the execution of the sentence. Of course no supervision would be provided if anyone were accorded the favor of a suspended sentence. The code apparently states that this suspended sentence can be invoked for first offenders alone and then only in cases of infractions, punishment for which does not exceed six months or a fine. However, there may be a concurrence of infractions. If the individual receiving this grace does not commit new crimes within the "probationary" period and for two years thereafter, the punishment is as if it had not been pronounced.

CÁRCEL IN QUITO AND THE COURTS

The court system of Ecuador follows the traditional pattern and includes, in order of ascendancy: the police court (*Comisario de barrio*); the *Intendence,* for misdemeanors; the *Juez del Crímenes,* for felonies; fifteen *Tribunales del Crímenes,* one in each provincial capital; and the *Corte Suprema,* with its seat at Quito.

The *cárcel* at Quito follows the traditional architecture of most South American jails. There is the central *patio* surrounded by two-storied buildings in which are shops, dormitories, administration offices and kitchen. The interior of the structure was unusually clean for such an institution. I should say it was cleaner than any other capital city jail I visited on the West Coast of South America. This is all the more remarkable since the penitentiary is in such a very bad condition. Many of the inmates were working either on trinkets or hats and shoes. Panama hats are made here and much of this work is exceptionally well done. Food is prepared in a primitive kitchen equipped with charcoal stoves and blackened kettles in which the food is cooked. The men sit down at their meals, a practice not found in the National Penitentiary. The inmates were a bedraggled group, similar to all such motley collections of humanity, but they seemed busier and less apathetic than in most municipal jails I visited. Cleanliness is at least possible of attainment in jails and prisons and the administration of this establishment can be congratulated on its efforts to realize this one phase of adequate treatment.

THE CARE OF CHILDREN

The courts that serve juveniles in Ecuador, as well as the institutions for the care of neglected and delinquent children, are under the direction of *El Ministro de Previsión Social.* There are two institutions for children in Quito, one for girls and the other, in the country, for boys. Neither is connected in any way with the Catholic Church, a most unusual situation.

The Code for Minors, adopted in 1938, provides for a special form of treatment for children under eighteen years of age. They cannot be detained longer than twenty-four hours without being turned over by the police to the *Tribunales de Menores,* which divest themselves of their legal aspect and make a psycho-pedagogical, anthropological and biological examination, after which disposition follows.

These *Tribunales* are in operation in each provincial capital and are headed by an educator, a physician and a lawyer who examine each case of delinquency on the basis of information given them by the *Policlínicos.* The examinations are made in what is called a House of Observation. Social workers also make an analysis of home conditions and the general economic situation. These visitors are also charged with the duty of supervising delinquent minors even in cases where they are reinstated in their homes.

Like so many provisions so proudly and courageously established in Ecuador in recent years, this special work for delinquents lags far behind the ideals set down on paper. A few work schools and child shelters have been provided but nothing thus far established by the government can compare with the work of the Brethren which was described earlier. Fortunately, the government has taken cognizance of this special type of work, so there is hope that it will not only be given support but expanded.

I visited two schools in Quito which might be called reformatories for delinquent children. Both are doing a good job although there is much still to be desired.

The girls' school is in a ramshackle building constructed along traditional lines many years ago. The personnel, naturally, are laymen and they are reasonably capable people. There is the conventional dormitory and the girls are occupied with the usual tasks: sewing, laundering, school, etc. There is a large *patio* or yard, in the rear in this case, where the girls may exercise. Also a large garden is maintained. But the girls stand up at their meals, at long tables. The inmates seem to be highly regimented.

Delinquent boys of Quito are housed in much more commodious quarters. The institution is located about fifteen miles from the city and consists of a quadrangular enclosure surrounded by a number of buildings. There are dormitories and workshops together with a school. About one hundred and fifty boys were present the day I visited the establishment. Many were lounging about in the enclosure, doing nothing, although there are excellent facilities for mass play. In the shops were several boys working at weaving and making shoes. The very small boys were employed at sorting out the wool from huge piles, a very monotonous task, which offers no incentives or satisfaction. They are given this menial task merely because they are young.

The director of the school was not present but his assistant showed us around. A great deal of statistical matter is prepared, the meaning of most of which was problematical. The statistician presented several charts in a wide variety of colors representing beautiful handiwork, and for this I complimented him. Here, again, the visitor sees meticulous paper work but fails to observe a program in action.

As stated earlier, Ecuador has dispensed with the influence of the Church in the treatment of delinquent children, an extraordinary achievement since in few places throughout the entire continent has this been accomplished. But the programs in operation in both the girls' school and the boys' reformatory leave much to be desired. There is little regimentation in the boys' institution; certainly less than in the girls' school in the city.

There is a social work training course in Quito known as the *Escuela de Visitadoras Sociales.* Opened in 1938, it is under the direction of *El Ministro de Previsíon Social.* While this school has financial difficulties, it is the only school of its kind in which the students enrolled are paid a small stipend. This amounts to the equivalent of three dollars a month and it is allocated to insure regular attendance and serious attention to study. Students entering this school must possess either a bachelor's degree or a normal diploma and must be at least eighteen years of age. The curriculum is two years in length.

Recent word comes that this school has been disbanded and that a new one, more in keeping with modern practices, has been organized.

CONCLUDING REMARKS

When a country possesses two liabilities of such magnitude as poverty and political unrest, little hope for a promising economic and social future can be predicted. Ecuador is certainly thus handicapped in spite of her latent resources and charming people. The post-war era may usher in a more prosperous period for the country, but it will take a long time before much attention can be paid to problems dealing with social melioration. Sanitation, roads, agriculture and manufacturing have a much higher priority than universal education, housing and crime prevention; but, of course, any improvement in Ecuador's economic life will have a favorable effect on all the people eventually.

In the meantime, however, there are some phases of a rational penal program that need not wait for more prosperous times. The government can launch forth on a program of cleaning up the National Penitentiary in Quito. This can be done, first, by appointing officials who understand something of modern penology and, second, by renovating the institution physically. Another important reform would be to capitalize on the excellent diagnostic clinic which is already in operation and supported by government funds. The work of this group can be clothed with much more dignity than it now enjoys and its findings translated into action in the *Panóptico*. A centralized commission of correction which would exercise control over all convicted criminals would accomplish much, providing trained penologists were appointed. The country's concepts of conditional release and probation should be overhauled and placed on a more enlightened basis.

In time Ecuador should establish a special institution for convicted females separated completely from those detained pending trial. If special provision were made for females more space would be available in the penitentiary. A program of agricultural colonies should also be recommended. Such colonies, however, should not be too far from the capital, as is the case today with the one in operation in the *Oriente*. The country can be commended for abolishing the deportation of criminals to the Galápagos Islands in the Pacific Ocean where for years they were sent.[2]

There are many well-informed persons in Ecuador who would be of much value to the country in developing a progressive prison program. All that is needed is the will to act on the part of the president and congress. If this can be realized, Ecuador may make a beginning in the achievement of a penal program that will compare favorably with her sister republics.

[2] Just as this book was going to press, word was received by the author that the Ecuadorian Government, by decree of May 23, 1946, had established a prison colony in Galápagos Islands. It is to be known as *Colonia Penal "Isabela."* Its purpose is "rehabilitation of young offenders," and is to be in charge of the Civil National Guard, according to reports.

V

Peru

THE COUNTRY

THE tropical verdure of Ecuador with its giant expanses of hardwood jungles presents a marked contrast to Peru which is, in the main, a bleak and barren land. The country is long and narrow consisting of three portions, all totally different. The western coastline is desert throughout its entire length, an area where rain rarely falls. What little land is cultivated must be irrigated by means of mountain trickles of melting snow. The central portion consists of the tremendous *cordilleras* in which are hidden away a few wide flat plateaus. The easternmost section of the country slopes off to the Amazon jungles.

There is a great deal of mystery associated with Peru. It is easy to visit the country and come away with the impression that it represents a lost civilization, in spite of the simulation of modernity found in its capital city of Lima. For even here, in this city built by Pizarro, now boasting of a population of half a million people, much of the culture, the life, the architecture, and the habits of the people, is distinctly Spanish colonial. The historian, Prescott, wrote of Lima: "Amidst the woe and destruction which Pizarro and his followers brought on the devoted land of the Incas, Lima, the beautiful City of Kings, survives as the most glorious work of his creation, the fairest gem on the shores of the Pacific." [1] Today there are modern buildings but they all seem out of place in this distinctly Spanish city.

This capital city, consisting of proud descendants of the Spanish *conquistadores,* but with more than a liberal sprinkling of equally proud and capable progeny of the Incas, held a dominant place in the New World long before any of our cities

[1] *History of the Conquest of Peru* (Philadelphia: Lippincott, 1874), II, 35–36.

of the United States. It fairly exudes culture and aristocracy as well as the mellowness of age. Perhaps typical of Lima is the historically famous Plaza de Armas, the locale of so many famous events. On the far side of the ancient square stands the ugly but massive cathedral built by Pizarro. Indeed, his mummy is still on display and for a pittance the sexton will light a candle and show the tourist the shriveled remains reposing under glass. Beside the cathedral is the archbishop's ornate residence with its overhanging balconies, never showing a sign of life. On still another side of the plaza is the Government Palace standing on the site of Pizarro's residence. It was here that the conqueror of the Incas was murdered by his greedy followers.

Thornton Wilder in his *Bridge of San Luis Rey* stimulated a real interest in Peru. Since his book was made into a movie we in the United States became familiar with the Bridge (which, according to some *limeños*, never existed), the fabulous *Perricholi* (for whom Viceroy Armat erected a palace, even though in a fit of anger he once called her *perra chola*, or half-breed dog), and San Marcos University, the oldest university in this hemisphere. This famous institution is a disappointment to the *gringo* since he expects to see some venerable gothic ivy-covered buildings. Instead he finds merely a square of adobe thrown around several *patios*. It was founded in 1551.

Lima's suburbs are the most beautiful in all South American capitals. Miraflores, Barranco, Chorrillos and Magdalena are resplendent with the homes of the rich. Flowers of exotic beauty are everywhere. The magnificent bougainvillaea with its riotous colors, one tree of deep purple, another of dark orange, presents a beautiful sight.

But it is Cuzco, the seat of Incan civilization, that convinces the visitor of the romance and drama, as well as the tragedy of Peru. Perched high in the Andes it is still somewhat inaccessible and off the beaten path of travel. A few years ago, however, there was an air route from Lima but that has been abandoned. The tourist from the States now usually goes by plane from Lima to

Arequipa and from that point takes the British-operated train to the ancient city of the Incas.

In Arequipa tourists usually stay at Quinta Bates, a charming hostelry operated by a friendly woman from Rensselaer, New York, known affectionately at Tía Bates. The great and near great have been stopping with *Tía* for over forty years. Her establishment at the end of Calle Jerusalén is an isolated and restful spot where one is sure to find warm hospitality and excellent cuisine. On the sunroof of Quinta Bates the guests assemble for their typical South American breakfast, consisting of rolls, marmalade and coffee, and enjoy the superb view. This consists of snow-capped, majestic *El Misti* towering to 19,200 feet. Known as *El Volcán de Arequipa,* it has a perfect cone like Cotapaxi of Ecuador. It rests between two mountain peaks, *Chachani,* 20,000 feet, and *Pichu-Pichu,* 18,000 feet. The city of Arequipa itself has an altitude of 7,600 feet.

The railroad from Arequipa to Cuzco passes through many Indian villages. At each station hundreds of excited natives mill about attempting to sell their wares to the passengers. These consist of food, knitted goods, fur pieces, pottery and souvenirs. One of the villages is Pucará. Here only can the *gringo* purchase the famous ceremonial bulls and horses, deftly fashioned from clay, used in celebrating the harvest.

After leaving Pucará, the elevation gradually reaches 14,000 feet. The train crosses a natural divide from which, on one side, water flows down toward Lake Titicaca and, on the other, to the Amazon and thus to the Atlantic Ocean. The highest point of the trip is at La Raya. Throughout this country large flocks of sheep, llamas and alpacas may be seen from the car window, attended either by the women in their unique dresses and pancake hats, or by small urchins who spend their entire youth in this monotonous but not too arduous occupation.

Cuzco is reached after dark. The train is swamped by Indian men and boys, shoving each other to "smash the baggage" of the few passengers from the first-class coach. Such travelers can be counted on not to carry their own baggage however light. For years the British have operated Hotel Ferrocarril (Railroad Hotel) in the station building and practically enjoyed a monopoly in furnishing quarters to visitors. In recent years, however, the Peruvian government has been in the process of building modern hostelries at various resort towns throughout the country under the management of *Compañía Hotelera del Peru.* In Cuzco, there is now the Hotel Turista, an ornate structure built of white gleaming stone, situated on one of the many plazas of the city.

Most of the inhabitants of this quaint and lonely city, with an altitude of 11,400 feet, are Indians, although there are many old families of pure Spanish descent still lingering on. English is spoken by a few of the residents, especially by some of the students of the University. One of these, Señor Gabriel Escobar, served as my guide to the many ruins that surround the city. The most famous of these are the Sacsaihuamán fortress, overlooking the city, the outlying forts of Kenko and Pucára and the Incan "tavern," Tambomachay (Inn of the Snake).

Cuzco, City of the Sun, is full of interesting remains of the Incas. The narrow streets, for instance, written about in all books of travel, measure up to their description. Tremendous stones, piled high on one another so tightly that, to quote the classic aphorism, it is impossible "to introduce even the blade of a knife between them," form the walls of these streets. Perched on top are whitewashed adobe shacks in which modern *cuzqueños* live out their sleepy existences. The main plaza, flanked on one side by the University and the cathedral, and on another by the ornate La Compañía, the church of the Jesuits, is typical of all small cities of Peru. In the center of a smaller plaza nearby is a figure of an Indian. But it is no representation of an Incan brave but rather, for some mysterious reason, a memorial to the North American redskin armed with bow and arrow, a weapon never known to the Andean highlands.

One of the most interesting sights within the city is the Temple of the Sun, now occupied by the Dominican order. The lower portion of this work of exquisite mechanical art was definitely constructed by the Incan craftsmen. Its circular stonework is a unique wonder admired by all who visit the shrine.

The derivation of the word Cuzco is still considered a mystery. The early Spanish writers referred to it as Cozco or Couzcou, but there are those who claim the word comes from *ccosco,* apparently a Quichua term meaning gold. Certainly gold was there in vast quantities when Pizarro conquered the city and its surrounding hinterland. But there is little of the regal splendor left. The natives give scant evidence of ever belonging to a powerful, proud and efficient race. They are no different from those found elsewhere throughout South America—stolid, apathetic, hardworking drudges.

Seventy miles to the north of Cuzco is the famous ruin of Machu Pichu, an Indian agricultural village discovered by Professor Hiram Bingham in 1912. Perched high up on the mountain fastnesses of the Urubamba valley, these amazing ruins probably represent the most perfect remains of that lost civilization. An entire village, capable of housing five hundred people, and made entirely of massive stones, may be seen in perfect order. After it was abandoned by its population, probably due to the failure of the precarious water supply, the village was overrun by jungle growth. It lay dormant for four hundred years unknown to the Spaniards and their successors until Dr. Bingham learned of its possible existence from native Indians and determined to bring it to light.

Machu Pichu was a mountain fortress, a hideout for a small tribe of people who needed protection from enemies. Up the steep mountain trails, accessible today only on the backs of mules, these frightened people fled and, with herculean toil, the like of which no race of people under the sun can match, they carved a home. They eked out their existence by terracing the steep slopes and growing whatever a niggardly nature would permit. They watered these pathetic truck gardens by means of aqueducts of stone through which they coaxed the scant supply of mountain water.

High on top of two surrounding crags—Huayna Pichu and Machu Pichu—they erected watch towers which commanded the valleys below. Stone walls, moats, crow's-nests, palisades—all were created for protection, which apparently they never needed. The uniqueness of this stupendous ruin is that it is practically intact except where vandals, fortunately to only a slight degree, have attempted to disfigure and steal. It is surprising to anyone who visits this majestic relic of an amazing civilization that its wonders are so little known to North Americans. But, even Peruvians know little of it and few have ever made a pilgrimage to it.

There is a small *autocarril* that runs from Cuzco to the valley below the ruins. Small groups of seven may charter a car that runs on rails and visit the ruins, returning the same day. A small hotel has recently been built nearby by the government but due to the remoteness of the ruins it is deserted much of the time except for the keeper. Reservations for food and lodging must be contracted beforehand, which indicates that comparatively few visit this survival of Incan or, as many think, pre-Incan civilization.

HISTORICAL NOTE ON PENOLOGY

Peru is well endowed with men of penal vision but few of them are in the government. They know what they want and they set down their principles in books, pamphlets and articles but up to the present time their influence has been slight. I met some of these distinguished scholars and was greatly impressed by their vision and knowledge of crime causation and modern principles of penal treatment. Eventually they will have their way and then Peru can show the world a modern system of penology which at present it certainly does not have. Plans for the future will be discussed later in this chapter.

In his *History of Penal Law in Peru,* Dr. Julio Altmann Smythe states that it is possible to see in the modern penal philosophy of the country the influences of three distinct periods: (1) Ancient, or Incan; (2) Spanish colonial; and (3) The period since Independence.[2]

However, he points out that the modern code shows little of the first pre-historic epoch. And since Peru has borrowed so widely from other countries, it is not yet possible to say that it has a code reflecting its own peculiar culture.

Following Independence in 1822 a number of constitutions were enacted but it was not until 1836, during the period in which Peru and Bolivia were confederated under the Supreme Protector, Andrés Santa Cruz, that it realized its first penal code. This code remained in effect until 1863 when a new one patterned along French lines was promulgated. In 1920 and in 1924, more modern codes were adopted. In 1928 a project, correcting many of the defects of the code of 1924, was executed by Dr. Angel Gustavo Cornejo, one of Lima's best-known professors of penal law. However, this was not adopted. In 1940 a new code of penal procedure, which is considered quite modern and up to date, was put into operation.

During colonial days the Spanish conquerors established *cárceles* in each province of the country. Discrimination against the native Indians characterized this period; few white people ever went to jail. This era is replete with injustice and inhumanity and need not be described here.

The administration of the prisons as well as the penal philosophy of Peru since the days of Independence may be divided into four periods: (1) From the establishment of independence in 1822 to the period of President Ramón Castilla whose term of office extended from 1845 to 1851; (2) From the reform era under Castilla, in which Señor Mariano Felipe Paz Soldán established the country's first penal system, to 1929, the year in which the office of Inspector of Prisons was created; (3) The period in which Drs. Augusto Llontop and Bernardino León y León were

[2] *Reseña Histórica de la Evolución del Derecho Penal*, Lima, 1944, p. 167.

Directors-General of Prisons, that is, until 1933; and (4) From the resignation of Dr. León y León to the present, which finds the prisons under the direction of Dr. Gabriel Seminario Helguero.

The first edict of the new country regarding prisoners was drawn up March 23, 1822, at the Palace Torre Tagle in Lima. Its "humane" character may be seen by its directive calling for two hours' exercise for prisoners, one in the morning and one in the afternoon. The remainder of the time they were kept in their cells.

In 1836 the Protector, Santa Cruz, stated in an edict that prisoners should be treated mildly and that the Indians should not be obliged to pay for their keep while in prison. In 1850 an edict, inspired by the reforms of one Señor D. Miguel Medina in the prison at Cuzco, called for work from all the prisoners except those who were sick, too old, or too young, the finished goods to be produced for private customers. The prisoners were to receive wages, a portion of which was to be impounded for their maintenance and a part to be withheld until release.

This edict further provided for the separation of prisoners on the basis of the length of their sentences; the separation of the sexes; privileges for well-behaved prisoners, one of which was the removal to a larger cell, another, permission to drink some non-alcoholic beverage once a week; floggings for prisoners who caused trouble; and a crude form of conditional release for those whose conduct was above reproach.

The prisons of the country during this early period were: the *Presidio de Casas-Matas,* a sort of fortress consisting of two large rooms, built originally for storing purposes and utterly unsuited for a prison, due to its dampness; the Isle of San Lorenzo in the harbor of Callao; the prison at Cuzco; the *cárcel* at Aquira, a sort of natural granite cave; the *cárcel* at Lima, known as the prison of Santo Oficio and often referred to as *el infiernillo,* called by Paz Soldán "a sepulchre of living beings"; and the *cárcel* at Cajamarca, in which province the great reformer, Paz Soldán, was judge.

In 1853 the government of Castilla instructed Paz Soldán to go to North America to study the prisons in operation there.[3] He returned to Lima and offered his findings to President Castilla who immediately gave orders for the construction of a penitentiary in the city of Lima. On January 13, 1856 the Gran Mariscal Castilla laid the first stone of this National Penitentiary, but it was not until July 23, 1862 that it was opened. The occasion was one of great solemnity. One month later, the first prisoners were admitted with Paz Soldán serving as its first director. It was built along the lines of the Philadelphia prison with a central rotunda from which four blocks extend, each consisting of three tiers. The new director established a régime of classification similar to that put in operation in the jail at Cuzco in 1850 by Sr. Medina, mentioned above. Children and women were separated in blocks designed for that purpose. There was also developed a system of punishments and rewards as well as work opportunities. The women were not taken from the prison until 1892 when the fervent pleas of Sister Ernelinda Carrera convinced the government that there should be a special institution for females.

In 1867 Paz Soldán resigned from his post to accept another position in the government. He was succeeded by Dr. Thomas Lama who, to quote from our own Dr. Enoch Wines, was a man of astute vision. At that early date, 1867, Lama was convinced that criminals were such from faulty education rather than from an inborn predisposition, as the Lombrosians believed. Both Lama and his successor, Sr. Aurelio Villarán, believed that work training presented the most encouraging method of reformation. Consequently they developed a prison labor program by which prisoners were permitted to learn trades and receive wages. Schools were also introduced during Lama's régime.

But about this time the prison fell on evil ways. Wines states that "order and discipline fell into confusion . . . communication was possible between the prison yards" and, as these were

[3] Paz Soldán visited Philadelphia and in November 1854 was made a corresponding member of the Pennsylvania Prison Society.

the days of the separate system, such conditions could not be tolerated.

In 1902 an order from the then Minister of Justice, Lizardo Alzamora, permitting the reward of *coca,* an herb from which cocaine is derived, for well-behaved prisoners, and providing the lash for incorrigibles, was considered in its two provisions a reactionary step in penal treatment. From that time forward, for many years, nothing commendable could be adduced for Peru's prisons. In 1925, the Spanish criminal lawyer who is South America's most penetrating penal critic could say that "in no jail or prison in Peru can a sentence terminate in the reformation of the criminal." It was this same critic, Dr. Luis Jiménez de Asúa, until recently professor of penal law at the University of La Plata in Argentina, who castigated Peru's penal apathy in the following words: "What is the use of a good penal code as you have in Peru if all the penitentiaries that exist in Lima are deplorable? The penal code exists to be applied and the science of penitentiary treatment makes this possible." [4]

Finally, in 1927, there was created the position of Inspector of Prisons. The new post was first occupied by Dr. Augusto Llontop who brought to his task an intelligent understanding of penal philosophy. Inspired by the organization of a School for Wardens and Guards in Argentina under the direction of Dr. Eusebio Gómez, Dr. Llontop set up a similar school for guards in Peru's prisons. In this same year, 1927, there was also developed a classification section for the prison and, in addition, a Bulletin of Criminology was published.

With these reforms serving as a backdrop, Dr. Bernardino León y León became Director-General of Prisons in 1928. As far back as 1924, Dr. León had advocated a system of progressive stages of advancement for the prisoner, terminating in liberation. Upon assuming his duties as Director-General, he called for a monthly classification of each prisoner based upon good conduct

[4] From manuscript material furnished the writer by Sr. Guillermo Zurita, Panamanian penologist.

in every phase of his program, with an intramural staff of officials being responsible for such evaluation.

But perhaps his greatest contribution to Peruvian penology was his establishment of an Institute of Criminology which had been provided for in the penal code of 1924 through the vision of Dr. Leonidas Avendaño. Such a clinic had been developed by the eminent Argentine, José Ingenieros, as long before as 1907, and its success had been recognized throughout both North and South America. So it was but natural that a similar organization should be recommended for Peru. By Supreme Decree, dated February 13, 1929, this clinic was established. It was to be under the direction of the Faculty of the National University of San Marcos. It is interesting, in passing, to note that only one or two states in our own country and the Federal Bureau of Prisons had experimented with the classification or diagnostic clinic by 1929.

The personnel of this Institute was composed of: Dr. Angel Gustavo Cornejo, Dean of the Faculty of Law, who presided; the Director-General of Prisons, Dr. León y León; the psychiatrist of prisons, Dr. Honorio F. Delgado; and the professor of criminology, Dr. Carlos A. Bambarén, secretary of the Institute. At the time of its inception, the only other such institutes in Latin America were in Buenos Aires (1907) and in Havana (1928).

Unfortunately, for reasons of economy, or for others not quite so obvious, the clinic was forced to suspend operations in 1932, after only three years. Dr. Bambarén, prominent psychiatrist of Lima, offered to carry on the work of the clinic without compensation, but to no avail. In 1937 the Decree of August 16, referred to as No. 97, provided for the reopening of the clinic but thus far it has not materialized.

Thus, in 1946, we find no clinical examinations in Peru's prisons. But it is clear to prominent students of the crime problem in Lima that no progressive penal philosophy can be realized without some such organization which has for its function the complete scientific examination of each prisoner coming to the institution. Only through the findings of such a group can an intelligent decision be made regarding conditional release, for example; nor can an inmate's program while in prison be developed without recommendations from a clinic whose responsibility calls for an analysis of his potentialities.

SYSTEM OF CRIMES AND PENALTIES

The penal code permits a wide latitude in penalties, perhaps more diverse than in any other South American country. It has been stated that the principles set down in the Peruvian code of 1924 are "judiciously precise." Running counter to the Franco-Germanic tripartite classification of offenses, it follows the conventional bipartite principle, recognizing felonies (*delitos*) and misdemeanors (*faltas*).

Felonies are divided into the following categories: (1) against life, body or health (*contra la vida, el cuerpo y la salud*) and includes homicide (*homicidio*), abortion (*aborto*), wrongs (*lesiones*), and quarrels (*riñas*); (2) against accepted customs (*contra buenas costumbres*) involving liberty, sexual honor, corruption, or violation of a person or his name, such as slander; (3) against honor (*contra el honor*) involving calumny, defamation or injury; (4) against the family, such as adultery or illegal matrimony (*matrimonios ilegales*); (5) against liberty, including rape of children or women and the violation of the home; (6) against property (*contra el patrimonio*) including robbery (*robo*), illicit appropriations, concealment (*encubrimiento*), deceit and other frauds, and usurpations; (7) against public security; (8) against public authority; (9) against the administration of justice; and (10) against public faith, such as falsification of documents.

The so-called measures aiming at the provision of security are internment (*internamiento*), penitentiary (*penitenciaría*), *relegación*, *prisión*, expatriation, fines, and the deprivation of civil rights (*inhabilitación*). Peru also recognizes and demands indemnity or reparation (*reparación*).

The prison system of Peru in July 1944 consisted of the following institutions:

1. The Central Penitentiary in Lima to which are sent prisoners from the entire country, sentenced to *internamiento, penitenciaría,* and indeterminate *relegación,* with the time fixed from one to twenty years.
2. The penal colony in the bay off Callao known as *El Frontón,* to which are sent prisoners sentenced to *penitenciaría* and *relegación* from one to twenty years.
3. Twenty departmental *cárceles* (jails) for prisoners sentenced to *prisión* from two days to twenty years.
4. One hundred ten provincial jails for the punishment of *cortas de prisión.*
5. The *Cárcel de Mujeres* (jail for women) located in the city of Lima for the reception of all females of the country sentenced to *internamiento* and *penitenciaría.*

It was impossible for me to visit many of Peru's penal institutions due to lack of time and their inaccessibility. However, I visited the Central Penitentiary in Lima, the penal colony of *El Frontón,* the *cárcel* in the city of Cuzco, and the institutions designed for children located in Lima. A description of these follows.

THE CENTRAL PENITENTIARY AT LIMA

As stated earlier, the massive central prison located in Lima was built in 1862 and is obviously designed with the Eastern Penitentiary at Philadelphia in mind. However, there are several modifications. It consists of four cellblocks, each three tiers high. At the time of my visit there were 320 prisoners. The entire institution was cold and damp, but it is to be remembered that I was in Peru during its winter season which is relatively mild compared to ours. Nevertheless, there is no provision made for heating the cells or any other part of the prison. This cannot be criticized since practically no private homes are heated in all of Peru, except by small stoves. There are no furnaces. The director of the prison at the time of my visit was Sr. Gonzalo Cabada Dancourt, who courteously received me and gave of his time in showing me his institution. I was accompanied by Sr. Ernesto San Martín, one of the architects attached to the Bureau of Prisons.

While the prison was not dirty, it is in very bad repair, which fact immediately gives the visitor the impression of its being in a rundown condition. This was explained by the statement that for the past several years there has been a prospect of abandoning it since it occupies a very expensive site in the central part of the city. It is reputed that the land on which it stands is worth two million dollars. There is no doubt that within the next few years it will be sold and other prisons substituted for it.

There is some productive work furnished the prisoners but not nearly enough for so large a population nor for a country as progressive as Peru is reputed to be. The occupations followed are shoemaking, carpet weaving and printing. Wages are paid and the usual partition is followed. One-fourth is allotted to each of the following: immediate use by the prisoner, the family, indemnity, and release.

There are some flower gardens in the prison yard but the inmates may not enjoy them. The chapel is very old and uninviting. There is a new school building, previously designed for other uses, where the equipment is well above the average. The very primitive eating accommodations consist of crude wooden tables standing in the corridors of the cellblocks.

In the rear of the prison yard is the isolation cellblock, surrounded by a garden. It is a dreary looking building built of stone and consisting of about eight cells. The men serving this initial isolation period wear a striped uniform and have all the traditional earmarks of convicts. It is a very obvious vestigial hangover from the old separate system of bygone days, totally out of harmony with modern penal philosophy. Each man is permitted two hours' exercise a day under special guard. It is strange, too, that two of them are permitted out at the same time. The cells are fitted up crudely with a cot, toilet and shower. These men are not permitted to read, but they may occupy themselves with handicraft labor. This feature of Peru's penal philosophy is certainly benighted.

The penal colony of *El Frontón* is a primitive place. Its good feature is that it is out in the open and away from the stuffiness of a large city. *El Frontón* is a small island in the bay of Callao, Lima's seaport, and quite close to another island called San Lorenzo. This island was used many years ago as a penal colony but was abandoned. It is now used as a naval base.

In July of 1944 there were about two hundred prisoners at *El Frontón* in addition to thirty-nine politicals (*Apristas*). More of these later. The weather in July is practically always damp and misty so that on the day of my visit it was extremely unpleasant. The prisoners have considerable freedom within certain limits of the island. Escape is difficult since there are treacherous tides that make swimming practically impossible. Yet there have been escapes. The prisoners work and go to school. A teacher comes out from the mainland two days each week. The prisoners are locked in their cells from six to six. In the early evening there is a radio program amplified so the entire population can hear. There are no movies, however. The cellblock is built against a ledge of rock and is long and low with no windows in the cells. There is an iron door to each cell but it affords little protection against the damp night air. The cellblock is a very crude housing device and should be abolished. In fact, the entire colony should be abandoned. One "dangerous" prisoner is kept in a single cell at one end of the small island under a special guard. He has complete freedom during the day within the definite limits of the tip of the colony. His cell door is open and he may come and go as he pleases. I had the impression that he enjoyed this special treatment. His was a particularly notorious case.

The political prisoners were housed in a special building. The commandant of the prison, a genial and no doubt capable man, advised me that this group was segregated from the others because they were "too dangerous." The group was composed of members of the *Apristas*, an outlawed political party which for many years gave the conservative Peruvian government considerable annoyance. The leader of this political party is the fiery genius, Victor Raúl Haya de la Torre, who John Gunther claims is one of the greatest personages in the Americas.[5]

When I was in Peru members of this outlawed party were being hounded by the police and many of them had been jailed. Haya himself was free from physical restraint but was under careful surveillance of the police. But some of his more violent followers had been arrested and spirited away to the fog-bound colony of *El Frontón*. I was solemnly told by officials that each of those arrested had actually committed some crime and been convicted in the constitutional manner and sentenced according to law. However, prominent *limeños* as well as *Norteamericanos* told me with tongue in cheek that if there were actual offenses they were made to appear as having been committed by these persons. Aside from the public officials I talked with, almost everyone was convinced that the thirty-nine sent to *El Frontón* were innocent of any crime and that their period of incarceration would be indefinite. These prisoners were men of ability including doctors, lawyers, students and others of similar attainments.

On June 10, 1945 the conservative régime of Dr. Manuel Prado was defeated in an exciting election and Dr. José Luis Bustamante, Democrat Front party candidate, was swept into office amid great rejoicing by the common people. While the members of the *Apristas* and their leader, Haya de la Torre, took no active part in the campaign, they gave strong support to the successful party. Many of the exiled party members returned to Peru, the hated Laws of Exception were abolished promptly and all political prisoners freed from prisons. But when I was on the island of

[5] For an analysis of the career of the leader of the *Apristas*, see Gunther, *Inside Latin America*. New York: Harper, 1940, pp. 208–14. In 1944 the name of the party was changed to *Partido del Pueblo*.

El Frontón there were political prisoners and I shall mention my experience with them.

My visit to their section of the prison was heralded by them with great enthusiasm. They shouted *Viva la democracia! Viva Roosevelt!* Before I left they presented me with their signatures appended to a statement which reads as follows: "En muestra de cordial solidaridad con la causa de la Democracia, entregamos este saludo de los prisioneros Apristas, defensores de la Libertad y la Justicia en nuestra Patria." [As a token of our cordial solidarity with the cause of democracy, we pay this salute to the Aprista prisoners, defenders of Liberty and Justice in our country.] In poorly written English they also wrote the following for my benefit: "We are political prisoners for our freedom democratic. We are many years in this concentration country for our ideas. Our leader is Victor Raúl de la Torre. Here we are living very much illness for cause of these meals. Here are intelligent men; doctors, lawyers, ingineers, poets, etc. We are sorry we can speak well language ingles." Here is a human document worthy of preservation. My impression is that Peru was a little ashamed of its treatment of the *Apristas*.

When I was in Cusco I had the opportunity of visiting the jail, or *cárcel*. There is nothing unusual to report about this institution since it is exactly like dozens of other such establishments throughout the West Coast countries. Its architecture is Spanish colonial and follows the traditional lines of the convent or monastery. Buildings surround a large bare *patio* which serves as the compound for the prisoners. I was accompanied to the jail by the postmaster of Cuzco, Sr. Roberto La Torre. We were met by the subdirector, Sr. Gavino Gamallo G. who was quite courteous. There was a certain air of freedom about the place although the inmates were of the same type as is found in small-town jails. They were practically all Indians. Many of them were busily engaged in weaving *ponchos* on looms set up in the jail yard. Perhaps the most interesting sight in a jail of the Andes is that of the inmates weaving their *ponchos* and blankets which they dispose of through members of their families in the markets of the city.

Dormitories in the Cuzco jail are the same as those in other jails. There were long rows of decrepit beds, or what passed for beds, with the bedding simply lying on pads of straw. The inmates were milling about, many of them following the visiting party, filled with an interesting curiosity and smiling when looked at. The visitor can easily get the impression that the treatment is kindly and the routine free and easy. The jail at Cuzco is undoubtedly a typical Peruvian jail, no cruelty, no program.

The women who run afoul of the law in Cuzco, and they are few, are cared for in the *Cárcel y Comisaría de Mujeres* operated by the Franciscan nuns of the Convent of Belén.

FIGURES ON CRIME

Statistical data are difficult to obtain and their interpretation is even more perplexing. However, the following data covering the year 1943 give a fairly adequate picture of the types of people who run afoul of the law in Peru.

During the year 12,475 persons were arrested and "sent to prison" which obviously means to detention jail only, rather than convicted. Of that number, 11,535 were men and 940 were women.

Of the total number, 6,988 were single; 4,873 were married; 587 were widows or widowers; and 27 were divorced. Of the total, 5,387 were illiterate; 4,125 had finished elemental schooling; 2,296 the primary; 562 possessed "medium" education; 99 had "higher" education; and 6 had technical training.

Out of this total arrested, 2,303 were recidivists and 10,172 were first offenders. As to occupations, 6,361 were agriculturists, cattle raisers or sheep-herders; 778 were merchants and workers; 1,279 were skilled; 1,517 were laborers; 562 were "drivers";

468 were "employees"; 1,462 had "other occupations," and only 48 were without employment.

Of offenses, 3,948 were "against life, body and health," 1,671 were "against morals," 5,359 were against property, and 1,497 were miscellaneous.

Of the total arrested, that is, 12,475, only 3,147 were awaiting trial and 1,081 were sentenced to prison, or "condemned."

From these scanty data we note that the bulk of those arrested for crime in Peru are single agricultural workers, illiterate, never before arrested, and committing either violent offenses or those against private property. And few of them find their way to the penitentiary.

CONDITIONAL RELEASE AND PROBATION

All prisoners have the advantage of conditional release with the principle of revocation explicit. It is granted, or may be, only after two-thirds of the sentence is served providing that sentence is over one year of *penitenciaría* or eight months of *relegación* or *prisión.* Evidence of potential rehabilitation together with a good conduct record, established before the *Tribunal de Conducta,* is necessary for consideration by the sentencing judge who alone can grant this privilege (for that is what it is, not a right).

There is *condena condicional,* the conventional form of probation, or the suspension of the execution of the sentence, but this, of course, is not probation as we understand it. The suspension applies only to those sentenced to less than six months, or to those who have been fined but who have not previously been before the court charged with a deliberate crime. There is no supervision during the suspension period.

CARE OF CHILDREN

Courts serving children were decreed by the penal code of 1924. Up to that time little was known in Peru about the scientific treatment of dependent and delinquent children. In that year there was formed a volunteer organization of women interested in the welfare of minors who called themselves the National Council. They made a survey of delinquency and dependency as well as treatment methods, calling upon the children's organizations and bureaus of the United States for help.

Equipped with this preliminary knowledge, the women of the Council started their work with a committee of twelve volunteers. Their next move was to apply to the government for official standing. This was granted, together with a slight annual stipend to cover part of their expenses. The name was changed to *Sociedad Especial de Patronato de Menores* in 1928. Their monetary grant was rescinded in 1930, but the organization was carried on, regardless, by means of subscriptions from its own members. Although its budget is relatively small, it employs two salaried assistants who have social work training. Most of the work of the society, however, is handled by volunteer members.

The work of the *Patronato* can best be described by material given to me by Señora Mercedes Gallagher de Park, of Lima, who has long been interested in children's welfare work.

Its work consists of semi-official duties of inspection of the reformatories as well as maintaining friendly coöperation with them. In addition it assumes the responsibility of properly disposing of those children whom the judge does not see fit to send to an institution, but who are homeless or suffering from destitution or unsatisfactory home conditions. The methods followed in this work are described by Señora de Park as "rough and ready," but the organization does its best to make its work efficient, adapt it to the peculiar conditions of the country and, above all, to avoid routine by giving the individual case intelligent and sympathetic attention and study, which is the keystone of the work. Orphans are, whenever possible, placed in a seaside orphanage on the outskirts of the city of Lima which is by no means an easy task since this institution is normally crowded to capacity.

However, the usual plan for disposing of the children is to

place them in carefully selected homes of families of the upper and lower middle classes where they do light housework for their maintenance.

Señora de Park admits that this procedure is far from being an ideal solution of the problem, but feels that in practice it works out satisfactorily, especially as the children and the housewives in whose care they have been placed are expected to report to the *Patronato* once a month, or oftener if anything unforeseen should arise in connection with the child's welfare. This they do with commendable regularity, both parties looking upon the institution as an ally and a help. These visits take place in the office of the *Patronato* and are conducted by one of the members who takes a turn at this work one day each week. The child and the housewife are interviewed separately and the resulting observations and decisions entered in a register so that the organization possesses a record for each child covering the period it remains under the vigilance of the society.

A child not seeming to fit into a household is at once changed to "a more congenial one" and, according to Señora de Park, the *Patronato* permits nothing to jeopardize the welfare and the reasonable preference of the child.

As great a measure of schooling as possible is carried on. Children suspected of imperfect health are immediately examined by a physician and either receive proper home treatment or are sent to a hospital. It is reported that the percentage of sickness and deaths is extremely low and that the "placed" children are in the main healthy, contented and well treated. Hundreds of children are thus saved every year from neglect, malnutrition and destitution.

A serious attempt is being made by the government as well as by the *Patronato* in Lima to develop institutions for the care and treatment of delinquent and destitute children, which will compare favorably with standards of other progressive countries. When I visited Lima I was taken to the boys' school, located in the city of Lima, and the girls' school, situated at the seashore near Callao, but of course not too far from Lima.

Up until a few years ago the boys' school was located in the open country at Surco amidst pleasant surroundings. But this site was requisitioned by the government for a flying field to train aviators so a removal had to be made. A new reformatory was conceived and was in process of being built when I was there. The new institution is situated on the seashore near Callao and is ambitious from an architectural point of view, well designed and thoroughly modern.

Meanwhile the boys have been housed in a set of buildings that were used by the Japanese prior to the outbreak of the war. The buildings are recognized by members of the *Patronato* as most unsatisfactory, although the boys are receiving a fairly good education and trade training under the auspices of the organization of the *Caballeros de la Gran Cruz de Isabella la Católica y de la Orden de "El Sol del Perú."*

Up until 1931, the boys' school was in charge of laymen who, according to my informant, were "extremely unsatisfactory because there is yet in Peru absolutely no way of training teachers for reformatory work." This lack of sympathetic personnel made it advisable to turn over the administration of the school to the religious organization mentioned above which has specialized in this work.

According to Señora de Park: "The Brothers have changed the Reformatory to an almost unbelievable extent. The discipline is very strict, yet it is enforced almost entirely by a system of enlightened kindness combined with firmness. The percentage of reformed boys is very high, a fact which under such treatment is partly due to the peculiarities of the Peruvian Indian race, which, in pure form or mixed in proportion, is that of the great majority of the boys. The boys are trusted as far as possible and rivalry in trustworthiness is most intelligently fostered. On Sundays the boys considered worthy of the distinction are allowed to go home for the day for a visit, and it is rare that one of them should not return."

Trades taught in this school are those of carpentry, locksmith, mechanics, leatherwork and shoemaking. Such production as there is, is privately purchased. Remarkably well executed hand-carved chairs are made of native hard woods. There is a band at the school which was practicing for the Independence Day parade, scheduled during the time I was in Lima. One interesting feature of the institution is the amazing interest of both the Brothers and the boys in pets. Hundreds of pet birds and rabbits were to be seen and the boys are taught, in caring for them, kindness and sympathy for animals.

The director, Brother Paulino Vicente, whom I met, is a kindly old padre who gave the impression of understanding delinquent and neglected boys, although he has all the earmarks of his conservative religious group.

The shortcomings of this school, at least those tangible ones that are obvious and easily detected, are readily admitted by those interested in the school. Nevertheless, to the visitor they are inexcusable. For instance, there are no beds; the boys sleep on the floor. Most of them were in their bare feet since they were "saving" their shoes for the big parade, mentioned above. I was told that they are given new clothes once each year just prior to this Independence Day celebration. By the end of the year they are usually worn out. Lack of funds in the school makes it necessary for the boys to be shabbily dressed and actually neglected so far as physical necessities are concerned. No amount of firm kindness can substitute for this neglect on the part of the authorities.

The girls' school was in the process of being erected, while the inmates actually carried on their day-by-day program. It is situated on an attractive site, located directly on the Pacific Ocean, although bathing is inexpedient since the current is too treacherous. However, the view from the front *patio* of the school is excellent. There are a few new buildings, small but attractive and functional. Each new cottage has the dormitory system which, of course, is universal. At present the cottages are excessively crowded. The institution is under the administration of a religious order and the school is called *Instituto Ernelinda Carrera,* in honor of the nun who organized the Women's National Council, from which arose the *Patronato.*

The problem of caring for destitute and abandoned children in Lima is an extremely serious one. As my informant stated: "There is a large floating population of children in the entire country due to the improvidence of the half-breed working classes and the irregularity and promiscuity of marital relations among them." This situation is described as "perhaps the gravest social problem confronting Peru and other Latin American countries."

The women criminals of Lima are housed in Santo Tomás, which is administered by the Third Order of Saint Francis of Assisi, founded expressly to carry on penal work by the same Sister Ernelinda Carrera mentioned above. The régime is described as "understanding and humane." Those who have babies are extended every facility for caring for them under wholesome and healthy conditions.

The women criminals are described as harassed and generally a hard-driven, devoted class. Their mates, however, "seem to be about evenly divided between two extreme types—the sober and industrious family man and the unprincipled and self-indulgent, irresponsible, whose amorous exploits leave a long and tragic trail of misery and squalor behind them." The latter type seems to be in the majority. I owe much to Señora de Park for patiently discussing with me the problems of juvenile delinquency and the general treatment of women and children. We visited the institutions and also the offices of the *Patronato.*

There is a school of social work in Lima known as *La Escuela de Servicio Social del Perú* created by Law No. 8530 of April 30, 1937. It is operated under Catholic auspices. Candidates for admission must be over 21 years of age and under 35; have completed secondary school or its equivalent; and, to insure good faith in the pursuit of the two years' curriculum, have deposited a small sum of money in addition to the tuition. Many of the students come from homes of the wealthy and have had private tutoring. According to the director, they usually make better social workers than those having a public school diploma.

In addition to the above entrance requirements, candidates must have had some experience in social or charitable agencies and possess a knowledge of home economics and household management. Instruction is continuous throughout the day, which precludes any part-time students from attending. After completion of an apparently busy two-year course, candidates must pass an examination supervised by members of the Ministry of Public Health, Labor, and Social Insurance, a delegate from the Council of Lady Patronesses, and the faculty of the school. If they are successful, they must spend one year in professional practice before receiving the diploma of *Visitadora Social.*

PLANS FOR THE FUTURE

Peru has long neglected her prisons. This neglect, I was told, was due to the attitude of her leading men who believed in the philosophy of "first things first." The government some time ago launched an ambitious road-building program which was obviously long overdue. Now that this has been completed, money can be diverted to other improvements. A prison program is one of the items on the agenda.

The Director-General of Prisons, Dr. Gabriel Seminario, has not been idle during the interim. He and his architects have been busy planning a series of detention houses for the several provinces, a number of small *cárceles* and prisons, and eventually the removal of the Central Penitentiary in Lima which has long since served its usefulness.

When I was in Lima I had long discussions with Director Seminario and his capable architect, Sr. Ernesto San Martín, in which they manifested keen interest in modern prison architecture. These men are not interested in the old Bastille type of prisons. They have designed small structures to house from one to seven hundred prisoners. The architectural style is quite similar to our own "telephone-pole" design with outside cell construction and administration buildings in the front. A communal kitchen is provided with small dining-rooms at the ends of each cellblock, food to be transported by portable steam-tables.

The Peru Congress, on November 24, 1944, through Decree No. 10,129, made an appropriation of forty million soles for the construction of these new penal units. In our money this is the equivalent of six and a quarter million dollars. Under the energetic leadership of Dr. Seminario, assisted by the sensible ideas of his architect, Peru should soon have a system of small penal establishments that will adequately meet her needs and place her among the first countries in South America so far as physical plant is concerned.

The plan of construction, as outlined by Dr. Seminario, calls for the following establishments: (a) 103 places of detention (*puestos de detención*) scattered throughout the provinces, ranging in size from those designed to house 80 persons to the smallest to provide for 10, the total cost to be 10,450,000 soles or about $1,672,000; (b) 12 establishments of the prison type of construction (*casas de inculpados*) for those who have been convicted of serious offenses, housing from one to two hundred, with one for the city of Lima to accommodate 700, the total cost to be around five million soles, or $800,000; 4 prisons, each to accommodate 200 prisoners, in the judicial districts of Apurimas, Ayacucho, La Libertad, and Piura, the cost of each to be 600,000 soles, or $96,000 or a total of $384,000; and 7 prisons, each to house 100, in the districts of Amazonas, Ancash, Huánuco, Huancavelica, Ica, Moyobomba and Tacna, to cost 400,000 soles each or a total of 2,800,000 soles, or $448,000; (c) work houses (*colonias de trabajo*) for those serving more than two years imprisonment and providing both industries and agriculture, to be of five different types based on population needs, one for each of the departments of Lima, Junín, Cuzco and Puno, each to house 400, and to cost 4,000,000 soles, a total of $1,920,000; one such establishment for the department of Lambayeque, to house 300 prisoners and to cost 2,250,000 soles or $360,000; two establishments for each of the departments of Arequipa and Cajamarca, to house 250 prisoners and to cost 2,000,000 soles each ($640,000 for both); one such prison for the town of Iquitos to house 150 and to cost 2,000,000 soles or $340,000; and one institution in the department of Madre de Dios, its location and cost to be later determined.

These ambitious plans also contemplate a program for women's institutions. A prison for females in Lima is to be built to house 80 inmates, the cost to be 250,000 soles or $40,000; seven work houses in the same departments where plans call for the same types of institution for men, except Madre de Dios, each to cost 100,000 soles, or $16,000; also a special institution for young men between the ages of 18 and 21 for the city of Lima, with a capacity of 100 and a cost of 350,000 soles, or $56,000. The overall plan also calls for a diagnostic hospital for the purposes of making studies in abnormal behavior to be located in Lima and to cost 500,000 soles, or $80,000.

While the total cost of this extensive building program exceeds the forty million soles appropriated by the recent Congress, it is proposed by Dr. Seminario that the ancient penitentiary now functioning in Lima, occupying a very valuable site, be sold. The proceeds would more than make up the deficit.[6]

With this ambitious building program realized, Peru will at least have a modern system of prisons, so far as plant is concerned. Such a development is obviously long overdue, as anyone who is familiar with the country's institutions can attest, and on its completion Peru may well be congratulated.

But personnel is another matter even more important. In the opinion of many observers in and around Lima it is this field of penology that most needs development. Custodial officers are none

[6] Since I was in Peru and with the victory of the Democrat Front party, Dr. Julio Altmann Smythe, well-known penologist, has been appointed director of the country's prisons, to succeed Dr. Seminario. Dr. Smythe, in a recent letter, states that he proposes to carry on the construction program with some limitations and, in due time, reinstall the prison clinic.

too well paid, so that men of high calibre rarely seek such employment, especially in the district jails. A program of improving personnel should go hand in hand with building construction so that upon the completion of the institutions high-grade officers would take charge immediately. It is my understanding that this officer-training program is contemplated by the Director of Prisons.

But, above all, Peru should revitalize its classification and diagnostic program by re-installing the Institute of Criminology which was so enthusiastically organized in 1929 and effectively carried on for three years under capable leadership. If these recommendations can be acted on and the ambitious building program realized, Peru will rank among the best in Latin America so far as penology is concerned.

VI

Bolivia

THE COUNTRY

THE vast tin country of Bolivia is well off the beaten path of ordinary travel in South America. Not only is it less accessible because of its great distance from the coast, but most of it is bleak and barren and thus does not attract tourists. Then, too, the altitude is so high that many people find it extremely uncomfortable to spend any considerable time there. Mountain sickness (*soroche*) attacks a great many tourists and it is not unusual for an occasional victim to be flown out of the dizzy altitude to the more comfortable lowlands.

The country attempts to support three and a half million people, almost ninety per cent of whom are of Indian extraction. Most of the natives are indescribably poor since there are few crops of consequence in most of the country. Nevertheless, the Indians of the capital city of La Paz are less miserable than those who dwell in the capitals of Colombia and Ecuador. There is less begging, for instance, in La Paz than in Bogotá or Quito. The Indian women are also dressed in gayer colors and carry fewer burdens than those of Ecuador. One amazing sight is Indians riding in taxis, something one never sees in the countries to the north. The dress of the women is similar to that of the natives of Peru, but most of them wear black or brown derbies which cost as much as twelve dollars in our money.

Travelers usually think of Bolivia as a country entirely bleak and mountainous. This is not altogether true, although few see anything but the drab country adjacent to the city of La Paz. But there is another Bolivia—the large portion that lies near the eastern jungle. Santa Cruz, for example, is a city of tropical verdure, in the center of an agricultural region. The primitive Chaco region, fought over with Paraguay a few years ago, is another tropical but little known area of the country.

My visit to Bolivia was brief, only one week, and covered the trip from the small lakeport at Puno, in Peru, across unforgettable Lake Titicaca to Guaqui, in Bolivia, and by rail to La Paz. The train descends a slope from the lake to La Paz, which is 12,500 feet above sea level, the highest capital in the world. The city lies in a valley rimmed by the *altiplano* or central plateau which is a full thousand feet higher. The train cautiously descends a breathtaking grade, round and round the ellipse of the city until in due time it arrives at the busy station.

The towering mountain peaks rising above La Paz immediately attract the visitor's attention, with stately Illimani surpassing them all with its twenty thousand feet. The city itself is, in many ways, quite metropolitan. Much of its architecture is modernistic although the Spanish influence is still very conspicuous. The rarefied atmosphere makes walking a burden and climbing the steep streets, some of which consist of steps, an almost painful experience. Yet the Indians can run up these inclines at a dogtrot with heavy burdens on their backs. The days are almost always sunny and comfortable but the nights are cold. Eighty per cent of Bolivia's population live above the ten-thousand-foot level and they have become inured to thin air and cold.

Misery and governmental intrigue are the two most conspicuous features of this country. The bleak mountain plateaus, with scarcely a tree and no grass in sight, make wresting a living from the soil a serious problem for the masses. Thousands of them work in the tin mines of southern Bolivia where they are unmercifully exploited. Illiteracy is very high. Most of the Indians cannot even speak Spanish but must converse in their old Indian dialect of Aymará.

THE PRISON SYSTEM

Of all the countries I visited in South America, I daresay Bolivia's system of prisons and penal philosophy is the most benighted. It would scarcely be accurate even to suggest that there is a prison system, let alone a philosophy. There are just prisons. It is true I had little opportunity of seeing what the country had to offer since it was difficult to contact anyone who could be of service to me in visiting the institutions, or with whom I could discuss the status of the country's penology.

After two or three days of attempting to negotiate some relationship with responsible persons I finally succeeded in visiting the national *Panóptico* in La Paz. I shall describe this prison later.

On the day before I left the city I had the good fortune to meet Dr. Manuel López-Rey y Arrojo, a well-known Spanish criminologist who, until recently, lived in Bolivia and taught at the University. He told me of the work he had done in connection with the newly proposed penal code which is outlined elsewhere in this chapter. He was also able and willing to answer my questions regarding Bolivia's penal system as well as contemplated plans for the future. However he did not speak in optimistic terms regarding either the present system or the future prospects of penology in this country. The instability of all Bolivia's governments is probably the reason for the lag that exists in penal matters. First things must come first in countries like Bolivia where a government must prove itself for at least a couple of years, and that is difficult, as witness the hectic recent history of the country.

In 1942 the government then in power passed an impressive decree which envisaged a complete reform of the jails as well as a more adequate plan of suppressing criminals. The decree called for the establishment or further expansion of three penal colonies to be distributed according to the geographic and climatic conditions of the country. The first of these would be the further development of the penal colony on the island of Coati in Lake Titicaca to take care of the criminals from the departments of La Paz, Oruro and Potosí; the second, to be constructed and located at some central point or area, for prisoners from the depths of Cochabamba, Chuquisaca and Tarija; and a third, to be developed at a point between Ichilo and El Chapare, for the criminals of Santa Cruz, Beni and Pando.

The decree further provided that the jails of the capitals of the various departments would serve for *delincuentes de carácter preventivo,* that is, for those against whom a mandate of preventive detention has been issued. Those sentenced to "arrest" were to be placed in the jails of the provincial capitals but in special annexes. A correctional school for children and a reformatory for women were also to be provided.

One interesting but dubious feature of the *Proyecto* is that in most of the establishments, men, women and children are to be housed in sections separated only by walls. I was shown a copy of the *Proyecto,* which probably will never be realized. On the title page appears this motto: *La Ley debe ser igual para todos, las celdas no* [The law should be equal for all; the cells no]. I gathered from this that various types of cells were to be utilized. No one could enlighten me on this departure from tradition. However, the wording may only be symbolical with the word punishment substituted for the word cells. I suspect that is one of the enigmas of Bolivia which has been described as a problem, not a country.

THE PANOPTICO AT LA PAZ

The National Penitentiary of Bolivia is called the *Panóptico,* following the South American tradition. It stands within a few blocks of the main section of the city on the top of a relatively steep rise of ground. It was erected in 1896, and from the outside, is quite colorless, since it looks not unlike dozens of jails and prisons throughout the world.

Upon entering the outer gates, one is confronted with a court in which there is a small nondescript fountain. I was told on good authority that it has been used frequently to duck political prisoners incarcerated in the prison. Beyond the court is a series of cellblocks assuming no special shape or architecture. The blocks are of two stories, each cell facing a central court or *patio* rather than a corridor, which is the usual type of construction. All cells are without windows, so that, aside from the door opening on a balcony overlooking the court, they might be called inside cells. Of course there is no plumbing in the cells, the night problem being met simply by the men knocking on their doors until relieved by the guards unlocking them and permitting the men to go to the outside toilet. This is characteristic of most South American prisons. There is no "bucket brigade" so familiar in old-time prisons in the States.

The cells are fairly commodious but very dark, the walls showing unmistakable signs of never having been painted. Each cell has a bed and some are supplied with an electric light, although this is the exception. Because many prisoners work in their cells, these rooms are equipped with little workbenches. Most of the inmates have decorated their cells with pinup girls and other lithographs, since this practice is permitted in Bolivia.

The shops of the prison are pathetic. They are small makeshift rooms, totally inadequate for a prison labor program. In truth, there is no such program. Some of the men who wish to work—there is no compulsion—make knickknacks, including ingenious toys, llamas of exquisite design of fur, inkstands, etc. There is a small shoe shop, a furniture factory and a rug-weaving shop. These are operated on the contract system. In Bolivia, the contractor may enter the prison and take charge of production. The contractor in charge of the rug shop is a Jewish refugee.

The prison authorities assist the inmates who wish to work on their own account by furnishing equipment and electric power. The men buy the raw material themselves. They may market their wares only in the prison to visitors who may be interested and they may keep all the proceeds. The others, working for the contractor, make fairly good wages, twenty per cent of which is withheld pending release.

The sex problem is not handled in any official manner, although I was told that in some cases prisoners might have their wives visit them in their cells. Since there is no policy regulating this, it is probably permitted as a special concession to privileged prisoners. Regular visiting day is on Sunday, in the afternoon from two to five o'clock.

There is a special wing for political prisoners in the *Panóptico*. It is slightly cleaner than the other wings and here may be found many political agitators and police who have been convicted of crimes. None of the political prisoners work.

Capital punishment is rare in Bolivia. It is provided for in the law of 1938 and may be invoked in three types of crimes: patricide, murder and treason. The method is the firing squad. Commutation, however, is quite frequent. The maximum penalty allowed by the penal code, aside from capital punishment, is ten years; commutation of the death penalty usually means double the maximum, or twenty years.

There were women and young boys of fifteen years of age and over in separate blocks in the prison when I was there. There is a so-called minor wing, and while I was told these children are separated from the adults, I saw some young boys working in the ships. Children of ages up to fifteen are sent by the courts to an institution operated by *El Buen Pastor*, a religious order. There are no juvenile courts in Bolivia and I was told there are very few delinquents. Nevertheless, petty crime is as prevalent in La Paz as in other South American capitals. It is committed by the same type of ragged urchins so familiar in the streets of most of the cities of South America.

Under the able direction of Professor Manuel López-Rey y Arrojo, an excellent course in criminology was developed at the *Universidad de San Andrés* in the School of Law and Political Science in La Paz. The outline of this course, as presented to me, is copious and comprehensive, including a historical background of the works of the Italian, Spanish, French and German schools, as well as the influence of criminologists in the United States. Both the biological and the environmental approaches are stressed. The contributions of the psychoanalysts, psychiatrists

Recreation: National Penitentiary
LA PAZ, BOLIVIA

Typical South American Jail: Weaving Ponchos
CUZCO, PERU

and endocrinologists are reviewed and the studies of identical twins are analyzed. The course ends with a discussion of criminalistics and efficient police work in the apprehension of criminals. On the whole, it appears to be a thorough and entirely satisfactory course in criminology, so far as can be judged from the outline. Dr. López-Rey is now living in Buenos Aires.

HISTORY OF PENAL LAW

Bolivia, like all South American countries, was ruled during colonial times by Spanish law. Sometimes these laws dealt specifically with Bolivian conditions, whereas on other occasions they were merely the general Spanish laws put into operation in the colony. They were obviously very unwieldy and unsatisfactory legal mechanisms, recognizing, only incidentally, local socio-economic conditions.

These laws, emanating from Spain, were often compiled in groups. One such important group was that drawn up by the eminent jurist, Encinas, in 1661, which was sanctioned by Charles II under the title "Compilation of Laws for the Kingdoms of the Indies." The seventh book of this code includes the penal laws of the time which, with few variations and additions, functioned until the Independence of Bolivia. This code was in many respects a harsh one, although it was in some respects humane and progressive, especially in its disposition of vagrants, gamblers and persons of ill-repute.

In addition to this code, there were in Bolivia, as well as in other colonies, local police regulations which dealt with purely local conditions. In the year 1805 a revision, known as the "Newest Compilation," was promulgated from Spain for all the Spanish colonies and attempted to deal with the conditions then existing.

In actual practice, however, it should be recognized that the Spanish penal code in operation all through the colonial period was used interchangeably with the vestiges of the Incan code, which obviously militated against homogeneity and equity so far as the people of various geographic areas or social classes were concerned.

After Bolivian independence was proclaimed in 1825, the Spanish code continued in effect until 1831. In that year, the Protector, Andrés Santa Cruz, the first president of the newborn republic, ordered a revision. This innovation, however, was based almost exclusively on an earlier Spanish code. Much dissatisfaction arose during the next few years since this reminder of Spanish rule was, in addition, considered unduly harsh as well as incompatible with Bolivian institutions. So, in 1836, President Santa Cruz ordered a revision which has been in operation until the present. While this revision is little different from the earlier one of 1831, it did make possible a better organization of the provisions of the law.

The first section of this code of 1836 deals with general dispositions; the second with crimes against the State; and the third with crimes against the person. A few modifications have since been made in this venerable code, most of them attempting to reform some of its archaisms or to recognize more modern conditions of life. As matters stand today, the code of 1836, according to Dr. López-Rey, fails to satisfy existing Bolivian conditions. This is attested to by professors of law, public officials and legislators.

In 1898 a law dealing with this phase of jurisprudence was enacted, none too wisely, sponsored by the College of Lawyers of the city of La Paz. It dealt specifically with criminal procedure, judicial police, special process and appeal, but did not provide for a jury except in special civil cases.

There is no parole, as such, in Bolivia, and the provisions of *libertad condicional* (conditional release) are quite vague and unsatisfactory. The approval of the "good time" provision which diminishes the original sentence for good behavior is purely subjective and is in the hands of the judge. The fantastic manner in which this procedure works is worthy of comment. The judge calls in two prisoners who have known the candidate in prison and asks their opinion of him. In addition, the warden of the prison or jail is also asked to render his opinion. On the basis of these reports, the judge grants conditional release. As Dr. López-Rey remarks: "If we remember that the prisoners, whose report is secured through simple friendship or companionship, have no training in criminology; that the warden of the jail is not an authority, since in Bolivia there is no trained group of prison wardens, we may readily conclude that the diminishing of the sentence is arbitrary and inadequate, granted merely as routine, and an act that is much criticized by Bolivian professors."

THE PENAL CODE OF 1943

In 1941 Dr. López-Rey was commissioned by the Bolivian government to develop a completely new penal code which would reflect the conditions peculiar to Bolivia. Two previous attempts were made to draw up a new penal code. The first was in 1857 by Don Melchor Urguidi. The text of this project is not known, but there is record that the code was presented to the Congress in that year. In February 1935 the government commissioned Don Julio Salmón, a professor of penal law and a judge, to write a new code. Eight months later it was presented to the Congress but was rejected completely on the grounds that it was totally inadequate for the country and because of its lack of penal technique.

The López-Rey code was presented to the National Commission in 1943 which examined and changed it slightly. It is considered in a most favorable light and has already been officially published (November 1943). It was submitted to the Congress with a presidential message asking approval. While there is little doubt that it will be approved, thus far it has not been adopted.

The new López-Rey project is divided into three parts. The first is dedicated to general concepts regarding crimes and penal sanctions including measures of security, special dispensation for the Indian population, judicial pardon, conditional sentence (probation), conditional release (parole), indemnity to the victims of crimes, etc.

Books two and three deal with felonies and misdemeanors (*delitos y contravenciones*). This is the first code that has ever taken into account the interdependence of the various countries of the continent in so far as security and coöperation are concerned. It also strikes a new note regarding crimes against the national economy.

This new code has received considerable praise both from within Bolivia and without the country because of its modern, flexible and scholarly attributes. While the agitation for a new code stemmed primarily from the former administration of President Peñaranda, which was overthrown in 1943 and replaced by a mixed civil and military *junta,* it is still considered likely that it will eventually be adopted. Such innovations are accepted slowly in Bolivia.

While I am not prepared to present an evaluation of this new code, my experience in South America convinces me that what is really needed even more than a new code is a complete overhauling of the court procedure as well as a renaissance in penal philosophy and treatment. However, it is not out of place to quote from one of our own reviewers concerning some of the provisions of the López-Rey project. Professor William S. Stokes of Northwestern University, writing in the *Journal of Criminal Law and Criminology,* says, both in praise and in criticism:

> Dr. López-Rey Arrojo's objective was to produce a simple, concise, workable criminal code based upon modern principles of law and penology which would be directly applicable to Bolivian problems. To his broad knowledge of criminal law, philosophy, and psychology, the author added the leavening influence of careful field studies and research in La Paz, Cochabama, Oruro, Potosí, Sucre, Santa Cruz, Coati, and other small centers. The resulting code leaves little to be desired. In organization and presentation it is clear and untechnical. . . . (He) rejects the mechanical philosophy of the classicists and insists on individual case studies of violators and wide latitude of punishment of offenders. The author wisely includes the Indian, who forms the bulk

of Bolivia's population, within the provisions of the code, thus avoiding the possibilities of a legislative dualism.

The enthusiasm of the legal student for the code as a juridical document must, of course, be tempered by thought as to its practical usefulness. In adopting the indeterminate sentence, the judge may vary the punishment according to the possibilities of the "juridico-social" readaptation of the individual. The success of administration of justice in criminal cases under such a flexible system is contingent upon a well-prepared, cooperative judiciary and the establishment of scientific principles of penology in all agencies of law enforcement. While the author admits these prerequisites, it is highly doubtful that such objectives will be realized at an early date in Bolivia.[1]

The news received from Bolivia concerning its political unrest does not offer much encouragement for any constructive reform in the fields of penal science or prison administration. It will doubtless be a long time before this mountain country will be in a position to entertain any new ideas in penology. While the new contemplated penal code is a step in the right direction, it represents a beginning only. Since a code constitutes in itself only a document to present to the world, its implementation with court procedure and prison administration is vastly more important.

1 35, September–October, 1944, p. 179.

VII

Chile

A LAND OF CHARM

CHILE is the land of copper and nitrates. It is also the land of excellent horsemanship. A visit to Chile is a rare experience since it has long been distinguished as a friendly country proud of its true democracy, its wine, women and unsurpassed scenery.

Any school boy knows that the contour of Chile takes the shape of a long narrow snake hemmed in on the west by the Pacific and on the east by a long range of Andean mountains. Its population is about four and a half million and, except for the southern portion, its people are mostly white. There are Indians in the southern lake region, the picturesque Araucanians, and there are some Negroes in the cities. While illiteracy is high, amounting to about fifty per cent of the population, it does not reach the fantastic height of seventy-five or eighty per cent as in Ecuador, Peru, Paraguay or Bolivia.

Chile is roughly divided into five parts. First and northernmost is the Atacama desert extending from Arica, on the Peruvian border, to the region around Copiapó and including the seaport town of Antofagasta. From this barren land, where the sun shines mercilessly and no rain falls, come the nitrates and copper which, in normal times, are a source of tremendous wealth to Chile. There are some olives cultivated in and around Arica but irrigation from mountain snows is necessary. The second part of the country is semi-desert and extends south to Illapel. Here some farming as well as mining are carried on, again with the aid of irrigation.

The central zone, which is the heart of the country, extends roughly as far south as Concepción, and includes the large cities of Santiago, Valparaíso, and the smaller Talca and Chillán.

While the summers are dry, there is plenty of rainfall in the winters. The farm land is intensely cultivated and yields vegetables and grapes in large quantities. It is in this part of Chile that life weaves a pattern of color and magnificence. The cities are distinctive and modern, characterized by a gaiety somewhat subdued in comparison with, say, Rio de Janeiro or even Buenos Aires, but certainly much livelier than the northern cities. There is considerable manufacturing in Santiago, especially in recent years.

The fourth part of Chile extends from Concepción to Puerto Montt and is known not only for its agriculture, but for its rich scenery. Here is the famous lake country of which all Chileans are justly proud. Here, too, are those great horsemen, the cowboys of Chile, known as *huasos*. Water sports and fishing in abundance make the area a playground surpassed by nothing of its kind in all South America. It is also a great farming section and is rapidly being developed by settlers from the northern areas of the country, dissatisfied with mining, which is precarious as a livelihood. It is in this area that most of the Araucanian Indians dwell, especially around Temuco where they exceed some one hundred thousand.

The most southern area of the country extends to the Straits of Magellan and is sparsely inhabited since the climate is tempestuous and the terrain very rugged. Much of the territory is virgin forest and still uncharted. However, there are great sheep farms in this area.

Fast streamlined trains run north and south, making it possible to go from the central cities to the lake country overnight in solid comfort. These bright red, silver-trimmed trains (made in Germany) are known as *flechas* (arrows) and are the epitome of comfort and riding luxury.

Chile reminds the *gringo* of his own country, in many ways. English names are prevalent, especially in Santiago and Valparaíso, where theatres, shops and hotels bear familiar labels. Of course, these show the British influence rather than that of the United States. The main street or boulevard in Santiago is Avenida O'Higgins, named for the famed Bernardo O'Higgins, one of the country's great heroes. Born of an Irish immigrant, he played a major role in delivering Chile from the Spanish yoke. This famous thoroughfare, best known as the Alameda, and the Plaza de Armas, are among the main promenades for *santiaguinos*.

A few words about Chile's cities are of interest. Arica, the country's northernmost city, is a dreamy place of 12,000 and its only bids to recognition, if not fame, are that it serves as Bolivia's only seaport, through treaty arrangement with Chile, and that it was the headquarters of the Commission of 1929 to settle the boundary dispute between Peru and Chile—the famous Tacna-Arica controversy. It was also the scene of a great battle between these two countries in their war of 1879. The Hotel Pacífico, an ornate structure too extravagant for the town, was built to house General Pershing and his aides when they arrived to negotiate the settlement mentioned above. The Pacific Ocean rolls into the little town over massive rocks and thus provides Bolivians a respite from their high altitude homes.

Aside from the gorgeous bougainvillaea flowering in extravagant profusion in the public plaza, Arica can boast of its little gingerbread church flanking the square. It was designed and its fabrication supervised by Alexandre Gustave Eiffel, the French architect who conceived it in such a manner that it could be assembled without aid of nails or bolts, save one. Made of sheetiron, it was transported across the ocean to quaint little Arica. But the workmen were unable to read the plans or guess the riddle of construction so it was put together with as many bolts as was found necessary.

Santiago is the capital and chief metropolis of the country. It has a population of about a million and is cosmopolitan and sophisticated, with beautiful boulevards and homes, excellent restaurants, a couple of good hotels, and a mass of poverty, just as in any other large city. It stands on a wide plain flanked by the snow-decked Andes. The city is crossed east and west by the Mapocho River which passes through an ingenious artificial stone channel 130 feet wide and is spanned by iron bridges. The city has been described as "a gem in a ring of gardens and snow-capped peaks, blessed with an almost perfect climate."

Those who visit Santiago in the winter season may well question the perfect climate. It rains a wet cold drizzle most of the winter months. And, of course, there is little heat anywhere and actually none in the public buildings. Public officials work at their desks all day long in their overcoats and college professors are obliged to bundle up when they lecture.

One interesting feature of Santiago's professional and social life is the famous volunteer fireman brigades, membership in which is coveted by the gay young blades of the city. These 1,400 fire-fighters actually pay dues to belong and there is a long waiting list. One of these organizations is known as the *Cuerpo de Bomberos Voluntarios* and its chief is a professor of criminal law at the University. It was founded as an aftermath of a horrible holocaust that occurred on the night of December 8, 1863, when the *Campañia* church caught fire and some 2,000 men, women and children died. The brigade has had a long and glorious history. It not only maintains a high level of efficiency but a most rigorous discipline.

Valparaíso, the largest port in the country, as well as nearby Viña del Mar, the playground sea resort, are well worth visiting. Long known as the Pearl of the South Pacific, Valparaíso is still doing business, but her great activity has been sharply curtailed since the opening of the Panama Canal. Built on a narrow ledge on which her business section stands, she has slowly and carefully ascended the surrounding hills to perch her homes there. Several miniature funiculars, or *ascensores,* ascend at two-minute intervals so, for a few pennies and a minimum of time and, perhaps for the first few times, no little courage, her citizens can go to and from their work down in the city. Much of the city was destroyed by a severe earthquake in 1906 but in recent years many-storied buildings have given a thoroughly modern air to the business section. Its colored sidewalks of brown and cream tiles are a distinctive sight.

Viña del Mar, one of the most beautiful seaside resorts to be found anywhere, is only six miles from Valparaíso. Here the citizens of Santiago come to play, providing they have enough money for train fare and roulette. The Casino at Viña is one of the most ornate and smart in all South America. Stately castles, fine residences, modest but tastefully built homes are conspicuous at Viña and flowering vines, notably the bougainvillaea, make the little resort a pleasing hideaway from the workaday world.

The cities of Talca and Chillán lie to the south in Chile, the former about one hundred fifty miles, the latter three hundred, from Santiago. Both are pleasant towns, each approximately fifty thousand in population. Both cities suffered greatly from earthquakes in the immediate past. In 1928 Talca was practically destroyed. In 1939 the entire region was visited by a devastating quake and 30,000 people were killed with 12,000 from Chillán alone. Both cities, however, have been practically rebuilt, much grander than before the catastrophe.

These two proud cities enjoy a culture of their own. Chillán, especially, is appealing. It is, for example, the birthplace of the famous revolutionist, Bernardo O'Higgins. The streets are full of proud cabelleros who ride sedately on their horses, arrayed in the gay *ponchos* of the *huasos* or the more subdued long black capes and broad-brimmed hats of the Spanish dons. Silver spurs, snappy whips made of bone and heavily inlaid with silver, sturdy horses, and magnificent saddles constitute the equipment of these distinguished equestrians, the pride of Chile.

One could continue indefinitely discussing the many charming and unique features of Chile. For example, the country has gone far down the broad road of socialistic enterprise. Through an elaborate system of *Cajas,* or bureaus, the country owns and administers much of the productive machinery. There are also many social benefits for the workers.

THE DEVELOPMENT AND ORGANIZATION OF PRISONS AND JAILS

Back in 1930 an article appeared in the magazine *Chile* which, at the time, was published in the United States, obviously prepared for our consumption. This article, by one A. R. González, dealt with proposed changes in the penal code of Chile. The author painted a glowing picture of the progressive penal reforms that were about to take shape in that country. He stated enthusiastically regarding the code: "This new code . . . introduces revolutionary yet soundly scientific concepts into the traditional notions of criminal procedure. Emphasis throughout is on reform and the prevention of crime rather than on mere punishment." [1]

In preparing material on Chile's prison system for my *World Penal Systems* [2] in 1944, the only information to be obtained was from this article by Señor González. I took it on faith, assuming that Chile had gone forward to take her place among the truly progressive countries in the domain of penal science. But if this project was introduced in the Chilean Congress of 1930, certainly it was not passed. The country still operates under the penal code of 1874, although every few years since that date modifications have been made to attempt to bring it up to date and to square it with modern conditions. There is at the moment much discussion in Chile suggesting a complete recodification of the laws but thus far no definite action has been taken.

In my visit to Chile in 1944 I found no one who was even aware of the proposed reforms of 1930 outlined so joyfully by Señor González. I also found that the country is extremely orthodox in its attitudes toward the criminal and, aside from some

1 "Chile's New Penal Code," *Chile*, IX (July 30), 19 f.

2 Sponsored by the *Pennsylvania Prison Society*, Philadelphia, 1944.

sporadic enlightened practices in dealing with children, it maintains a system of prisons that is backward and highly conventional.

The first legal system under which Chile operated followed the old Spanish code which was known as the Code of the Seven Parts (*Siete Partidas*). After independence was obtained, the same code was operative until 1874 when a new one was adopted which adhered closely to the Classical traditions. Since that time, as stated above, there have been many modifications, some of which have introduced concepts other than those of the Classical tradition. Penal lawyers in Santiago are hoping that a new project will be on the agenda in the not too distant future, but this reform will probably not come for some time if we may judge from the lethargy in official circles in that country. It is much easier merely to add to the frame of the older code. This was done only recently—in August 1944—when the new law regarding the suspended sentence was adopted for adults.

In the early days of Chilean history, her convicts were sent to a penal colony in the Tierra del Fuego country where the present city of Magallanes now stands. In 1908 another colony was started on the island of Más Afuera in the Juan Fernández group but this was abandoned in 1913. No act was passed by which this colony was abolished; it just happened that no more prisoners were sent there.

The penal colony idea takes hold easily in Chile. In 1943 the Minister of Justice (he has only recently resigned) started a colony in Santa María island, forty miles off the coast from the city of Concepción, in the Pacific. Prisoners sent from the National Penitentiary in Santiago are in the process of constructing this colony and it is expected to be opened soon. The late President Ríos did not like penal colonies—at least not the words—so after much debate it was decided to call the new establishment Santa María Rehabilitation Colony; but it will still be a penal colony shut away from the prying and critical eyes of the public.

Unlike most South American countries which follow the bipartite system of classifying violations of the penal law (felonies and misdemeanors, or *delitos y contravenciones*), Chile adheres to the Franco-German system which is characterized by a tripartite classification. Offenses are divided into crimes, misdemeanors and disorderly conduct (*los crímines, los simples delitos y las faltas*).

Short sentences up to sixty days are served in the municipal jails or *cárceles;* medium sentences, from 61 days up to five years, are served in prisons known as *presidios* which are located in a number of cities and towns throughout Chile; and long sentences, over five years to life, are served in the National Penitentiary located in Santiago.

Chile also has the death penalty, executed by a firing squad at the penitentiary in Santiago. The victim is taken from his death cell, blindfolded and strapped to a chair. The guards making up the firing squad wear slippers to muffle any sound. The captain of the guard gives no audible commands but merely drops his hand as the signal to fire. In case the bullets miss their mark it is the unpleasant duty of the captain to give the *coup de grâce.*

However, the death penalty is seldom carried out, the average being one a year. There are many reprieves by the president in spite of the final court recommendations. A prisoner sentenced to life has the privilege of applying once a year to the president of the country for pardon or grace. If pardon is granted by the president the Minister of Justice is called upon to add his signature to that of the chief executive.

When I visited the National Penitentiary in Santiago there was only one man in the death house. He had already had two reprieves and was awaiting the results of his third review. He was a dejected person in spite of the fact that he was provided work in his little apartment-like cell. His life's handicaps were enormous. Orphaned at an early age he was also the victim of stuttering and had a hare-lip. He had killed a couple of people and, at his trial, had slashed the judge with a knife. Certainly he deserved the death penalty, if anyone did; at least in the eyes of the general public. Yet his case had received and was still receiving sympathetic consideration from the officials. The prison staff were also understanding. They recognized that this man had never had a chance in life, weighted down with a complex of handicaps so that it was impossible for him to become anything other than what he was. This interest in so unfortunate a person was most revealing and speaks volumes for the social understanding of public officials so far as the death penalty is concerned.[3]

Court sentences are divided into two types: complete deprivation of liberty and limited freedom. Three types of sentence under the latter category are recognized and imposed. They are: *relegación,* by which a convicted person may be sent to a special town or city where he must remain and, while there, report once a week to the police or to some other authority; *deportación,* by which a convicted person is sent from one place to another of his choice, providing he does not return to the city in which he was sentenced; and *destierro,* banishment from the country for a period of time. This last usually applies only to political prisoners.

Aside from the *cárceles* attached to each local community, Chile maintains some twenty prisons known as *presidios,* scattered throughout the country in the various departments. Among these are the institutions at Antofagasta, La Serena, Talca, Chillán, Los Andes and Rengo. I visited two of these prisons—those at Talca and Chillán—and shall describe them below.

But all long-term prisoners are sent to the National Penitentiary at Santiago. It is a huge structure dating from 1843 and covers many city blocks not far from the main business district of the city. In its early days the treatment of its prisoners presented a paradox to travelers. One investigator, writing in 1893, stated that in one part of the prison the inmates were employed usefully and under humane conditions. However, in another portion of the establishment the solitary system of treatment repre-

[3] This man, one "Che" Galdamez, has since been executed in spite of official interest in his case.

sented a punishment far worse than the "prompt infliction of the death penalty." He describes the solitary treatment in these words:

> In this splendid "model" institution there are noisome, slimy cells, where daylight never enters, in which human beings are literally buried alive. . . . There are inner cells, two feet wide by six feet long, and destitute of a single article of furniture. Until recently, those confined in them were walled in, the bricks being cemented in place over the living tomb. Now there is a thick iron door which is securely nailed up and then fastened all around with huge clamps, exactly as the vaults are closed in the Santiago cemetery, and over all the great red seal of the Government is placed—not to be removed until the man is dead, or his sentence has expired. . . . Low down in the door, close to the ground, is a tiny sliding panel . . . so that food and water may be slipped in on shallow pans and the refuse removed. Twice in twenty-four hours this panel is operated, and if the food remains untouched a given number of days, it is known to a certainty that the man is dead, and only then can the door be unsealed, unless his time is up. . . . Not the faintest sound nor glimmer of light penetrate those awful walls. In the same clothes he wears on entering, unwashed, uncombed, without even a blanket or handful of straw to lie upon, he languishes in sickness, lives or dies with no means of making his condition known to those outside. He may count the lagging hours, sleep, rave, curse, pray, long for death, dash his brains out, go mad if he likes—nobody knows it. They told us that only one man has ever survived a year's sentence, there.[4]

While the system of separate confinement, practiced as it was throughout most of the world in the nineteenth century, was rigorous and perhaps cruel in many countries, this description of penal treatment in operation only fifty years ago in Santiago represents the epitome of apathetic official indifference to the sufferings of prisoners. Fortunately such treatment no longer exists.

My visit to the National Penitentiary was a most pleasant experience although I was none too favorably impressed with the institution. It is architecturally not unlike the Philadelphia prison and, save for the prison at Rio de Janeiro which was built in 1837, is the oldest on the southern continent. It was opened for

[4] Quoted from William Tallack, *Penological and Preventive Principles*, London: Wertheimer, Lea & Co., 1896, pp. 78–79. The investigator was F. B. Ward.

the reception of prisoners on July 19, 1843, but it has been remodeled to some extent since that time.

Seven cellblocks radiate from the central oval which, instead of being a rotunda as is the case in most prisons thus designed [*e.g.*, Philadelphia, Bogotá, Quito], is a plaza interspersed by flower gardens and little pools. This part of the prison is quite attractive. The cellblocks are two tiers high and the cells are fairly large although quite unattractive due largely to the age of the institution.

The shops (*talleres*) are built on the outside perimeter of the blocks but within the walls. They are dark and gloomy although some of them, especially the printing and electric shops, are well equipped. Over one hundred men are employed in the prison's print shop. It does a thriving government business (known as *fiscal*) and is, by far, the best and most promising of all the industries. About seventy men work in the chair factory and another twenty in the paint room. Sixty men make shoes on contract for the armies of Colombia and Bolivia. Other shops employing small numbers of men are: mechanical, slipper, tiling, foundry, brush and broom, and electric. This last shop is a recent one and was designed primarily to teach those interested in the electrical trade.

There is a large "self-work" shop (*taller por su cuenta*) where over 150 men are engaged in handicraft work. Each worker has his little space allotted to him and a wide variety of trinkets and handmade objects are turned out. It is in this vast shop that much of the prison trouble breeds. It is a difficult matter to resolve the petty personal problems that arise here from both real and fancied wrongs, or from petty pilfering of tools or materials from which the products are made. The men who work here are wild and undisciplined without a skilled trade but possessing a high degree of native craftsmanship. It is the only organized shop of its kind in all of the prisons I visited in South America. While it provides employment for a large number of men it is handicapped by lack of orderliness and system as well as by

National Penitentiary
SANTIAGO, CHILE

the temperament of the men who make it their daily rendezvous.

The wages earned by the men in this prison are divided as follows: 10 per cent is retained for release; 15 per cent is used for the support of the prisoners' families; and 75 per cent is given to the men. There is no indemnity or restitution in Chile.

There is a fine spirit among the personnel in the National Penitentiary. The warden, the captain of the guards and the guards themselves seemed to me well above the average. Nevertheless, they have a difficult job because of the size and age of their prison. It seems a mistake to bring together in one prison so many of the country's serious offenders when it should be possible to distribute them to the various smaller prisons in the hinterland. Maximum security units might well be designated in three or four geographic localities where *presidios* are already in operation.

One unique problem existing in the prisons of Chile is the universal habit more indigenous to this country than to others in South America—that of wine drinking. Chile is a country that produces exceptionally fine wines and practically everyone drinks freely since it is cheap and well loved by the citizens. Prisoners are denied this indulgence so that it makes smuggling a serious institutional problem. The inmates have money and the guards are seriously tempted to bring wine into the prison to sell to those who crave it. I was asked what solution I might offer to this problem. There is only one answer, it seems to me; give the men a certain amount at their meals, either free of charge or for sale, preferably the former. This may sound dangerous to those familiar with conditions in the United States but one must really understand the folkways of Chile to see the implications of the problem.

By all odds the best feature of the National Penitentiary is the outstanding *Instituto de Criminología,* or diagnostic clinic, which functions under the able direction of Dr. Israel Drapkin, noted South American penologist. This clinic was established in 1936 and is composed of a director, who must be a physician; a psychologist; a psychiatrist; an anthropologist; a lawyer; two social workers who are women; and two stenographers. The warden of the prison sits in on the proceedings and serves as chairman.

This clinic enjoys the distinction of being the only one in the world, so far as I know, of having female social workers who enjoy equal standing with other members.[5] This, of course, refers only to men's institutions. Dr. Drapkin has long been an admirer of the work of Dr. José Ingenieros, the distinguished Argentine who founded the first diagnostic clinic in the world, and his successor, Dr. Osvaldo Loudet. Drapkin spent some time in the United States in 1942 where he visited a number of prisons in which classification and diagnostic clinics operate. He returned to Chile and injected new life as well as new ideas into the organization. In the opinion of this writer, the clinic which he heads is potentially the best all-round diagnostic service in South America.

My reason for making this statement is that in this clinic we find all types of analysis undertaken. Its director thoroughly understands the role played by the socio-economic forces in criminal causation and thus provides for social investigation of each prisoner. While the personnel of the clinic is heavily weighted by those following the biological approach and in this respect parallels the conventional clinic in South American prisons, it is nevertheless balanced by the presence of two social workers and the good judgment of the director.

But here, as in other South American countries, the recommendations of the clinic are practically ignored. The final decision regarding the new prisoner's disposition rests with the warden. Occasionally its suggestions are scrupulously adhered to but generally they are ignored or, at best, carried into effect in a half-hearted manner. The clinic makes investigations of candidates for conditional release but, as there is no requirement by

[5] As stated in the *Introduction*, female social workers are now found in a few of the prison clinics in the United States but this situation arose only because of the shortage of trained men during the war.

law that its judgments be considered, it receives no encouragement from official circles in this important matter.

However, I am convinced that this clinic is of a superior nature. Dr. Drapkin enjoys the confidence of the prison officials and what he does is understood by them. But there exists a tragic lag somewhere between the prison and the officials in the government that is difficult of analysis. For example, the Director-General of Prisons, Sr. Julio Olavarría Avila, an estimable gentleman, finds it difficult to develop a scientific régime in his prisons. His difficulties undoubtedly stem from official inertia as well as from lack of funds. I had the good fortune to talk at length with the Minister of Government, Don Oscar Gajardo Villarroel, who has since resigned. I found him overburdened with problems but sympathetic to the introduction of reforms in the country's penal structure. I told him frankly what, in my judgment, should be done in Chile, in so far as I could diagnose the trouble. He received my suggestions warmly and with interest. I came away feeling that some of my suggestions would bear fruit. However, he is no longer Minister and I fear that Chile will go along with its habitual apathy and official inertia.

But to get back to the National Penitentiary. It is old and run down. Perhaps the most amazing part of the institution is the chapel. Here, of all places, one would expect cleanliness and an atmosphere of reverence. It is just the reverse. It shares the same dirty dilapidated building in which moving pictures are shown. It is dark and depressing. The priest himself walked through this building with me and when I commented unfavorably this worthy said nothing. At first I sensed his attitude was one of mortification. But as I discussed the matter with prison officials I concluded that he, too, was merely apathetic. A more resourceful and militant cleric would never have permitted such a sorry state to exist in the one place where decency should prevail. The Minister was shocked that the chapel was such a disreputable and neglected place and promised that he would see that it was renovated at once. Again, I feel sure nothing has been done to remedy this situation.

I visited two departmental *presidios* or small prisons, one at Talca and one at Chillán. As they are both quite similar I shall make one description do for both. They were both built about 1926; that is, new front additions were placed on older structures and then the work stopped. They are little more than common jails now. One conspicuous feature of these establishments is the housing for the men at night. There are no cells as such; merely compartments built against a wall, open at the front and used only for sleeping purposes. They have the appearance of catacombs. Only those occupying the first tier can enter their cubby-holes without the aid of a ladder. In all my prison travels I have never seen anything like this bizarre arrangement. These "cliffs" are only wide enough for a narrow bed; the men's clothes hang on hooks in the back wall. Toilets and washing facilities are at one end of the corridor but to use them at night, the inmate must take to his ladder and if it isn't handy, call a guard to assist him to and from his sleeping car bunk, as one in an upper berth on a Pullman car must do.

There is little constructive work provided in these prisons. There is some shoemaking by hand—in fact, all the work is handicraft. Inmates make a wide variety of articles from cow horn and many are of excellent workmanship. Since these jails are in the cow country of Chile, a large number of whips made of bone, halters and harnesses fashioned from rope, are manufactured by the prisoners.

I was cordially received by the wardens and physicians in both the Talca and Chillán prisons. They are understanding men but their equipment and administrative duties prevent them from developing more progressive measures than they now follow. These prisons, as no doubt is true of all prisons in Chile, are mere cogs in a penal system that badly needs overhauling. Leadership in high official places is lacking, so far as prison philosophy and administration are concerned.

I also visited the *cárcel* in the city of Valparaíso. Parts of this venerable institution date back to the days of the early Spanish colony. In fact, the dungeon-like structure within its walls, in which the alcoholics are herded at night, is distinctly colonial Spanish. No beds are provided the wretched inmates in this miniature bastille; they merely lie down on the cold stone. There were once wooden floors provided but the drunks ripped them up and burned them to keep warm. There is no heat in the jails of this country, nor in any other in South America. Consequently it is quite understandable that prison inmates, in a frantic effort to keep warm, must burn anything in sight that is inflammable.

The deplorable condition of these alcoholics in the Valparaíso jail beggars description. At the time of my visit these derelicts sent to this jail by the court, were crushing bricks into dust for use in the roadway running through the jail. I was told, as an aside by one of the employees of the prison, that their hearty diligence was for my special benefit; that these men ordinarily did nothing. I daresay I was the victim of much window dressing in South America. But, then, this is a universal device, to "cover up," not excluding our own prisons in the United States.

The Valparaíso jail is a big institution; that is, it houses around five hundred men. There is practically no work for the inmates, but there is a school. It is almost impossible to keep the place clean; not because there is a shortage of man power but because there is no sustained policy of cleanliness and sanitation. Here is an example of this fact. There are no toilets in the cells. The inmates simply urinate on the floors during the night and this refuse runs out of the cells and into the corridors. There is no real attempt made to stop this disgusting practice nor for that matter, to keep the corridors clean and healthy. They may be swept or even flushed with water but I doubt if they are ever disinfected for the odor is nauseating.

But of all the miserable penal establishments I had the dubious pleasure of visiting in South America, the Santiago city jail was the worst. Located in the heart of the capital city, it houses on the average about one thousand men. It is a huge establishment divided into various departments. There is, therefore, some degree of segregation or classification, although, aside from a *pensionado,* the section in which those from the upper social classes may purchase their accommodations and maintenance, there actually seemed to be no separation. Hundreds of inmates mill about, giving the impression of pure bedlam.

The jail is unbelievably dirty and gloomy. The inmates are a miserable and dejected lot. They are practically all of the white race, and in this the institution differs from the large municipal jails I had seen previously, in which the bulk of the population is Indian.

As we passed through the various blocks the inmates eyed our party with hatred and suppressed fury. The lack of even a bare minimum of accommodations is enough to elicit such unwholesome attitudes. Certainly one does not expect to find comfort in a jail, but there are basic needs that should be provided, at least on a minimum level. Decency in the preparation of food, of sleeping quarters, of toilets, of medical care, and the like, represent such a minimum. None of these is provided, as a rule, in hundreds of jails in the United States or anywhere else. Certainly the Santiago jail represents degradation on a vast scale where these minima are totally ignored.

True, the men do eat; and they must sleep. But I have seldom seen such unwholesomeness anywhere. I have no hesitation in labeling it the worst *large* jail I have ever been in. I told this to the Minister of Government and to other responsible persons in Santiago. I suspect I told them nothing they did not already know, but I felt that coming from a *gringo* it might startle them into some sort of remedial action. If it hasn't done so by the time this book receives publication, I hope it will soon swing some official group into a much-delayed action.

In 1935 a school for the training of police was founded in Santiago but it was not until 1942 that a "chair of criminology" was established. Dr. Drapkin holds this post and lectures in the school twice each week. I had the pleasure of speaking to the candidates of this school and found them receptive to the ideas of the new penology as well as to the modern responsibilities of the police to the community.

In the month of June 1944 there was inaugurated in Santiago the first Pan American Congress of Criminalistics. Members of our own Federal Bureau of Investigation were in attendance. The conference discussed such matters as police methods, coöperation between police and medical and other scientific laboratories in the analysis of clues, schools for police, improvement in personnel and the like. This meeting presents a hopeful sign that police methods throughout the continent will be improved by an exchange of ideas. It may even lead to the elimination of much indifference on the part of the police in some countries and even of brutality that is unquestionably practiced in more than one country to the south.

Since my visit to Chile there has been inaugurated a training course for prison guards, an idea that Dr. Drapkin has been working on for several years. The Minister of Government told me that he was convinced that this was one of the most important aspects of modern penal treatment and was happy to inaugurate this course.

The *Instituto de Ciencias Penales* of Santiago was founded in 1937 by Dr. Drapkin. It is composed of persons who possess an interest in criminology or penology so that it is much esteemed among professional groups of the capital city. Penal lawyers, social workers and government officials make up its membership. To the best of my knowledge this is the only organization of this kind in the Americas. I had the pleasure of appearing before this group and I found sympathetic response although my topic dealt with the divergencies of Latin American criminology from that practiced in the United States. This organization publishes the *Revista de Ciencias Penales,* which appears quarterly and is devoted to subjects dealing with the penal law and crime causation. Its president is the eminent Dr. Luis Cousiño MacIver.

CONDITIONAL RELEASE

The law creating conditional release (*libertad condicional*) in Chile was passed in 1925. First offenders who have not committed serious offenses may apply for release after they have served one-half of their sentences; recidivists or first offenders convicted of serious crimes may not make application until they have served two-thirds of their sentences.

Four conditions must be met before release is granted: the time element; good conduct while in the institution; the guarantee of a job upon release; and the ability to read and write.

Twice each year a committee presided over by the President of the Supreme Court and consisting of all the judges of that court as well as the members of the Court of Appeals and the magistrates of the local courts of crime, make a tour of the penal institutions within their jurisdiction. In addition to appraising the penal establishments, this committee considers applications for conditional release submitted to them by the wardens and directors of the prisons. From these lists of eligible candidates the initial selections are made. They are then presented to the Minister of Justice who issues a decree calling for conditional release. It is not valid until he and the president of the country sign it.

Upon release the prisoner must present himself once each week to the prison in which he served his time. This is a mere formality since he is obliged only to sign his name. However, if he fails to do this twice in succession or three times altogether, he must be returned to the prison to serve out his uncompleted sentence. Since 1940, in the city of Santiago only, there has been some supervision of conditionally released prisoners by social workers. If the social worker feels that he is not maintaining good behavior, she may recommend his return to the prison. It is estimated that in Santiago there is about five per cent recidivism since this supervision has been provided.

Each prison maintains a *Tribunal de Conducto* which passes on all disciplinary problems. It is composed of the warden, who is chairman; the Director of the Institute of Criminology, who must be a physician; the teacher or director of the prison school; the captain of the guards; the chief of the shops; and, if a social worker is on the staff, she may be included but may not vote.

Chile also maintains a device for the control of ex-convicts. It is known as accessory sentence, its administration being in the hands of a body known as the Accessory Authority. It maintains a desultory supervision over all prisoners released through the conditional process or outright through expiration of sentence. The Authority stipulates a period of time which prisoners must serve under its jurisdiction.

THE STATUS OF PROBATION

Probation in Chile offers nothing new nor different from what has already been described as being in operation in other South American countries. It is not probation, as such, but merely the suspension of the execution of the sentence, pronounced by the judge. Action of this sort, dealing with minors only, was taken in the year 1928. It permits the Judge of Minors to dispose of the case of a delinquent child in any one of the four following ways: (1) by permitting the child's parents to continue their custody (this method was previously considered as an amnesty and was known as *Amonestación Previa*); (2) by sending the child to a reform school (in Santiago the school is known as the *Politécnico para Menores* and is located in the suburb, San Bernardo); (3) by turning the child over to the authority of the Director-General of Protection of Minors which disposition is the closest to probation philosophy found in Chile because social workers have charge of supervision; (4) by sending the child to a foster home selected by the Judge of Minors.

It is worthy to note that Chile was the first country in South America to develop a philosophy that approaches our own theory of probation in dealing with children, dating in its incipient form, from 1906. However, so far as adult procedure is concerned this was inaugurated only in August 1944, just a few days before my arrival in the country.

No social workers or other types of trained supervisors are resorted to in handling adult cases. There is a *Patronato* but, being a private agency, its vigilance is little more than superficial, if it is even that effective.

The provisions under which a sentence may be suspended for adults are as follows: (1) in cases of a first offense; (2) when the sentence is only less than one year; (3) when the background of the candidate is favorable; (4) when the type of crime and its motivation are not vicious; (5) when there are good prospects of adjustment in the community. Under such rigid conditions few adults are granted this privilege and, since the supervision in the few cases so granted is so poor, there can be little doubt as to its futility.

THE TREATMENT OF WOMEN AND CHILDREN

The female prisoners in the Santiago city district are incarcerated in a large convent-like institution administered by the nuns belonging to the religious order *El Buen Pastor*. The establishment is divided into two departments, one for misdemeanants and the other for felons, all convicted by the courts. In the former section are those detained for trial.

The institution is clean and, to a degree, wholesome, but there is the same atmosphere of religious repression so characteristic of such places. The nuns are a kindly group and without a doubt are most helpful to the inmates in preparing them for a more socially acceptable life upon release. In the misdemeanant section there is no segregation. The women eat, sleep and work together. However, in the department constructed for the felons, presumed to be a more dangerous group, each woman has her own individual cell, or room, a condition favorably recognized by all progressive penologists.

Those in South America who have an interest in the female

offender, and there are very few, feel that this group is woefully neglected. I sensed this feeling as I went from country to country. They are "pushed around" in detention quarters while awaiting their hearings, almost always attended by men; they are seldom furnished with decent housing facilities or the necessities peculiar to their sex; and, aside from a very few establishments, they are treated as sinful Magdalenes and constantly reminded of their guilt. Hence, feelings of shame are accentuated to such a degree that they appear humble and remorseful.

Santiago and other centers in Chile could do much to make the lot of the female offender less humiliating by developing separate institutions on the cottage system, similar to the famous *Ciudad del Niño* which I shall now describe.

This children's institution is situated on the outskirts of Santiago and was opened quite recently—in December 1943. Its setting is superb. It occupies a large level tract of land which has for its backdrop the snow-covered Andes.

The school is patterned after Father Flanagan's "Boys' Town" in Nebraska and was sponsored by the personal interest of the late President Ríos and his wife, Señora Marta Ide de Ríos. However much credit is tendered the president and his wife for their genuine interest, other noted *chilenos* also played a leading role in making this excellent institution possible. Certainly, the former Minister of Justice, Don Oscar Gajardo Villarroel, to whose vision and interest in penology I can testify, played an important part in making the school possible. Also Sr. Juan Lagarrigue, Director-General of the Council of Defense of Children, deserves credit for his dynamic energy and human interest in the project.

It would be no exaggeration to compare this institution with the best we have in our own country and to place it alongside the best schools of the same type in both Argentina and Brazil. The plant is, of course, new. It is composed of the usual administration buildings, hospital, chapel, school, and the like, and cottages housing no more than thirty or forty boys—all properly equipped and classified according to the age of the children. All buildings are of clapboard, one story high, painted white, each bearing the name of a country.

The personnel is of high grade, professionally trained and from what I observed, sympathetic and human. The children, all boys, are a healthy and bright-looking group. They wear uniforms similar to our Boy Scouts. These are made of the best material.

Each cottage is in charge of a married couple, most of them quite young, appointed for their ability to train children. I was quite impressed with their understanding of the problems of young boys. The equipment of each cottage consists of attractive furnishings, gay curtains at the windows, of which there are plenty, and throughout there is a warmth and gaiety that reflect the wholesomeness of the régime. Unfortunately the dormitory system prevails here also. Some of the personnel agreed that separate rooms would be much more valuable but felt that the advantages were scarcely worth the additional expense involved.

There are several other features of *Ciudad del Niño* worthy of comment. First, mention should be made that here trained social workers are employed in investigating each boy's background. I talked with two of these workers and can state that they are among the most understanding, compared with what we expect our own social workers to be, of all I met in South America. They were, for example, conversant with the role case work technique plays in dealing with juvenile delinquency.

Another phase of the program is its music. The boys have a good band and an excellent *a cappella* choir, both of which I heard. The instructors in these branches of music are well trained for their work and it is obvious that they are achieving most satisfying results. The athletic program is good as well as the manual training and the education in general.

It is true that most of the boys sent to *Ciudad del Niño* are abandoned and neglected, rather than delinquent. However, aside from serious delinquency, the children brought before the

Judges of Minors are usually assumed to be neglected and unfortunate rather than delinquent. Most of the boys are homeless or come from depraved homes so that the training they receive is regarded merely as an insurance in good citizenship. In this, Chile, or at least Santiago, accepts its responsibility.

Near the *Ciudad del Niño,* but not an integral part of the school, is a day care center which caters to the children of a large congested neighborhood. Boys and girls, from nursery school age to adolescence, come here for free instruction, recreation and health care. The entire school, quite large in extent, operates on a high level. A well-equipped nursery school, progressive in all details, is operated; kindergarten and early school curriculums operate along progressive lines; and, for older boys and girls, manual training and what we call domestic science are provided.

Of course, these schools cannot begin to reach the child population of Santiago needing this type of training. What they accomplish is unquestionably admirable but they are inadequate in solving the problem of the neglected child. If a few more *Ciudades del Niño* were created throughout the country, perhaps not necessarily so elaborately equipped, but staffed with equally as capable personnel, Chile would find such an investment profitable indeed.

SOCIAL WORK

As was already stated in the first chapter dealing with penology in general throughout Latin America, it was Chile that first developed social work training in these countries.

The desire to initiate training for social workers was first translated into action in April 1924 when it was proposed to open a two-year course. A grant of 30,000 Chilean pesos was obtained from the *Junta de Beneficencia,* the state organization for social assistance, and the school was opened in March 1925. The first director was Madame Jenny Bernier, a graduate of the Ecole Centrale of Brussels. Since that time the school has had several directors, most of whom received their training in Europe.

The technical organization of this school is considered quite superior. It has a large faculty which is appointed by the *Junta de Beneficencia,* the organization which directs the school by means of a council of five members. The school has increased its curriculum to three years and courses are given daily with field work and practice reserved for Fridays and Saturdays. There have been some contacts between this school and some of our own in the United States and scholarships have been granted for post-graduate work in the New York School.

In 1929 a Catholic school was opened as a memorial to the wife of the president of the Chilean Senate and former ambassador to the United States. This school is known as the *Escuela de Servicio Social "Elvira Matte de Cruchaga."* Señor Cruchaga received his inspiration to found this school from the National Catholic School of Social Work in Washington, D.C.[6]

In addition to the excellent work accomplished by this school throughout Chile, it has served as a model and an inspirational force for other Latin American countries. This is largely due to the fact that it has been designated the American representative of the *International Catholic Social Work Union* which has its headquarters in Brussels. The first director of the Santiago school, Fraülein Joerissen, was supplied by the International Union.

This school maintains a rural social welfare center as well as a settlement house in Santiago. Many of its graduates find positions as welfare workers on the *fundos,* or large estates in rural districts. It also finds outlets for its graduates in labor and industrial establishments throughout the country.

Since the *Junta de Beneficencia* has charge of all public hospitals, clinics, health centers, day nurseries, maternity homes and similar institutions in Chile, it is quite natural that the graduates of the former state-sponsored school should find employment in such agencies. However, there is no discrimination shown gradu-

[6] See Rebeca Izquierdo Phillips, "Social Service and Legal Assistance in Chile," *Pan American Bulletin,* LXXX (June 1946), No. 6, 334f.

ates of the Catholic school in hiring workers for state-supported agencies.

The country of Chile has for many years accepted the social work technique in assisting in the solution of the problems of social and economic maladjustment of its people. Consequently these two schools cannot meet the demand for trained personnel. This demand comes primarily from the large rural areas and the public health centers. A great need is expressed for the establishment of schools of the *polivalente* type, that is, combination training centers for social workers and public health nurses. However, there is some criticism from trained social workers of such a proposal since they claim girls from wealthy families are looking for positions which pay well without accepting the responsibilities of hard work.

During the year 1944 one of the schools of social work has permitted Dr. Israel Drapkin, director of the diagnostic clinic at the National Penitentiary, to give a series of lectures to the thirty students of the senior class on the subject of penology. Three students became interested in this field and wrote their theses in that subject or in criminology. This represents the first "penetration" of penology into a school of social work in Latin America. There seems to be the same resistance to this field in those countries as we have found in the United States.

CONCLUDING REMARKS

When one views the signal progress made by the government of Chile in the social and economic fields and contemplates the healthy state of democracy throughout the country, he is frankly disturbed that so little has been accomplished in the area of progressive penology.

Certainly, if the proposed reforms described by Sr. A. R. González in the article referred to earlier had actually been formulated into law, Chile would have gone down in penal history as one of the most advanced countries of the world so far as its philosophy of criminal treatment is concerned.

This ill-fated code of 1930, according to González, was spectacular in all its details since it broke with most of the concepts of traditional criminology. It called for the abolition of the death penalty. It attempted to resolve the old conflict between free will and determinism, which problem arises to bedevil all penal lawyers when developing a new project. As González writes: "Crime is no longer defined. For the old interpretation, 'a voluntary action or failure to act punishable by law,' leads to confusing controversies on free will and determinism. The new code recognizes that from the standpoint of the individual and his relation to the community it matters not whether his will is free or predestined; crazy or sane, master of his fate or slave of circumstance, he is a member of society, and if he becomes a menace to that society, it must be protected against him."

In brief, the salient parts of this reform measure of 1930, according to Sr. González, were:

1. The fundamental purpose is prevention of crime, not vengeance.
2. The criminal is to be reformed, not punished.
3. Prison sentences are indeterminate, depending on the reformability of the subject.
4. The death penalty and life sentences are abolished.
5. Fines are imposed according to the prisoner's ability to pay.
6. Adultery is no longer a crime for the woman and not the man.
7. Psychological, sociological, biological causes of crime are to be considered determining factors in every case, and reform is based on modern scientific knowledge in these fields.

This proposal also called for higher qualifications for judges and magistrates. They were to be versed not only in the law but in psychology, sociology, criminal anthropology and history of crime and punishment.

Fines were made relative in an ingenious provision. As González states: "Fines are imposed according to the income and financial obligations of the subject, and their standardization is one of units rather than of amounts." If two persons, for example, have committed the same crime and have each been fined thirty units, the judge may interpret a unit in one case as ten pesos, and in another as thirty pesos, the one consequently paying a fine of 300 pesos and the other, one of 900 pesos. This procedure represents an amazingly enlightened doctrine, one that is perhaps found nowhere throughout the world.

It is highly regrettable that this progressive code was not adopted in Chile. As the situation is now, the country is traditionally hidebound in all its aspects of criminal law and penal philosophy. The strangest situation concerning this reform measure is that no one I met in Santiago knew anything about this attempt to streamline the prevailing code of 1874. I went over each reform measure with persons familiar with conditions in that country and found to my surprise that none was in operation. The mystery of this project of 1930 has not yet been cleared up. In fact, none with whom I talked had ever heard of Señor A. R. González.

There are many recommendations that may be suggested for the country of Chile. Its only bid to fame, so far as penal treatment is concerned, is its one outstanding school for children, the *Ciudad del Niño*. But even this progressive institution can handle merely a fraction of the children needing decent care and supervision in the city of Santiago alone. Many more such establishments must be developed throughout the country.

In the treatment of adults, much is left to be desired. In Santiago, it is of the utmost necessity to provide for adequate quarters for those awaiting trial and a thorough housecleaning of the municipal jail. This institution is a disgrace to Chile.

Jails throughout the country can stand improvement. A realistic jail program, based on adequate standards of sanitation, work program and housing, is essential as soon as possible. The jail in Valparaíso is little better than the one in Santiago, while those throughout the provinces have little to recommend them so far as decency is concerned.

The penitentiary in Santiago should be torn down since it is over a century old and cannot be satisfactorily renovated. The work program in this prison is fair, although more government contracts are desirable if more prisoners are to be employed.

The diagnostic clinic is excellent. However, as stated above, it seriously needs implementation so that its recommendations can be carried out by the prison officials.

Perhaps the most important reform that can be suggested is a complete overhauling or scrapping of the antiquated penal code of 1874. There are plenty of capable penal lawyers in Chile who are able to draw up a sensible code that will raise Chile to the front rank in penology, a place that she merits when we think of her progressive concepts in other fields of human endeavor.

VIII

Argentina

THE COUNTRY

OF ALL the Latin Americans the Argentines probably dislike most those who are often called "parachute" *yanquis*—visitors from the States who spend a short time in their country and go home to pose as authorities on some phase of their political, economic or social life. They are undoubtedly justified in this attitude, yet in fairness to the "hit-run" student it should be stated that it is possible to learn a great deal about a country in a short time if the right people are met and conferred with. My short stay in Argentina was packed with activity, thanks to the letters of introduction that preceded my arrival and the courtesies extended me by the Director-General of Prisons, Dr. Eduardo Ortiz, and his capable staff, as well as by Dr. Jorge Eduardo Coll, prominent authority on child welfare.

It would take months to see all of Argentina, so vast is the country. It is some two thousand miles long and, at its widest point, about a thousand; its total area is over a million square miles. In spite of the fact that most of the country consists of flat *pampas* there are many high mountain peaks, some of them extending well over twenty thousand feet. The population is approximately fifteen million, about one-fifth of which live in the federal district of Buenos Aires. The city of Buenos Aires is well over two million. Argentina ranks with Uruguay in being the most literate country in all of South America.

One of the most thrilling air trips in all South America is that between Santiago and Buenos Aires *via* Mendoza. The plane must climb to a twenty-thousand-foot altitude to clear the high snow-covered Andes which, from the plane, look like a bleak storm-tossed waste of country. School children from the United States have become almost as familiar with the picture of the huge statue of the "Christ of the Andes" as of some of their own native monuments, since practically every elementary geography textbook comments on it.

Perched 13,750 feet up the mountain on the border between Chile and Argentina, it was constructed of melted cannon and erected in 1903. Dedicated to peace, its inscription is worth recalling at this particular time when suspicion and fear grip the people of more than one country of South America: "Sooner shall these mountains crumble into dust than the people of Argentina and Chile break the peace they have sworn to maintain at the feet of Christ the Redeemer."

The chief natural divisions of Argentina are, first, the Andine, consisting of the eastern slope of the *cordillera* separating Chile from the country; second, the Gran Chaco or northern lowlands spreading off to the northern boundary facing Bolivia; third, the Mesopotamian fork lying between the Paraná and Uruguay Rivers; fourth, the Pampas which represents the economic heart of the country and consists of the vast central plains; fifth, the Patagonian or southern plateau lying south of the plains region; and sixth, the Tierra del Fuego region forming the toe of the country and extending down to the Straits of Magellan and Cape Horn.

Many books and innumerable articles have been written on Argentina and her people during the past few years. Most of these have dealt with the controversial political issues that have literally torn the social and economic life of the country asunder. Our relationships with this people have been precarious and, at this moment, there seems little hope that a good healthy feeling of neighborliness can be developed. Our policies regarding Argentina have been most inconsistent, a fact that baffles not only the Argentines but all the people of Latin America. The tortuous paths of diplomacy have no place in this book, but no citizen of the United States can travel in South America without experiencing some embarrassment when the name Argentina enters into conversation.

The people of this wealthy country are proud and astute. They are more like ourselves, for good or bad, than any other people in Latin America. They are proud of their country and of their achievements, and they simply will not be patronized by anyone, either from the States or from Europe.

Buenos Aires is without doubt one of the most remarkable cities of the world. Few metropolitan areas can equal it for grandeur, sophistication and beauty. Its avenues assume tremendous proportions and its public buildings are superb. The people who promenade its streets are well-dressed and possess a jaunty air. The downtown section of the city gives one the impression of a dozen Fifth Avenues and Park Avenues rolled into one. The most aristocratic street in Buenos Aires is Calle Florida which, unlike most of the other principal streets, is quite narrow, and is roped off for pedestrians every afternoon from four to seven o'clock. Swanky shops line both sides. Thousands of smartly dressed women and immaculately groomed gentlemen promenade this thoroughfare, stopping to chat or entering the many smart tearooms for cakes, tea and gossip.

But the beauty of this imposing city may best be seen in its plazas and many wide boulevards, such as the Avenida de Mayo, a tree-lined street 120 feet wide, at one end of which is the famous Plaza de Mayo and at the other, the Plaza del Congreso on which is situated the Capitol building; or the Avenida Alvear, a boulevard passing through a number of small parks and leading to the polo grounds and race track; or the new and imposing Avenida 9 de Julio which has been cut through the heart of the city by demolishing entire city blocks; or Diagonal Norte at one end of which stands the Boston Bank Building which houses the embassy of the United States.

It is quite easy for the tourist to stay in one of the luxurious hotels of Buenos Aires, eating his meals at the many excellent restaurants and steak houses, and see no poverty or slum areas.

Perhaps in no other capital in all of South America, unless it may be Montevideo, are there so few beggars or hawkers as on the streets of the capital of Argentina. Yet this city has its *pobres*. Vast slum areas are to be found if the tourist wishes to look. They are inhabited by whites; there are no Indians in the city and, aside from the Patagonians far to the south, none in the provinces. Argentina is strictly a white man's land. The upper and middle classes live very well and food is much cheaper than in most of the other countries. Argentina is proud of its beef and justly so. Almost every schoolboy talks cattle. Restaurants vie with one another to serve the choice cuts of beef and a T-bone steak of large size, with all the trimmings, may be bought for less than half a dollar—two pesos.

Argentina, without a doubt, is a thrilling country and it is regrettable that we know so little about it. One method of cementing the tenuous ties between this country and our own would be to teach something of its history, life and customs to our own children.

PENOLOGY

No one can write of penology or criminology in Argentina without paying tribute to three noted men of that country associated with these two fields. They are José Ingenieros, founder of the first diagnostic clinic in the world; Juan Vucetich, pioneer in the technique of finger-printing; and Juan José O'Connor, the indefatigable fighter for penal reform and, in a real sense, the father of the country's modern prison system.

The first two of these men are internationally known for their unusual contributions. Dr. O'Connor, who died only a few years ago in the prime of life, bids fair to be remembered as one of Argentina's most remarkable men. It is possible that if he had labored in some field other than that of penology he would have ranked even higher than he now does. The field of penal reform is rarely acknowledged to be of much importance by the general public or by those who select candidates for halls of fame.

José Ingenieros (1877–1925) is best known in South America, in general, and in the Argentine, in particular, as a prolific writer on social and economic questions. In the field of criminology he is best remembered as the founder of the world's first diagnostic clinic which he established in 1907. Ingenieros also established two technical journals. The first, *Archivos de psiquiatría y criminología y medicina legal,* made its initial appearance in 1902, ran through twelve volumes and succumbed in 1913; the second, *Revista de filosofía,* is still published. The development of the Argentine clinic as well as its functions will be discussed below.

The world of finger-printing, or dactyloscopy, pays homage to Argentina's second pioneer, Juan Vucetich. There are many claimants to the development of this amazing and revolutionary technique of identification and criminal detection. We know, for example, that Sir William Herschal, a British executive stationed in India, made it his habit to impress the thumb print of all natives on contracts they made for employment. He urged his government to adopt the practice for mere identification purposes, but it was cool to his proposal. In 1888, Francis Galton, who had long realized the possibilities of finger-prints, developed the system of arch, loop and whorl patterns and succeeded in getting the government to supplement the famous earlier Bertillon method with finger-prints.

Prior to 1891, Vucetich had finger-printed and classified many criminals and on September 1 of that year made his first identification. He is generally regarded as the first person to make practical use of the technique in criminal identification. The system he developed is now in use in Argentina. The United States uses another similar system known as the Henry system. Vucetich published the mechanics of his system in his *Comparative Dactyloscopy* in 1904.[1]

The work of Dr. Juan O'Connor, however, is more relevant to

[1] Cf. Rollin M. Perkins, *Elements of Police Science* (Chicago: Foundation Press, 1942), pp. 144–46.

this discussion since penal reform owes much to this intrepid man of vision. Born in Colón, in the province of Entre Ríos, August 24, 1890, he was quite obviously of Irish ancestry, although none the less Latin in his outlook and culture. At the time of his death, on May 5, 1942, he was juvenile judge (*Juez de Menores*), to which office he had been appointed in 1937. His prison régime extended from 1923 to that year. It is primarily with his work in this connection that we are especially concerned.

Up until 1923, and even for some time thereafter, nothing was expected of the custodians of the thirteen local *cárceles* in operation at the time in Argentina but security of the inmates who happened to be thrown into them. Dr. O'Connor, after assuming the responsibility of reorganizing the prison system of his country, visited these jails and indicted them as "centers of corruption and vengeance." In 1925 he proposed the construction of five new jails (*cárceles*) for the provinces, the work to be done by inmates. O'Connor believed in men and in their ability to absorb gradual, but not abrupt, reformation. This was his conviction and by means of its practical application in his penal program, he accomplished much. During the early years of his incumbency he transformed the provincial jails from what was termed a national disgrace into a system of "decent and habitable" establishments. This was accomplished by means of small subsidies and inmate labor.

In 1933 a comprehensive law was passed (No. 11,833) which had for its purpose the regulation of all the penal institutions of the country. It called for the creation of a Director-General of Prisons and Dr. O'Connor was tendered the post. In addition to the Director-General the law called for the creation of an advisory council and a technical-administrative staff.

On the Council, presided over by the Director-General, are a professor of criminal law from the University of Buenos Aires, named by the government; the president of the parole board; the director of the classification clinic or psychiatric annex; and the Chief of the National Register of Recidivism.

As stated above, Dr. O'Connor resigned his post as Director-General to become judge of the children's court and was succeeded by Dr. José María Paz Anchorena, professor of law in the University of Buenos Aires. He had for many years been identified with prison work, serving on the Council and being a member of the diagnostic clinic. Dr. Paz Anchorena resigned in 1941 and was succeeded by the present incumbent, Dr. Eduardo M. Ortiz, on November 24, 1943.

The law which created the advisory council also called for a progressive stages system of treatment consisting of five steps: (a) observation; (b) internment in which the convict works inside the prison; (c) orientation, in which the convict may work outside the establishment; (d) trial or test period, in camps permitting semi-freedom, which may be in sections of colonies, farms or industrial prisons; (e) reintegration, or release under supervision and under the control of the "parole board" in cases of conditional release.

In order to insure rehabilitation within the prison three different régimes were created by this same law of 1933, as follows: (a) a moral régime with practical education; (b) a régime of technical apprenticeship of trades; and (c) a disciplinary régime.

The new law also projected into the future an ambitious building program calling for several types of penal establishments including: penal colonies, industrial prisons, semi-freedom camps, prisons for adult females, prisons for those awaiting trial in conjunction with the criminal courts of the Federal District of Buenos Aires and for each province, and, in addition, quarantine sections and a psychiatric annex. Special establishments for recidivists and for rebellious convicts were also contemplated.

Today Argentina's system of prisons and *cárceles* is complete and modern so far as construction is concerned. Aside from the National Penitentiary in Buenos Aires, all establishments are located in agricultural regions with the result that farming and allied work constitute the main occupations of the prisoners. The system of prisons and jails is as follows:

PRISONS AND PENAL COLONIES

Name	*Province or Territory*	*Population in 1941* males	*females*
National Penitentiary	Buenos Aires	702	
National Prison	" "	612	
Women's Prison	" "		104
Santa Rosa Penal Colony	La Pampa	216	
General Roca Penal Colony	Río Negro	157	
Rawson Penal Colony	Chubut	110	6
	Cárceles (Jails)		
Ushuaia	Tierra del Fuego	500	
Posadas	Misiones	205	7
Formosa	Formosa (capital)	166	3
Resistencia	Chaco	478	
Santa Rosa	La Pampa	82	9
General Pico	" "	27	
Neuquén	Neuquén (capital)	133	6
Viedma	Río Negro	179	13
Esquel	Chubut	84	
Río Gallegos	Santa Cruz	77	
(In custody of police) *		689	
	Totals	4,417	148

* In the prison reports this category is not explained. From an answer to a letter of inquiry, my understanding is that this group represents minor offenders, such as vagrants and those detained on suspicion.

THE NATIONAL PENITENTIARY IN BUENOS AIRES

My short stay in Argentina made it impossible for me to visit any of the country's prisons except the one in Buenos Aires known as the National Penitentiary. However, Dr. Eduardo Ortiz, Director-General of Prisons, and his staff took me to a projection room in the city where we saw a film depicting life at the penal colony of Santa Rosa in the province of La Pampa.

The National Penitentiary was erected in 1877 and, at the time, was located in the country near the city. However, today

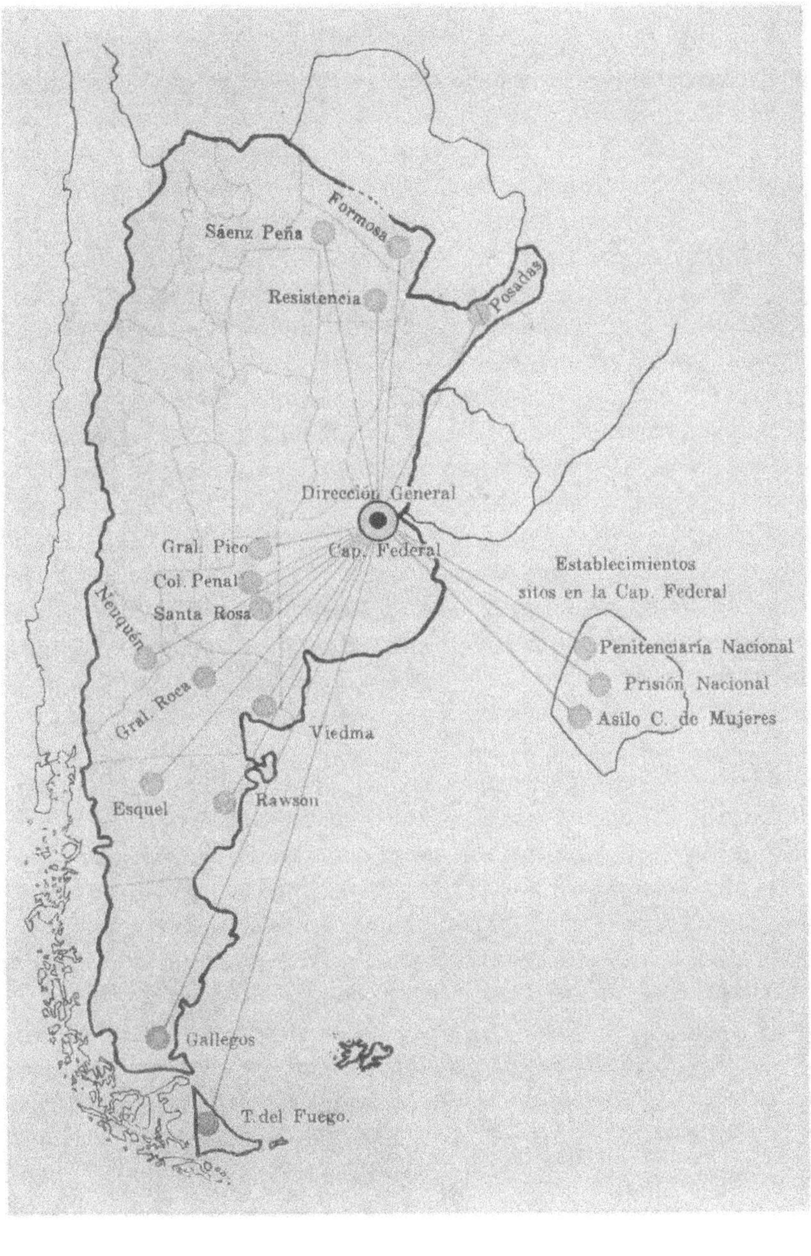

Location of Penal Institutions
ARGENTINA

it may be seen in the midst of crowded thoroughfares and, like so many of our own penal institutions, is outmoded and totally unsuited for progressive penal treatment.

The architect of this prison was Ernesto Bunge and the builder, Valentín Balbín. It is even today a most imposing structure, covering a very large area and kept in scrupulous condition. The total capacity is 704 without doubling up, a situation which has not yet been resorted to. However, the total number of prisoners is usually approximately the same number as the cellular capacity. The present director is Sr. Pietro Siricura.

Immediately inside the walls and beyond the administration building there are two small cellblocks (*pabellones*) each accommodating 52 inmates. Beyond these and radiating from a center are five larger blocks each accommodating 120 inmates. On the perimeter of the wall, in separate buildings, are the shops (*talleres,*) eight in number. Housed also in separate buildings are a modern and superbly equipped hospital and the *Anexo Psiquiátrico,* or diagnostic clinic.

There are some interesting features conspicuous in this penitentiary calling for both favorable and unfavorable comment. I was especially impressed with the cleanliness of the establishment. While the institution is old, it is not so ancient as many of our own penitentiaries, but it definitely belongs to that period when it was the fashion to build fortress-like prisons. The problem of housekeeping in such institutions is a serious one. But in this prison the management does a very commendable job. Then, too, this prison has long been famed for its paintings and murals. Along all the corridors—though not in the cells—are works of real art, executed by former inmates and attractively framed. As one writer has described them:

> And the pictures! The oil paintings which decorate the walls! Everyone is the work of a convict. There was no unrecognized master among them, no sentenced Gauguin or Van Gogh, but the intention and gusto were astonishing. Rustic comedy of a *paisano* being thrown from a lively Creole horse; gaunt portrait of San Martín, the national liberator, star-

ing from his equestrian heights toward a shrunken version of the Andes —rural and patriotic motives nearly all. But the fact that these men should have bothered to paint pictures here, should have cared to decorate the background of their constrained lives, is indication enough that they keep their self-respect.[2]

So far as I was able to learn, painting is no longer encouraged. More serious work is pursued in the elaborate shops, and even within the walls and between the *pabellones* of the prison are large open spaces devoted to the growing of vegetables.

There are features of this prison, however, that mar the progressive vision of its administration, as judged by a penologist of the United States. There is a deadly monotony present with altogether too much military precision. The monotony also reflects itself in the hideous prison garb worn by the inmates. It is the old-time stripes, but here, instead of being our conventional black and white, it is yellow and blue. Even the walls of the entire prison are painted in a monotonous shade and, of all colors for decorating a prison, orchid was chosen. Even in the bakery, which is modern in every respect, the walls are also of orchid and the large windows are daubed with the same colored paint. My reaction to this extravagant use of such a bizarre color was one of depression. If this condition prevailed in a prison of the United States one might be tempted to accuse the warden of exercising an ingenious device to punish the inmates. Certainly a surfeit of purple tints should be enough to provide ennui of the worst sort.

But aside from the above criticism I found this penitentiary well equipped and staffed by understanding personnel and efficient guards. Argentina has long maintained a school for guards, this service having been organized by Dr. Eusebio Gómez in 1925, the same outstanding scholar who, with Dr. Jorge Eduardo Coll, drew up the proposed new project of a penal code in 1936. Much credit is due Dr. Gómez for his excellent services in developing prison administration in his country.

[2] Rupert Croft-Cooke, "Prison Reform in Argentina," Pan American Bulletin, 1937, 71, 695–97.

The hospital, too, deserves special mention since it ranks with the prison hospital in São Paulo in Brazil as the best I saw in South America. This hospital was created and brought to its present state of medical and sanitary efficiency by the former Director-General of Prisons, Dr. Paz Anchorena.

There are many well-equipped shops in the National Penitentiary where the traditional prison products are manufactured for state-use (*fiscal*) and for private contract (*particulares*). Clothing, shoes, printing and other products are in demand from the various state-supported agencies although I was unable to ascertain the extent of production. The law calls for an eight-hour work day and, aside from several groups of prisoners standing in line, apparently for some type of inspection, all of the inmates I saw were employed or at least occupied. Many of them were working in the vegetable gardens between the blocks.

The prisoners are paid a wage which is divided into four parts. These are for indemnity or restitution, for the maintenance of dependents, for their own maintenance in prison and for an account which is payable to them upon release. What the various percentages are I was unable to learn. Nor did I learn just what wages the inmate workers receive. But judging from the practice found in most of the countries as well as in our own states, the amount is probably negligible.

The prisoner entering the National Penitentiary for the first time goes through the traditional initial ritual such as a bath, exchanging his clothing for prison garb, meeting the director, who outlines the purpose of his incarceration and analyzes the rules, penalties, etc. Then he is taken to his cell. He is gradually examined by the various members of the clinic or institute of criminology and, if necessary, by the personnel of the psychiatric annex. What use is made by the prison administration of the diagnosis made by the specialized personnel I was unable to learn. The fact that I was ushered through the prison in Buenos Aires by the Director-General of Prisons, Dr. Ortiz, and some of his staff members, made it somewhat indelicate for me to ask too many questions in so short a time. While my questions were answered with great courtesy I had the feeling that some of the prison services were either taken as matter-of-fact or were not functioning too efficiently. When I asked about the classification clinic I was told with considerable pride that there was a splendid clinic; but how it functions I could not learn. I suspect that it is staffed by capable men and that thorough examinations are given every inmate. But I further suspect that no individual prison plan is worked out for the inmate as we find in our best clinics in the States.

There is functioning in this prison a *Tribunal de Conducto* composed of the sub-director of the prison, the Chief of the Penal Section and the director of the school. It holds sessions to consider discipline from the first to the tenth of every other month. Prisoners are classified by this tribunal into the following categories based on their conduct: exemplary, very good, good, regular, bad and very bad. It arrives at its decisions through the reports on the prisoner covering his conduct in the cellblocks, the shops and the school; his cooperation in shop and class; his progress as a worker and as a pupil; and his disposition and character in so far as they can be ascertained by the guards.

There is a system of rewards and privations or disciplinary measures. *A La Buena Conducta* (good conduct) permits the withdrawal of books from the library, use of a heater in the cell, privilege of visits from family, permission to spend some of the money earned in the prison factory for herbs, tea, coffee, sugar and tobacco; *A La Muy Buena Conducta* (very good conduct) the same as those above in addition to the free use of chocolate; *A La Conducta Ejemplar* (exemplary conduct) same as above and, in addition, an hour more light in the cell each night, privilege to wear one's own clothing and to receive articles from home on visiting days.

The privations or penalties deal only with the withdrawal of those privileges stated above. There apparently is no dark cell nor corporal punishment.

There is a publication printed in the prison for the inmates.

It is called *El Domingo* and has the format of a small newspaper rather than of a magazine.

It is obviously clear to anyone who comes in contact with the Argentina penal system that the genuine vision of Dr. O'Connor, its creator and guiding spirit, still inspires the present director and staff members in developing a progressive penal philosophy. Then, too, the policy that has permitted O'Connor's successors to be chosen from that scholarly group associated with the University has borne fruit not only in maintaining the gains made by the first Director-General but also in carrying on a modern program of construction and treatment.

The present Director-General, Dr. Eduardo Ortiz, is a man of enthusiasm and solid worth. He has associated with him trained personnel in a variety of fields and a spirit of harmony and constructive thinking obviously prevails.

THE PENITENTIARY CLINIC

Since the diagnostic clinic in the National Penitentiary of Buenos Aires is the oldest of its kind in the world, a few words concerning its history and function are relevant.

In the year 1905 Dr. Antonio Ballve wrote a letter to the president of the republic suggesting that a "technical office" or service should be opened in the National Penitentiary for the purpose of making a scientific study of each prisoner. The Minister of Justice was impressed and in due time created an "Office of Psychology and Anthropometry" for the prison. By a decree dated June 6, 1907, Dr. José Ingenieros was made the director of this newly created bureau or office. Under his leadership and energy this new service took on the character of an Institute of Criminology. To quote from one writer: "Así nació el primer organismo oficial de esta naturaleza, totalmente independiente del cuerpo médico del penal." "Thus was born the first official organization of this nature, totally independent of medicine and law." [3]

[3] Julio Altmann Smythe, *Reseña Histórica de la Evolución del Derecho Penal*, Peru, 1944, p. 156.

Ingenieros was convinced that the prisoner should be studied in all his personal phases and thus he set up three sections in his new Institute. They were: *Sección de Etiología Criminal* (criminal causation), which dealt with the anthropology of the criminal as well as the factors associated with the crime; *Clínica criminológica,* which attempted to ascertain the degree of social maladjustment and criminality of the inmate by studying his psychopathological attributes; and *Sección de Terapéutica Criminal,* which studied treatment of the inmate as well as recommended types of preventive legislation and measures of reforming penal treatment.

Ingenieros was succeeded by Dr. Helvio Fernández and he in turn by the well-known Dr. Osvaldo Loudet. In April 1942 Loudet was succeeded by Dr. Carlos A. Videla who is the present incumbent.

Under the supervision of Dr. Loudet many improvements were effected and additional services introduced. On February 18, 1938 a diagnostic laboratory was created (previously approved by the law No. 11,833 of 1934) and called the *Anexo Psiquiátrico Central.* It is the function of this *Anexo* to examine and treat all inmates who present psychopathic manifestations more or less transitory (*más o menos transitoria*). According to the description of its duties it makes an analysis of the factors constituting the personality of the delinquent inmate and assumes the responsibility placed upon it by society and the judges for providing social security. Approximately five hundred criminal histories are prepared by the clinic annually.

CONDITIONAL RELEASE

The penal code under which Argentina functions was adopted in 1922 and superseded the older one of 1887. In 1937 an up-to-date project was drawn up by Dr. Jorge Eduardo Coll and Dr. Eusebio Gómez, known as "El Proyecto Coll-Gómez," but it was not adopted by the government.

Conditional release is none too specifically defined in the code of 1922 although it is recognized under certain stipulations which are as follows. Prisoners sentenced to life imprisonment who have served twenty years; those with a sentence of more than three years who have served two-thirds of their time; and those sentenced to less than three years who have served eight months, may apply for conditional release if their conduct has been exemplary while in prison.

The director of the prison submits the petition to the judicial authorities and, if granted, the following rules must be observed: (1) that he live in the place determined by the judicial regulation which frees him; (2) that he observe all the rules stipulated, especially the obligation to abstain from alcoholic beverages; (3) that he adopt a trade or occupation if he has no means of subsistence; (4) that he shall not commit new crimes; and (5) that he shall place himself under the care of some patronage indicated by competent authorities.

The *Patronato*, the supervising agency, was founded in 1918 in Argentina by a small group of "interested gentlemen" called together for the purpose by Dr. Jorge H. Frias who has been interested in the plight of the condemned man for many years. However recent this semi-official organization may be, concern for the released prisoner reaches as far back as 1820 when organizations similar to the *Patronato* functioned throughout the country.

THE SUSPENDED SENTENCE

Just as in other South American countries, probation appears only in its incipient form. It follows the familiar pattern of suspension of the execution of the sentence and if there is any supervision it is quite sporadic at best.

The penal code of 1922, in Articles 26 and 27, specifically defines the conditions under which the suspension of the execution of the sentence may be granted by the judge: "In cases of first offense or of a sentence to imprisonment not exceeding two years, or of fines, the tribunals may order that the serving of the sentence is to be suspended. This declaration will be based on the moral personality of the convict, the nature of the crime and the circumstances surrounding it in so far as they may be able to assist in understanding such personalities. The tribunal will require the information which it deems pertinent in forming an opinion. In the cases of recurrence of crimes, conditional serving will result if the sentence to be imposed does not exceed two years of imprisonment, or fine." And further: "The sentence will be regarded as not having been pronounced if within the term of the prescription of the punishment the convict does not commit a new crime. However, if he does commit a new crime he will suffer the punishment imposed in the first sentence and also that which is imposed on him by the second crime according to the laws of the accumulation of punishments."

TREATMENT OF JUVENILE DELINQUENCY IN ARGENTINA

During the past fifteen years Argentina has made significant strides in dealing with her neglected and abandoned children. Her system of cottage-type institutions, *Colonias-Hogares,* is known far and wide for its progressive insight in training children up to eighteen years of age.

The penal code stipulates that children under fourteen are not punishable for their delinquencies. Such children may be placed under the care of their parents or, if this is not feasible, they may be sent to a correctional institution until they have reached eighteen. No child under eighteen can be sent to a prison.

Argentina, following the tradition found in all South American countries, looks upon the delinquent child as neglected, not depraved. All forms of neglect including the dependent, the abused, the abandoned and the delinquent are assumed to be victims of someone's neglect, if not society's failure to guarantee a wholesome childhood. Hence, all such children are treated alike and come under the protection of the great organization of the *Patronato Nacional de Menores.* This organization is headed by Dr. Carlos de Arenasa with headquarters at Santa Fe, 880 in Buenos Aires.

The pioneer in this work is Dr. Jorge Eduardo Coll, mentioned earlier in connection with the Coll-Gómez project, who has long been interested in the neglected child. He is the author of the project of 1929 which created the *Patronato Nacional de Menores* and was its first president. He is also a former Minister of Justice of Argentina. While today he holds no public office, he still maintains a keen interest in the work of the institutions created for the protection and training of the neglected child. He is also professor of law in the University.

Perhaps the most famous of the schools which care for the children coming under the guardianship of the *Patronato* is the pioneer *Colonia-Hogar "Ricardo Gutiérrez"* located about twenty-five miles from the city of Buenos Aires but within the Federal District. Named in honor of a prominent physician who took a particular interest in children, this school, or colony, was opened in 1924. It has thus served as a model for subsequent schools.

Its director, Señor Felipe M. Giana, is a prominent educator, a man who understands boys, but one who also comprehends the grave responsibility to society in returning his charges to the workaday world better prepared for life's battles in centers of industry or even in colleges and the professions. He considers the function of the school as being to give the boys a well-rounded course of training. Each boy is treated as an individual. The old philosophy of mass training has long since been abandoned since it has become established that every boy and girl is a unique personality. This is accepted as axiomatic in this colony school.

The visitor to *Ricardo Gutiérrez* is immediately impressed with the commodious grounds, the plant and the equipment, after he has approached the school under the long avenue of giant old shade trees. The buildings are small but modern and especially attractive, from the comfortable administration building, which the new boy sees first, to the various cottages, school, theatre, and chapel.

The institution's population, on the average around five hundred, ranging from eight years in age to seventeen, is divided into small groups according to age and occupation. A homelike atmosphere pervades the entire establishment. Each cottage is supervised by a married couple whose main function is to maintain a home for the small number of boys assigned to them.

The only criticism possible in connection with the living accommodations of the boys is the ubiquitous dormitory. While the large rooms devoted to sleeping quarters in the various cottages are scrupulously clean, it is obvious to anyone trained in child care that the absence of privacy in the life of the child is much more to be deplored than a little evidence of carelessness in housekeeping in homes where individual rooms are provided. Those who accompanied me to this institution actually scoffed at the idea of individual rooms for children. This is the only country I visited where no interest whatsoever was demonstrated in the reasons why the dormitory is less desirable than individual rooms.

The new boy, upon entering, is submitted to the usual tests; medical, psychological, psychiatric, and social, following the best procedure found in similar institutions in our own country in the various states. A complete day-by-day record of the boys' achievements in school, shop and athletic field is maintained so that the director can see at a glance which boys need more individualized or specialized care. The entire staff has a fundamental and personalized concern for each boy which is obvious to the visitor.

The school building, modern in every respect and most attractive both inside and out, is staffed by understanding teachers who follow the progressive method of individualized study. Each classroom is gaily decorated with flags, paintings and statues, with attractive curtains at the windows. While most of the pupils are boys, there is a fair sprinkling of girls, daughters of staff members and of neighbors living in the vicinity of the institution. This, in itself, is evidence of the wholesome philosophy underlying the institution.

It is evident that the children like their courses of instruction. One interesting activity in the school is puppetry. This is understandable since the master of marionettes of the Argentine, Javier Villafañe, has created so much enthusiasm during the past ten years that over five hundred schools throughout the country make this form of self-expression an integral part of their curriculum.[4]

The colony of *Ricardo Gutiérrez* is especially proud of its athletics. It is equipped with a large outdoor gymnasium and playing field. Football, basketball, track and aquatic sports are an essential part of everyday living. Keen rivalry exists among the cottages, and athletic heroes are awarded special recognition for their prowess. Drill, wand exercises and calisthenics executed to band music is an inspiring sight for the visitor although this aspect of the program is a little too regimented in so progressive a school. The school paper, *Nuevo Rumbo,* an attractive sheet, features the athletic events of the school.

In addition to the regular school, shop work presents the serious side of the institution. Attractively designed shops, well equipped, light and airy, are beehives of activity a large portion of the day, especially for the older boys. Skilled instructors teach the trades—tailoring, ironwork, ceramics, printing, wagon making, and plumbing. But agriculture and animal husbandry are also major occupations. Boys are taught modern methods of farming and the raising of purebred cattle, so close to the hearts of all Argentines. Poultry, beekeeping, and the production of honey are all a part of the school program.

And the art work, including painting, sculpture, and the decoration of china ware, manufactured in the ceramics department, is a high spot in the course of instruction. Scenes from the *pampas,*

[4] See *Inter-American,* June 1944, "Argentine Puppet Master," by Vincent Pascal.

from the lives of the native *vaqueros,* Argentina's indigenous cowboys, furnish strong *motifs* for the boys, many of whom come from the rural areas and know at first hand the life of the cattle country.

Discipline seems to be no problem in this school. True, boys sometimes get into trouble but, unless they persist, they are handled by means of sympathetic councils. Those who continue to be wilful are transferred to the annex known as *El Retiro,* separate and distinct, but near by. Here a more closely supervised régime attempts to straighten out those who cannot appreciate the joys of normal group living. My short stay and my difficulty in conversing in Spanish made it impossible for me to see intimately just how problems of discipline were actually handled. The home-like atmosphere of cottage life as well as the definite evidence of progressive educational philosophy belie, for example, the slight tint of military precision in mass calisthenics or the abruptness with which the subject of individual rooms for the boys was brushed aside. My judgment is that both progressive education and mild regimentation exist in this school, paradoxical as it may seem.

But there are other *Colonias* besides *Ricardo Gutiérrez.* There is, for example, the sister school of *Santa Rita* for girls, at Boulogne, not far from the city of Buenos Aires. Located in the country, this school can accommodate about 150 girls between the ages of six and eighteen. Another school for girls is *Santa Rosa,* located on Calle Belgrano, within the city. Weaving, sewing and the domestic arts, in addition to regular graded school instruction, make up the curriculum of these schools, with some gardening in the former.

Since the establishment, under the act of 1929, of the *Colonia-Hogar, Juan B. Alberdi,* in 1932, many of these progressive institutions have been developed. Today the number of children cared for in the various schools directed by the *Patronato Nacional de Menores* is around 1,500. Besides those mentioned above, there are *Carlos Pellegrino* at Pilar; *Mariano Ortiz Basualdo* at Las

Armas; *Cayetano Zibecchi* at Juárez; a School for Artisans; and a new colony just recently opened, *Los Arenales*.

The programs of these schools are essentially the same. They were designed primarily to train the country's youth who have been handicapped by poor homes, social indifference, or sheer neglect, so that they may be equipped to take their places in industry and the arts.

Embryonic social work finds its place in Argentina. The first school was organized in 1930 and is known as the *Escuela de Servicio Social del Museo Social Argentino.* Aside from the regular students a special group of auditors recruited from the young society women of the city is admitted for the purpose, to quote from the director of the school, "of creating a more liberal point of view among these upholders of ancient philanthropic traditions." The faculty is drawn from the health department, the juvenile court, the University and the *Museo Social Argentino.* The curriculum consists of three years, but evening classes only were held as late as 1940.

Another Buenos Aires institution is that of the *Escuela Católica de Servicio Social* founded in 1940. The school operates in the headquarters of the *Instituto de Cultura Religiosa Superior Femenina* and is under the patronage of the Archbishop of Buenos Aires. Young people of seventeen who "have an education and culture which, in the judgment of the directors, is sufficient and adapted" may be admitted for the three-year course.

CONCLUDING REMARKS

So far as new and modern prison construction is concerned, Argentina stands in the foreground of all the countries of South America. She has done even more than Brazil since many states of this latter country still maintain old prison plants. Argentina's leadership can be attributed to the fact that prior to the days of Juan O'Connor there were no prisons except the National Penitentiary in Buenos Aires. As it stands today, this prison is antiquated as compared to those throughout the provinces. In fact, there have been many serious attempts to dismantle this institution and erect a new prison for the Federal District in the country. It stands on a most valuable residential site, a strange anomaly since few, if any, prisons throughout the world are in other than slum areas of a large city. The surrounding streets are filled with the homes of the comfortable middle-class and, as one writer describes the section, it is one of the "verdaderos jardines de la Metrópoli."

As stated above, I did not have the pleasure of viewing any of the provincial penal establishments. From pictures I saw, however, they are of modern lines, emphasizing a maximum of sunlight and fresh air. One of the prison architects attached to the staff of the Director of Prisons, Sr. José Pirovano, proudly stated that all of his country's prisons were outside cell construction and were totally unlike the prisons of the United States. Sr. Pirovano has spent some time in the United States and undoubtedly was making his comparison with our prisons of the Auburn era.

If one may be permitted to judge the philosophy of Argentina's prison system by the administration of the National Penitentiary in Buenos Aires, he would stress its efficiency almost to the point of strict regimentation, its apparently adequate work program and its excellent medical service. Perhaps, added to these features, should be listed the complete initial examination which features primarily the physical characteristics of the incoming inmate.

There is little evidence of any real individualization of treatment such as may be found in some of our more progressive prisons. The striped uniforms are obvious proof of this neglect. Another proof is the military precision apparent everywhere.

The personnel, however, seemed to be on a high level. Dr. Ortiz, the Director-General of Prisons, enjoys an excellent reputation throughout South America. He possesses a pleasing personality and is a capable administrator. The prison guards in the National Penitentiary are well trained and are undoubtedly of higher calibre than those found in most of the prisons of Latin America.

Supervision of those released from prison conditionally is none too adequate. The best efforts of the semi-private *Patronato* can be no more than superficial on the adult level. Probation also is not well developed.

Argentina, however, is doing remarkable work in the treatment of dependent and delinquent children. The *Colonias*, described above, are of first rank in any comparison throughout the world. Here, the *Patronato* is rendering exceptional service and deserves unstinted praise. Many of the country's most socially minded men and women contribute their time and energy in making this phase of penology the success that it is.

IX

Brazil

THE COUNTRY

THERE can be no doubt that Brazil is a land of wonder. Larger than the United States of America and occupying almost half of the land space of South America, it has a population of less than fifty millions. But her wealth is amazing; in fact, her untapped resources are unpredictably rich and boundless. Her mineral wealth alone is referred to as the greatest untapped storehouse in the world. The greatest iron deposits in existence are located within her vast reaches. The agricultural possibilities of the country prompt Brazilians to make the claim that their country could support almost a billion people.

With a coastline of over four thousand miles, this country consists of two sharply contrasted sections, a table-land of rolling plains and mountains in the east and south, and the great jungle area of the Amazon in the north and west. Two reasons why Brazil's vast resources have not been exploited are the cruel resistance of the impenetrable jungle and the inadequate transportation. Both of these hindrances to commercial development are slowly being removed because of the war (which permitted no difficulties to stand in the way of its successful termination), and the development of air transportation.

The people of Brazil are perhaps more mixed than those of any other of the South American countries. Only about one-third of its people are white. The remaining two-thirds are of Negro extraction, Indian, and mixed breeds. Negroes predominate in a far greater proportion than in any other South American republic. The Indians number only slightly more than a million and none of these are domesticated in the sense that they form a part of the country's economy as in Colombia, Ecuador or Peru. Most of them are hidden away in the far reaches of the Amazonian jungle.

Literacy is low in Brazil, but this situation is nothing unusual for South America as we have seen in our review of other countries. Aside from Argentina and Uruguay, illiteracy runs from fifty to ninety per cent in all Latin American countries. In Brazil it runs about sixty to seventy per cent. Primary schooling is provided in most of Brazil's twenty states, but attendance is not compulsory. The health hazards are tremendous, but heroic efforts are constantly being made to reduce these to a minimum.

The language of Brazil is, of course, Portuguese. However, in the larger cities of Rio de Janeiro, São Paulo and a few others, English is understood by many of the people. This is especially true since the war when so many soldiers and sailors from the United States were stationed in the coast towns and gravitated to the larger cities on furlough. Most Brazilians are fond of the people of the United States; in fact, this friendly feeling is much more noticeable here than in any other country of South America.

My stay of three weeks in Brazil made it possible for me to visit São Paulo, Rio de Janeiro and Bello Horizonte. A few observations on the first two of these cities are perhaps in order.

São Paulo is a city of dignity, culture and wealth. It is the great coffee city of Brazil, the collecting center of the country's greatest crop and the shipping point from which it leaves for the nearby port of Santos. Year in and year out some fifteen per cent of this valuable coffee crop is burned in order to keep the price stabilized. But so diverse a city is São Paulo in her industries and products that one may visit the city and actually see no signs of coffee. It is a great industrial center and has been compared to Chicago and Pittsburgh. Its population is close to a million and a half and its rate of growth is prodigious. In many ways it is much more progressive than Rio, its natural rival. Its buildings are much larger and higher. One gets the feeling of great strength when in São Paulo whereas in Rio he thinks more of glamour and romance. Even São Paulo's new library is a twenty-four-storied skyscraper, perhaps unique in library architecture.

Wealthy as is São Paulo, the city has its poor in large numbers. While they are not so miserable as those in Rio they do find life extremely dull and harsh. Approximately fifty per cent of the city's inhabitants live in sub-standard dwellings. Francis Violich in his extremely useful work, *Cities of Latin America,* gives us a thumbnail description of the *corticos* and *vilas* of the city which leaves no doubt concerning the overcrowding and other miseries of the masses. The *corticos* are the poorest of the slum dwellings and, translated, means beehives. Family congestion in a limited area describes these rookeries. The *vilas* are single-family units of two or three rooms each, all in a row and sharing the same roof.[1]

Rio de Janeiro is far enough east of New York City to be two hours later in time. It is the capital of the country but not of the state of the same name. That distinction belongs to Niteroi, a city of some one hundred thousand people and situated across the bay adjacent to the Federal District and to Rio.

Most of us have seen pictures of the famous Santos Dumont airport in Rio de Janeiro, an architectural gem that satisfies both functional needs and aesthetic taste. It is only two minutes by taxi from the business center, the only airport in the world so conveniently located. It is a spacious area reclaimed by filling in the bay and is equipped with facilities for all types of land and seaplanes. It is named for the Brazilian inventor who is credited with flying the first airplane publicly as early as 1906. He is called the Father of Flight by his countrymen.

When one thinks of Rio he immediately associates the city with romance. But it is the traditional romance of gaiety, superb coloring, dreamy nights, festivals and carnivals, not the romance of commerce and trade. Yet the city is also blessed with these. In fact, the real romance of Rio de Janeiro is its amazing building program with the creation of new architectural forms. Con-

[1] New York: Reinhold Publishing Corporation, 1944, p. 78.

ventional architects of our country would do well to emulate the daring city planners of Rio, idealists who have actually put their dreams into stone, concrete and glass. Perhaps the most unique structure thus far to rear its majestic torso into the clouds is the Ministry of Education and Health building. One wall of this eighteen-story building is practically all glass. Another wall is a mass of movable horizontal louvers which serve as a means of regulating the warm rays of the sun for heating purposes. Pioneering zeal in city planning is a definite part of modern Brazil.[2]

Nor can a *gringo* overlook the beautiful and graceful mosaics that form the sidewalks in Rio. Made of delicate small tile, their black and white designs are a never-ending pleasure to the tourist.

But the joy of Rio is its colorful setting, perhaps the most admired in all the world. The city extends a half dozen miles or so along the broken seafront set on a narrow plain between the mountains and the bay. The famous granite cone, the *Pão de Assugar* (Sugar Loaf Mountain) rises over a thousand feet and is known by its picture to practically every school child in our own United States. *Corcovado* (Hunchback), a mountain peak of over 2,300 feet, rises amidst the houses of the city to add its superb coloring to the setting.

The promenade facing the bay is of white marble and is five miles long. The many romantic features of this promenade and its immediate environs include Avenida Rio Branco, the Fifth Avenue of the city, over a hundred feet wide and lined with trees and the smart shops of the city; and Copacabana Beach, the pride and joy of all *cariocas* who regard it as the most beautiful bathing playspot in the world.

There is great wealth in Rio. But, again, there is much poverty. The slums are much greater and a little more miserable than those of São Paulo. Francis Violich describes the *favellas*, the lowest type of housing that might conceivably pass for such! He tells us that they make our Okies' camps in California look like

[2] For the full story of Brazil's architectural renaissance see Philip Goodman, *Brazil Builds*, New York: Museum of Modern Art, 1943.

garden cities.[3] They are to be found in a conspicuous confusion on the slopes of the hills which dominate the city throughout. In general, the inhabitants of the slum dwellings pay about one-half their incomes for rent, which is obviously excessive. The *favellas* have no color line; whites and Negroes squat side by side in these sub-standard hovels.

Both São Paulo and Rio have gone in for social work training during the past ten years. The *Escola de Serviço Social* was organized in São Paulo in 1936, the pioneer school in Brazil. It was founded by the *Centro de Estudos e Acção Social* (Center for Social Studies and Social Action), and was given official recognition by the State of São Paulo in 1939. The school is under Catholic auspices and is a member of the International Catholic Social Service Union with headquarters in Brussels. The curriculum is on a high level and the graduates find no difficulty in locating employment, most of them in public work or in state offices.

There are several schools in Rio de Janeiro. The first one to be organized was the *Instituto de Educação Familiar e Social;* this was in 1937. It is Catholic and, in fact, was given the approval of the Archbishop of Rio. The director keeps in close touch with our own National Council of Catholic Women and the National Catholic School of Social Work in Washington. The school functions as an extension service of the University of Brazil but has avoided governmental support for fear of becoming involved in politics. It enjoys an excellent reputation so far as standards and training of its students are concerned.

A second school in Rio is that of the *Escola Technico de Serviço Social,* founded in 1938 by the Judge of Minors who needed social workers for his court. It enjoys recognition by the Ministries of Labor, Industry and Commerce, and Education and Health. Many of its graduates find employment supervising the employment conditions of women and children, as well as in the various courts for minors.

[3] *Op. cit.,* p. 77.

Other schools are the Training Course in Social Work of the Anna Nery School of Nurses, the *Instituto Carlos Chagas,* and the Municipal School of Social Work which has recently merged with the Red Cross School.

There is considerable evidence that Brazil gives serious thought to the development of social work. Its schools are on a high level and their graduates are gradually being absorbed into practically all types of welfare work, both private and public.

HISTORIC NOTE ON BRAZIL'S PRISONS

Brazil is the only country in South America that operates a decentralized system of prisons. Each of its twenty states, as well as the Federal District of Rio de Janeiro, has complete autonomy so far as penal administration is concerned. The more populous states in the east-central part of the country have naturally given more thought and practical action to developing their penal programs, although in other scattered sections to the north and south the prisons and their management are well above the average found in most of the other South American countries. One would be obliged to remain for some months in the United States of Brazil to acquire a thorough knowledge of the concepts and methods of dealing with the crime problem throughout its vast area.

On the whole, then, Brazil has made major strides in the field of penal administration since the days when our own Dr. Enoch C. Wines described some of her prisons in his work, *State of Prisons.* At the time he wrote, in 1879, Brazil was an empire ruled by Dom Pedro II and the only central prisons were the military establishments, most famous of which was the island of Fernando de Noronha set up in 1859. This colony lay three hundred miles off the coast of the city of Recife, capital of the state of Pernambuco. Other such military prisons were located in the bay off the city of Rio. These were the Ilha das Cobras, built in 1736, Villegaignon and the Fortaleza de Santa Cruz. These were substantially built fortresses where recalcitrant prisoners led a monotonous and drab existence. These prisons were under the control of the Minister of War up to 1877 when they were transferred to the Ministry of Justice.

It is historically interesting to record what Dr. Wines had to say about the penal régime in the large penal colony of Fernando de Noronha around 1879. There were some sixteen hundred prisoners condemned to hard labor from all the country's provinces. They were divided into twelve companies, of which eight were engaged in agriculture, one in the trades of cooperage, smithery, carpentry and shoemaking, and the remaining three in the domestic service of the establishment. All prisoners were paid for their labor.

In 1891, by special decree, this colony ceased to be used as a central prison and was turned over to the state of Pernambuco as a prison colony for that state's convicts. At the outbreak of the recent war this island was developed as a military base as part of the defenses of the Western Hemisphere. Therefore the state of Pernambuco found it necessary to establish a new penal colony, which it did on the island of Itamaracá, about twenty miles from Recife. A few words about this colony will be included later in the description of some of the country's prisons.

Aside from these military prisons of early days, all other penitentiaries and jails were provincial, many of which were built during the early days of Portuguese colonization. Perhaps the most thorough and scholarly account of the prison systems of Brazil is that written by Dr. Lemos Britto in 1924–26, a three-volume work entitled *Os Penitenciários do Brasil.* Dr. Britto enjoys a well-earned distinction in his native country for a life of public activity as well as for his energy and progressive vision in his chosen field of penology. At present he holds the post of President of the Penitentiary Council for the Federal District in Rio de Janeiro.

It is from Dr. Britto's volumes of penal facts that one may acquire historical background concerning the places of detention for criminals from the days of the founding of the first jail in the country—at Bahia (São Salvador) in 1549—to the modern and well-known penitentiary at São Paulo established in the year 1922. The construction of more recent institutions is described in the various issues of the *Arquivos Penitenciários do Brasil,* official publication of the penitentiary council of the Federal District.

In 1890, the then Minister, Campos Sales, described the philosophy of penal treatment in Brazil's prisons as that of "the system in operation in Philadelphia [solitary] combined with that of Auburn [silent] and modified by the Irish system of Sir Walter Crofton." Such was the widespread confusion of concepts, although the same could be stated of our own forty-eight states at that time. Dr. Britto calls attention to the same persistent confusion existing in 1922 throughout the prisons of Brazil where he found a wide variety of philosophies of penal treatment. There were, for instance, some prisons where cellular separation was restricted only to nights; some where the inmates both ate and slept in isolation, while working in common during the days; a few where the rule of silence was merely relative; at least one in which small groups of two or three were "isolated" together; and a few where the silence rule was rigorously enforced. In short, there was no uniformity whatsoever.[4]

It may be seen from the above that decentralization and autonomy have their handicaps in Brazil. This, of course, is equally true in our own country with forty-eight different administrations added to the Federal System. In 1879 it was proposed in Brazil to unify the country's penal establishments so that their control would be national rather than provincial. Dr. Wines pointed out at that time that many advantages would accrue from such centralization. His words have interest even today: "It is beyond question that the unity of the penal law demands as its logical sequence uniformity in the penitentiary system of the country

[4] Lemos Britto, "Evolution of the Brazilian Penitentiary System During the Past Twenty-five Years," *Revista Penal e Penitenciária,* São Paulo, 1943, III, 36–37.

where there is a single criminal code, since the execution of the penalty is a part of the penalty itself."[5] There is, of course, more reason for Brazil to centralize than our own country since one penal code governs the entire country. But it takes more than a uniform code to facilitate such centralization. Sectional rivalry and political jealousy militate against it, especially since some of its advantages are somewhat dubious.

Regardless of the desirability of uniformity, the fact remains that today Brazil permits her various states to maintain practically complete autonomy over their prisons. In 1924, Decree No. 16,665 was inaugurated which established Penitentiary Councils in the Federal District and in the various states. These are composed of the Attorney General of the Republic, a representative of the local Public Ministry and five other officials, three of whom are professors of law and two physicians. These Councils handle all matters dealing with conditional release, pardons and penal discipline of all types of prisoners.

NEW PENAL CODE

The penal code in operation throughout Brazil, replacing the one of 1890, went into operation on January 1, 1942. It represents the culmination of a long and sustained effort dating from 1893 when the project of the deputy Vieira de Araújo was rejected by the Chamber of Deputies, through 1911 and 1927 when the respective projects of Galdino Siqueira and Bulhões Pedreira were turned down.

In 1936 the Conference of Criminology, meeting in Rio de Janeiro, dedicated its proceedings to an examination of the criminal code then in operation and, subsequently, in 1938, a new project was drawn up by Dr. Alcántara Machado, a professor of penal law at the University of São Paulo. In due time a Revision Committee was appointed to study and revise this project. This

[5] Wines, *op. cit.*, p. 555.

Commission was presided over by the Minister of Justice, Dr. Francisco Campos, and included three prominent jurists, Drs. Vieira Braga, Nelson Hungría and Narcelio de Queiroz. Associated with the Commission was a representative of the Public Ministry, the distinguished penologist and professor of law, Dr. Roberto Lyra. Others who also made definite contributions were Dr. A. J. Costa e Silva and Dr. Abgar Renault.

The new code is satisfying since it meets the needs of this vast country in every particular. It is a forward-looking document, devised with meticulous care and one which takes cognizance of modern social and economic conditions. Offenses follow the usual nomenclature found throughout South America: serious crimes, with a maximum penalty of twenty years, and misdemeanors, carrying only a brief sentence in a prison. Long-term imprisonment is known as *reclusão;* short-term as *detenção.* The code also calls for fines or *multas.* The death penalty is not referred to in the penal code although it was reinstated in 1938 after having been abolished in 1891. Its reinstatement was "for cases of extreme perversity only." Such crimes are determined by the Tribunal of National Security and include those which interfere with the national economy such as usury and excessive speculation in price-fixing of necessary consumer goods. However, there have been no executions in Brazil since this penalty was revived.

CONDITIONAL RELEASE

According to the provisions of the new penal code which bear upon conditional release from prison, a ceremony, perhaps unique in penal practice, accompanies the granting of the concession. The members of the Penitentiary Council are all present when the candidates appear for their coveted certificates of release. The prison population is assembled and a program, opening with the playing of the national anthem by the institution's band, is solemnly carried out. Each successful recipient of release is apprized of his responsibilities to society and must take a pledge by which he promises to observe all the conditions assigned to his release.

The penal code states that, for first offenders, conditional release may be applied for upon the expiration of one-half of the sentence; for recidivists, the time is three-fourths. The following items are taken into consideration: literacy, good conduct record, possibilities of reformation; work history showing adaptability; assurance of a job; and good relations with family. Candidates make application to the Penitentiary Council and, if deemed eligible, recommendations are made to the sentencing judge who is vested with the final authority.

There is no supervision comparable to that connected with our parole. However, the released prisoner must keep a notebook which he carries at all times. He must periodically present himself before the judge or the director of the prison from which he was released. Until the end of his trial release he is under the constant surveillance, or "official guardianship," of the police. If he violates any of his obligations his release is revoked by the judge and he is returned to the prison to serve out the remainder of his sentence.

It is somewhat of an anomaly that Brazil provides so wisely for a solemn occasion for officially granting conditional release and then countenances such a haphazard method of supervision. I can vouch for the impressiveness of the exercises connected with the granting of conditional release since I attended such a meeting in the penitentiary [House of Correction] for the Federal District at Rio de Janeiro. The prisoners were all assembled and the Penitentiary Council sat on the platform of the auditorium. Dr. Lemos Britto, president of the Council, spoke of the importance of release to society and to the prisoner. Each man walked to the platform, was given his release papers and Dr. Britto shook hands with him and made a few encouraging remarks.

Students of penology will agree that the released prisoner

needs more than a godspeed from the prison. He has little to look forward to, in so far as guidance and sympathetic help are concerned, if he must rely on nothing but close surveillance by a police system. It is here that Brazil is failing its released prisoners as well as society in general.

PROBATION

Only a few words will be necessary to describe adult probation in Brazil. The country maintains probation of the usual Latin type—the suspension of the execution of the sentence. This provision dates from 1893. However, it was put in operation only in 1924. While I was unable to determine the conditions of this so-called probation in Brazil, Professor Timasheff lists them as follows: for first offenders only, the suspension limited to one year only, and refusal to grant it in cases of offenses against the honor of families.[6]

PRISONS

If the expansive and highly progressive country of Brazil has failed to refine her methods of conditional release and probation, she may heartily be commended for her prisons, at least for those in some of the more populous and wealthy states. It would be difficult to choose between Brazil and Argentina in selecting the foremost country in South America in prison construction and penal administration. And I am not overlooking Colombia, which country, in some respects, surpasses all in recognizing many of the implications of the progressive era of the New Penology. For instance, Colombia's rational program of productive prison labor gives her a valid claim to top-rank status. But so far as prison construction is concerned she cannot hope to compare with either Brazil or Argentina.

[6] N. S. Timasheff, *One Hundred Years of Probation*, New York: Fordham University Press, 1943. Part II, pp. 63–65.

As stated above, Dr. Lemos Britto, veteran penologist of Rio de Janeiro, has produced a three-volume work on the prisons of his country and from it one may gain an excellent picture of the construction of prisons throughout the years. Many states have done very little in bringing their penal treatment into line with modern standards. In all too many penitentiaries there may still be found the black and white stripes on their prisoners—zebras, Dr. Britto calls them—and one may gather that much of the administration resembles the older nineteenth-century repression. But starting with the prison of the state of São Paulo in the city of the same name, some of the more progressive states have definitely accepted the responsibility of developing modern prison standards both in construction and administration.

Time prevented me from visiting many penal establishments in Brazil. The vast distances between centers of population and the transportation problem, especially during wartime, compel the visitor with little time at his disposal to restrict his visits to the cities of São Paulo and Rio de Janeiro. Aside from the penal institutions in these two metropolises I also had the good fortune to see a most interesting prison near Bello Horizonte, the state penitentiary for Minas Geraes, at Nevez. There can be no doubt that these three prisons represent the best to be found throughout Brazil from the standpoints of construction, administration and program. According to what I have been able to gather from the literature sent to me since returning home, few states aside from São Paulo, Minas Geraes and the Federal District of Rio de Janeiro have gone far down the road of the New Penology. However, there are new modern prisons in other states aside from those mentioned. I shall now describe these three institutions and add a few comments on some of the institutions that merit favorable mention but which I was unable to visit.

The penitentiary of the state of São Paulo was built in 1922 and has long been recognized as a modern and progressive institution. *Paulistas* with a knowledge of penology refer to it as one of the best penal establishments in the world. Such extravagant praise would be gilding the lily since it has obvious faults both in architecture and administrative philosophy. But to a person unfamiliar with the newer types of prison architecture that have been accepted since 1922—notably the "telephone-pole" plan found in many of our own institutions—or to one who looks upon all criminals as products of heredity almost exclusively, such a panegyric can be excused.

I was accompanied to this institution by the secretary of the diagnostic clinic officially known as the *Instituto de Biotipologia Criminal,* Senhor Rodrigues de Meréje, and Dr. Rex Crawford, Cultural Relations Attaché of the Embassy of the United States.

The structure is an imposing one with a massive façade, resembling in many of its architectural details a typical prison of the United States constructed along the conventional lines of the past century. I commented that it is regrettable that when this prison was planned more research in modern prison architecture was not pursued since even at that date—1922—penologists were beginning to abandon the conventional Auburn type of architecture.

Over the main door of the prison are these words: "Here, work, discipline and kindness mend the error committed and restore the offender to the status of the social community." These are brave words and there can be no doubt that work, discipline and, perhaps, even kindness are to be found here. But whether the prisoner is actually restored as a respectable member of society may be questioned. Certainly this laudable objective is not realized in most prisons, regardless of worthy motives.

While the São Paulo prison is scrupulously clean, modern so far as security is concerned—it has all the automatic gadgets to be found in our "best" prisons—, has outside cellblocks and ample provision for modern work shops, it still clings to the old traditional four-tier blocks. This alone stamps the prison with the curse of mass treatment in spite of the excellent services rendered the individual prisoners.

The former director of this institution was the outstanding

chief of police, Dr. Acácio Nogueira, but upon his death in 1943 Dr. Flamíno Fávero, professor of medicine in São Paulo University, succeeded him. Unfortunately the director was not present on the day of my visit but from what I could learn from residents of the city he is well regarded as a man and as a penal administrator.

It is a rare penal administrator, indeed, who is flawless. For an outsider who has never administered a prison but who has visited many of them, it is always easy to criticize. Hence, there are some features of the São Paulo prison, aside from the architecture, that call for critical judgment. Two are worthy of mention. The front corridor is filled with framed paintings, or lithographs, depicting the evils of drunkenness. I was reminded of the old pictures of temperance days in our own country which attempted to frighten the youth by graphically conveying the terrible results of chronic drinking. Another interesting sidelight that demonstrates the highly moral philosophy of the prison, or its director, is the conspicuous presence of small placards hung at various places throughout the prison warning the inmates to "Be Quiet."

Perhaps it may be regarded as unfair to make such carping criticism in the light of the excellent work being accomplished in this institution, but the skeptical penologist cannot overlook even the vestiges of the philosophy of expiation or retribution in an otherwise modern prison. Modern penal treatment cannot go far when fine moral undertones are permitted to permeate the prison program.

Perhaps the most progressive feature of São Paulo prison is its excellent diagnostic clinic, known throughout South America as the *Instituto de Biotipologia Criminal,* headed by the capable Dr. João Carlos da Silva Telles, a man who is an astute student of crime causation. This clinic was established in 1939 through the initiative of the former director of the prison, Dr. Acácio Nogueira. The first director of this clinic was the eminent psychiatrist, Dr. Pedro Augusto da Silva, who assumed his duties in

1941. He was succeeded in 1942 by Dr. Silva Telles. It is interesting to note, in passing, that the first criminal laboratory in Brazil was created in Rio de Janeiro in 1932 by Professor Leonidio Ribeiro. It was known as the *Laboratório de Antropologia Criminal do Brasil.*

The clinic in the São Paulo penitentiary was, in the beginning, referred to as *Servico,* but that term is no longer used. Nicola Pende, the disciple of Lombroso and the founder of the constitutional school of criminal investigation in Italy, is given credit for the word "Biotipologia." He defined it as "the science that concerns itself with each particular complexity of life—anatomical, moral, functional and psychological—by which diagnostic synthesis we are able to recognize the structural type of each individual; how he differs from all others especially through anatomy, physiology, psychology and statistics." [7]

The São Paulo clinic includes the traditional biological services. It is divided into various sections headed by the following specialists: Medical Director, Dr. Silva Telles; assistants, Dr. Salvador Rocco and Sr. Rodrigues de Meréje; Anthropometric Section, Dr. Rocco; Psychiatric Section, Dr. Tomaz de A. Collet e Silva Filho; Sociological Section, Dr. Arnaldo Caleiros Sandoval; Endocrinology Section, Dr. Alvaro Pedro dos Santos and Dr. Artur de Aguiar Whitaker; Psychology Section, Dr. Cicero Carhaldo Lage; Librarian, Sr. José da Silva Mendes; Statistician, Sr. José Augusto de Carhalho; Laboratory Technicians, Sr. José Amancio de Morais and Sr. Deocleciano A. Vieira. In addition, there are several secretaries and assistants. The clinic publishes an annual journal of distinction. It is entitled the *Revista Penal e Penitenciária.*

In so far as I was able to ascertain this clinic represents the most ambitious diagnostic service I saw in South America, although I must state that it stresses the biological aspects of the criminal and ignores social work. While it possesses a sociological section I was unable to learn its duties. Because of the biological

[7] Quoted in *Revista Penal e Penitenciária,* São Paulo, 1942, II, 419.

emphasis here, I contend that the Santiago clinic, which I described earlier in my material on Chile's prisons, is more complete and compares more favorably, as judged by our own concepts of a diagnostic or classification clinic.

However, there is evidence that the findings of this group of specialists are more acceptable to the prison authorities than those of the Santiago clinic under the direction of Dr. Israel Drapkin. There seems to be an excellent relationship between the professional staff and the administrative authorities in the São Paulo penitentiary. For this reason, then, there is much to be said in praise of the São Paulo clinic.

Solitary confinement for an initial period is maintained in all the prisons of Brazil since this is prescribed by the penal code of 1942. However, this period may not exceed ninety days for long-term prisoners [*reclusão*]. In practice, the period usually lasts from fifteen to thirty days, at least at the São Paulo institution. At the expiration of this solitary period, during which time the diagnostic specialists make their preliminary examinations, the inmate is either transferred to the agricultural colony at Taubaté or is kept in the prison.

The work program at São Paulo is excellent, having a wide variety of trades and industries. The shops maintained are: cabinet, shoe, mattress, bakery, mechanical, photographic, linotype, book binding, carpet weaving, tailor, broom, and tin. Wages are extremely low, amounting to seven cents a day. In this respect the São Paulo prison parallels our own state prisons.

There are those in the city of São Paulo, familiar with the management of the penitentiary, who criticize some of its policies. This is especially true regarding the work program. They claim that higher wages could be paid the prisoners since, at present, there is little incentive on the part of the inmate workers to be productive. These critics also maintain that many inmates are given work and even taught trades who have no intention whatsoever of following an industrial life after release from the prison.

Since São Paulo state is agricultural and the city capital—

with a population of over a million and a half—is largely industrial, it would seem that men sent to prison could choose whether to be farmers or industrial workers and thus receive the type of training they need.

Both the medical equipment and the academic school are most adequate in this prison. A well-equipped hospital capable of handling eighty cases at one time is proudly displayed to the visitor. Few institutional hospitals are as complete as this one at São Paulo. The operating room is also equipped with the latest mechanical operating tables and instruments.

The primary work of the school is that of teaching the large percentage of illiterates who come to the prison. However, there is further academic training for those capable of absorbing it. In addition, there are fine classes in oil painting and sculpture. The prison has a large studio in which are displayed hundreds of excellent paintings and etchings executed by former, as well as present, inmates. The penologist from the United States cannot help being impressed with the work done in the arts in many South American prisons. Here, at São Paulo, busts and portraits of Brazil's famous leaders as well as paintings of native landscapes are on display. The officials are quite proud of this phase of the training program and justifiably so since it is a form of therapy which we have thus far failed to grasp in our own treatment philosophy.

The prison inmates are afforded the privileges of radio programs and movies. At the time I visited this prison, on a holiday, all the prisoners were in the movie studio. There is also an excellent band of about one hundred pieces. It has professional direction and reminds one of the fine university musical aggregations in our own country. The men are snappy in their colorful uniforms and modern instruments and their rendition of stirring marches reflects the time and thought devoted to it by the officials as well as the personnel.

The women's department is an adjunct of the prison but time would not permit a visit to it. I am in no position to venture a judgment except to state that women should be provided separate institutions administered by women trained in modern penology.

The Jail in the City of São Paulo

While in São Paulo I had the opportunity of visiting the jail (*cadeia*) for those awaiting trial and also for certain types of minor offenders. It is a huge structure, parts of which are quite antiquated, dating from the seventeenth century. The population is large and, like so many institutions of its kind in South America, it is badly overcrowded. Yet, in spite of this handicap, there was evidence that the management was efficient and handled its onerous duties reasonably satisfactorily. I met the Director, a man of understanding, who labors under no illusions and who offers no excuses for his institution.

There were many interned Germans, some of them convicted spies, in the institution. They were segregated in cramped quarters but apparently were decently treated. Since the day I visited the jail was a holiday, many visitors, members of the prisoners' families, were present. What little production there is in the jail was halted for the day and the prisoners milled about the yard, most of them dressed in white. Some, however, wore the conventional gray uniforms. There was also a band playing.

Sleeping accommodations in this jail are none too modern, the dormitory being the method of housing the inmates. The older part of the prison, in which the prisoners sleep, is built of solid stone a couple of feet thick and destined to stand for another four or five hundred years. In spite of its age, the São Paulo jail is scrupulously clean and in good order. There is apparently no program, such as a student of the jail problem would like to see, but since so few of our own jails have one, it is certainly not fair to quibble over this shortcoming. The dispensary and medical equipment are reasonably modern but, naturally, do not measure up to that found in the penitentiary.

The Prisons of the Federal District at Rio de Janeiro

The present penitentiary, or House of Correction as it is called, was authorized on June 19, 1939. It is built on the site of the old prison which dated from 1837. Some of the older prison still stands, mute testimony of the crying need for a complete overhauling of the penal administration of the Federal District.

A word about the old prison will be of interest. Its design provided for cellblocks four tiers high with a modified inside cell construction. The narrow cells were naturally dark with little sunlight or fresh air making their way into them. A second group of cells was constructed in 1856. The plan of the prison followed certain features found in both the Pennsylvania and Auburn systems and, in examining the historical literature dealing with the institution, one may see that both the silent and separate systems were constantly in the minds of those who designed it.

The famous Italian criminologist, Enrico Ferri, visiting this establishment in 1908, said of it: "I visited this penitentiary which is at the present time well administered, but which in its structure represents the period of its building and the ideas that were dominant at the time with respect to delinquent men, in whom people saw principally the delinquent, and not the man."

To this outmoded structure was assigned in 1937, the well-known Captain Victorio Caneppa, a man who has for many years been regarded as one of Brazil's most eminent penal administrators. He had been director of the famous Correctional Colony of Dois Rios on Ilha Grande (Big Island). This island colony—now an agricultural annex to the House of Correction, or penitentiary—had long been referred to as Brazil's "Devil's Island." Opened in 1908 it served for many years as a sort of dumping-ground for male and female misdemeanants, alcoholics of both sexes, and young culprits beyond twenty-one years of age. Throughout much of its long career it had been under the control of the Chief of Police of the Federal District and did indeed enjoy a most unsavory reputation. Captain Caneppa made many reforms in the administration of the colony so it was not unusual that he should be asked to take charge of the old House of Correction in Rio de Janeiro.

Shortly after assuming his new duties, Captain Caneppa realized that with the old plant and its reminders of an old dispensation, little could be accomplished without a complete renovation of the institution. Not only did he find it necessary to convince the public officials of the necessity of a new prison, but he was obliged to "sell" his idea to the people of Rio. Dr. Francisco Campos, the Minister of Justice, aided the new director in his ambition. In 1939 the new prison was begun. It was planned by Captain Caneppa and the architect, Luiz Hildebrando Horta Barbosa. It was built gradually with the sections of the older prison giving way as the newer were realized. As one enters today he may still see many vestiges of the old plant which will not finally disappear until the complete plans are consummated.

Before describing the new House of Correction it should be stated that it is destined to be the House of Detention for the city of Rio rather than the penitentiary for convicted prisoners. A new penitentiary is soon to be erected in the country at Bangú. I shall refer to this later.

The buildings in the new House of Correction have been carefully designed. In them may be found many architectural features that square with scientific penology in spite of the fact that the prison is quite conventional in its larger aspects. The cell-blocks are three tiers high but all cells, aside from those on the disciplinary block, are of outside construction. Each block can accommodate 240 prisoners, sixty to each gallery. The cells are rather unique. They are divided into two sections with a metal partition, waist-high, with a passage between. In the larger section are the folding bedstead, table with a set of drawers, bench and table lamp; in the smaller compartment, nearer the window, are not only individual toilet and wash bowl, but a shower. To the best of my knowledge this is the only prison I have ever

Ilha Grande Prison Colony
NEAR RIO DE JANEIRO, BRAZIL

seen anywhere that provides individual showers for its inmates.

Each cell is provided with an outlet for radio and a push button which is connected with a light in the corridor outside for the purpose of calling a guard if help is needed. The doorway is designed in such a manner that the inmate must step higher to enter or leave the cell. This subtle device is insurance against a prisoner rushing a guard as he opens the outer door.

Other sections of the prison, located in the front, provide for reception of the prisoners, visiting rooms for families of the inmates and for sex visits, elaborate board room and office for the director, offices for members of the diagnostic clinic, record room, library, guards' lodging, and other administrative functions.

There is an excellently equipped hospital providing for every conceivable type of medical service: large wards for various types of diseases, an autopsy room, a morgue, X-ray room, a section set aside for ear, nose and throat examination and treatment, operating room and convalescent salons.

It should be stated here that in both Argentina and Brazil may be found exceptionally well-equipped hospitals which provide the latest techniques in diagnosis as well as treatment of the ailments of their prisoners. It would be difficult for a non-medical person actually to evaluate the hospital and medical equipment and services in Brazilian prisons but I cannot refrain from testifying that the three penitentiaries I visited in Brazil—at São Paulo, Rio de Janeiro and Bello Horizonte—and the National Penitentiary in Buenos Aires, are remarkably well equipped and, as I understand, as adequately staffed.

One unusual practice in the Rio House of Correction is that of placing all new prisoners in an isolation hospital ward during the initial period of quarantine. Their clothes are taken from them and in their place they are given hospital garments. The prisoners literally remain in bed for two weeks or longer except for those periods in which they are being examined by the members of the diagnostic clinic.

I have before me a mimeographed description of this prison,

written by Mrs. Helen Cooper, who is most enthusiastic about the equipment, the program, the personnel and the objectives. She writes: "The system used in the Central Penitentiary today is neither the Auburn nor the Pennsylvania system; it is a new one, truly Brazilian." She then proceeds to describe the diagnostic clinic or the classification process, so familiar to all penologists, and then adds: "This is true individualization."

One must remember, at the outset, that it is difficult to individualize penal treatment in a prison built along the old conventional lines. The desire to develop such a type of treatment may be present but to realize its objectives in cellblocks of three and four tiers cannot be done.

So far as the classification procedure is concerned, this institution is not different from many in our own country except in its emphasis on the biological rather than on the social factors in criminality. If the procedure is "truly Brazilian" it may be for the following reasons. First, there is a sane visiting program. As Mrs. Cooper writes: "The prisoner receives visits far from the prying eyes of the guards, and can at the time of these visits hold his loved ones in his arms, for the odious system of separating the visitor from the visited does not obtain here." She might have added that there are individual rooms in the front of the main building where the inmate may meet his wife in seclusion, himself holding the key to the door.

Second, Director Caneppa believes in bringing to his institution citizens of Rio, drawn from the professions, high-ranking society, or as Mrs. Cooper remarks, "ladies of the best *carioca* society," so that they may know what is being done to redeem criminals for the society to which they are bound to be returned. In addition, Captain Caneppa has enlisted the managers of the city's night-clubs to provide an occasional entertainment for his inmates. These are amazing evenings. I had the privilege of attending one of his *soirées* and shared with the seven hundred prisoners some of the best entertainment currently playing in Rio. Comedians, dancers, musicians, jugglers and singers provided an hilarious evening. It was all on a high moral level and demonstrated the genuine interest Director Caneppa has in his men.

Third, a system of self-government which, while not unusual in a prison, is always worthy of comment if not of unqualified praise from the uncritical. As Mrs. Cooper comments on this feature: "His [the prisoner's] breaches of discipline are judged by a board consisting of three of his fellow-prisoners; there is another board, also composed of prisoners, elected in the same way, which is charged with the responsibility for the whole prison régime, which represents the body of prisoners in their relations to the director, and which can argue for anything that appears to it just and in the interests of the welfare of the prison population." While we in the United States are frankly quite skeptical of any form of self-government in a prison, knowing full well its many dangers—gang politics, demagoguery, ballot-box stuffing, intimidation of prisoners by "top" men, and the like—the Director of this institution is enthusiastic about his system. Certainly Captain Caneppa deserves more than stilted praise for the many fine things he has done in his institution and if his self-government really works, he deserves genuine congratulations. I talked with him about it and voiced cynicism of any such system, but he maintained that it works in Rio de Janeiro.

The other features of this penitentiary are not unusual in any progressive prison but it is gratifying to find them, nevertheless. They include: a good system of education with fulltime teachers working in shifts from seven in the morning until nine in the evening with the curriculum providing for the illiterate and the academically well advanced and a provision for correspondence courses; six workshops in which some prisoners, possessing skill, are able to make wages that compare favorably with free laborers; permission to write and receive letters in generous numbers; the daily newspaper provided in an ingenious manner—hung on small chains at various places throughout the prison where the inmates are accustomed to collect, such as on the way to meals, outside the school room and in the recreation compound; small dining-rooms where the inmates eat four meals daily and with the provision that they may sit with their friends within their own unit. I talked with a couple of prisoners who knew English and they convinced me that they were quite satisfied with the régime and the treatment given them in this prison.

Director Caneppa is a man of forceful and yet very pleasing personality.[8] He is familiar with progressive penology, as is also Dr. Lemos Britto, who is President of the Penitentiary Council for the Federal District of Rio de Janeiro. They, together with Dr. Roberto Lyra, outstanding penal lawyer, writer and student of social problems, were my sponsors in Rio and I had ample opportunity to discuss penology with them all. These three men are extremely well versed in the modern interpretations of the field. Dr. Britto, for instance, was sent as a delegate from his country to the International Penal Congress at Prague in 1930. Dr. Lyra holds views regarding crime and criminals that would be regarded far out in the vanguard in our own country. For example, he writes: "The real prevention of criminality depends upon the just and effective distribution of work, culture and health, the participation of everyone in the benefits of society; in short: social justice." He is the author of over thirty books in his chosen field of penal law and criminology.

As was stated earlier, this prison which I have just described will eventually supplant the old House of Detention or city jail which has been in operation since 1851. The new penitentiary has actually not been realized as yet. The site has been selected and purchased and it is expected that construction will soon begin. The large area earmarked for this new institution is located at Bangú, about twenty-five miles from the city and adjoins the women's prison and tubercular sanitorium for prisoners. All of

[8] Captain Caneppa, in 1945, visited the United States where he inspected many of our prisons. Unfortunately, upon his return home he found he had been replaced as director by a political friend of the new Brazilian president. It is hoped that this new appointee will be able and willing to maintain the high level of administration of his capable predecessor.

these institutions are under the direction of Captain Caneppa although the women's institution is actively administered by the religious order of the Sisters of the Good Shepherd D'Angers.

It is claimed that the women's prison, officially known as the *Colonia Reeducacional de Mulheres,* is the only one in the world without bars; but in spite of this no inmate could escape without great trouble and a high degree of stratagem. Mrs. Cooper, quoted above in connection with the men's prison, speaks of this establishment as a "true home" and of the good Sisters as persons "who spare no efforts or sacrifices in working for the reform of the women." Instruction is given in the household arts, gardening, embroidery, singing and learning to read and write.

The institution is built somewhat like a convent, self-enclosed and quite modern. The architect was Dr. Horta Barbosa, the same who drew the plans for the new House of Correction. It was originally designed with dormitories, but it has since been found expedient to provide individual rooms—at least for most of the women. At the time of my visit there were only about fifty women in the prison.

The atmosphere might conceivably be described as "homelike" but the disciplined investigator easily sees below the surface of the traditional furnishings such as attractive curtains at windows, scrupulously clean dining-room and spotlessly white dormitory beds. The ministrations of members of a religious order are often kind, but truly severe. I was convinced, for example, that in this institution the inmates were encouraged to generate a sense of guilt. The women were too humble. I saw samples of their writing, copies of letters sent to loved ones at home. All of them emphasized the highly moral platitudes such as "how fortunate" they were to be there; "how lonely" they were but realizing that it "was good for them"; and how wonderful were the opportunities "to learn to be good" in this "kind home" due to the "patience of the nuns."

Here, again, is an instance of what I found in practically every country where the treatment of the wayward and delinquent women is allotted to the Church; firm but kind, religious and highly moral regimentation instead of trained female laymen analyzing the individual social and economic needs of each inmate. Brazil's progressive penology for males has far outstripped its philosophy of institutional treatment of her females.

Also located at the Bangú reservation but completely separated from the women's prison is the excellent sanitorium for tubercular prisoners and there are many of them in Brazil. This disease has a very high incidence in the country and heroic efforts are being taken to stamp it out. The sanitorium is quite new and when I visited it much of its equipment had not yet been installed. Its medical director, Dr. Gabriel de Lucina, is a most energetic gentleman, well-trained for his duties, outgoing and dynamic—a man of great personal charm and technical qualifications suited for his task. Eventually all the tuberculous in the city's prison and jail are to be transferred to this institution, and when the new penitentiary is built at Bangú it will aid materially in treating those afflicted with this dread malady.

The Penitentiary of the State of Minas Geraes

Adjoining the Federal District of Rio de Janeiro is the prosperous state of Minas Geraes. Its capital, Bello Horizonte, has long enjoyed the reputation of being a model city so far as architecture and layout are concerned. Wide streets, parkways, modernistic public buildings and civic pride are its virtues, so that any visitor to Brazil who can possibly spend the time is urged by her officials to make a pilgrimage there. Thanks to the good offices of Dr. Lemos Britto I was the guest of the government and transportation was furnished me so that I might spend some time at the state's new penitentiary at Nevez, not far from Bello Horizonte.

This modern institution, headed by Senhor Espedito Perdigão, is located in a remote agricultural section about forty miles from the state's capital. It supplants the older penitentiary of Ouro Preto. Its construction is quite modern with some features that

Model for New Penitentiary
FEDERAL DISTRICT OF RIO DE JANEIRO (BANGU), BRAZIL

reveal a close proximity to our "telephone-pole" type of construction. Cells are all outside, two tiers in height, roomy and light. Cell windows are large and, in fact, the impression is more of a room than a cell. There is more informality present in this institution than in any other prison I have ever visited. Perhaps this informality is its principal feature.

The former director, who supervised the construction of this model prison, was Dr. José María de Alkimin, a man of penal vision. The present director is carrying on in the traditions of his predecessor. Dr. Alkimin conceived his institution as one approaching the ideal set by the great French judge, Frédéric Auguste Demetz, at his colony of Mettray. In fact, the Nevez institution is usually spoken of as the agricultural penitentiary of Nevez. The prison proper, however, is surrounded by a wall and there are work shops within the enclosure. But much is made of agriculture. Dr. Roberto Lyra, well-known penal student of Rio, speaks of this prison as *"All Aperto"* signifying its approximation to the famous Italian penal colonies which have gained such a high reputation in recent years.

Perhaps the most significant feature of this colony was the initial introduction to the reservation of several of the families of prisoners. They were housed in small domiciles outside the prison proper and, at one time, there were perhaps as many as fifty families living there. When I visited the institution I was told by the director that only two such families were there and that the practice was slowly being abandoned. Enthusiasm for this type of penal-communal living has apparently died down in Minas Geraes.

The Nevez prison is admirably well equipped with an excellent school, modern shops, diagnostic clinical laboratories, kitchen, small dining-rooms, and library. The present director has recently begun to experiment with small tables, each seating four inmates, in the attractive dining-rooms, which were originally designed to serve only the inmates housed in the small blocks adjacent to them. Sr. Perdigão was selected for this position as director because of his long and successful career as superintendent of a juvenile reformatory. He feels that he can transfer much of his philosophy to an adult prison. He is a man of dynamic energy and is a great believer in the dignity of the individual. He wears a smock rather than a uniform and his staff wear light gray gabardine with silver buttons—the most attractive guard uniforms I have ever seen in a prison.

My stay at this prison was all too short and, to add to the handicap, it was on a Saturday afternoon when the shops were not working. The inmates were milling about the yards, some playing games and some merely sitting in small groups, smoking.

Outside the walls of the institution is a small community of attractive homes which serve as domiciles for the guards and their families. Since the institution is so far from the city it is necessary for all members of the staff to live on the reservation. While this practice seems, on the surface, quite satisfactory, there can be no doubt that in time such a restriction on the lives of the guards tends to reflect itself in their treatment of the prisoners. Outside contacts away from those with whom one works each day are necessary for the wholesome development of personality. When such are denied prison guards they often compensate for their frustration by treating the inmates harshly.

From this altogether superficial visit to the Nevez institution, this is the only criticism I can register. On the whole, however, its philosophy, its administration and its program are worthy of favorable comment.

Other Prisons

From recent volumes of the *Archivos Penitenciários do Brasil* and from remarks made to me by some of the Brazilian penologists, a few features of some of the other more progressive institutions may be ascertained. For example, the penitentiary of the state of Rio Grande do Sul, located at Porto Alegre, is considered quite modern. This state also maintains an agricultural colony known as *General Daltro Filho* located on a small island,

Ilha do Leão, and a prison for women at Hungría, referred to as *Nossa Senhora.*

The new penitentiary in the state of Pernambuco, located on the island of Itamaracá, elicited favorable comment from those who are familiar with the various prisons of the country. One penologist told me that in his opinion it is perhaps the most modern in Brazil. It is only four years old. It is located not far from Recife and close enough to the mainland to be reached by a bridge. Many of the prisoners are housed in small buildings, some accommodating no more than four inmates. However, from pictures I saw there is also larger cellblock construction. This colony has been experimenting with family groups similar to those in the penitentiary at Nevez, described above, and apparently the administration is well satisfied with the results. About 180 prisoners are in this colony. There is a good hospital and a well-equipped school. The prisoners are given a form of script which serves as money. Following is a list of the various prisons and colonies throughout the country of Brazil.

THE PENAL INSTITUTIONS AND AGRICULTURAL COLONIES OF THE VARIOUS STATES

State	*Type of Institution and Location*	*Agricultural Colonies*
Alagōas	House of Correction Alagōas	none
Amazonas	Penitentiary Paricatuba	none
Bahia	House of Correction Bahia (São Salvador)	none
Ceará	Penitentiary Fortaleza	Russas, Joazeiro, Senador Pompeu, Sobral
Espirito Santo	House of Correction Vitória	none
Goyaz	Penitentiary (modern) Goiãnia (Walfrido Campos)	none

PENAL INSTITUTIONS AND AGRICULTURAL COLONIES (*Continued*)

Maranhão	House of Correction São Luiz	none
Matto Grosso	none	Fazenda das Palmeiras
Minas Geraes	Penitentiaries Ouro Preto Neves (Bello Horizonte)	Neves
Pará	House of Correction Belém	none
Parahyba do Norte	none	none
Paraná	Penitentiary Ahú	Accioly Filho
Pernambuco	Penitentiary Itamaracá (Recife)	Itamaracá
Piauhy	House of Correction Therezina	none
Rio de Janeiro (State)	House of Correction Niteroi	none
Rio de Janeiro (Federal District)	Central Penitentiary Rio, Bangú (under construction), Female Prison, Bangú	Ilha Grande
Rio Grande do Norte	Penitentiary Aracajú	Dr. Jõao Chaves
Rio Grande do Sul	Penitentiaries Porto Alegre (males) Nosso Senhora (females) at Hungría	General Daltro Filho
Santa Catherina	Penitentiary Florianópolis	Florianópolis
São Paulo	Penitentiary São Paulo (Carandirú)	Ilha Anchieta Taubaté
Sergipe	House of Correction Aracajú	none
Acre Territory	none	none

CHILDREN'S INSTITUTIONS

Delinquent offenders in Brazil come under the jurisdiction of the Courts for Minors, or juvenile courts, which were decreed by the law of October 12, 1927. These courts have jurisdiction over all youth up to and including eighteen years of age. The courts in Rio de Janeiro and São Paulo, at least, make use of social workers in connection with the investigation and disposition of cases.

Probation consists, according to Professor Timasheff, "in returning the minor to his parents and entrusting him to a guardian, a trustee, or a willing employer approved by the judge, or in placing him in a welfare institution under the supervision of the judge. . . . Supervision cannot be continued beyond twelve months." [9]

In the large cities there are private agencies dealing with the dependent, abandoned and neglected child. One of these, in Rio de Janeiro, which attempts to be of special assistance to small newsboys who are homeless, was initiated by the wife of former President Vargas. It is called *Casa do Pequeño Jornaleiro.* A small home is maintained for the boys and they are free to come and go as they please. Since their street work is irregular, they have access to the home at all times. Clean sleeping quarters and simple meals are provided them. Other private homes are maintained and are known as *Asilos.*

Through the courtesy of Dr. Noé Azevedo, professor of law at the University of São Paulo, I had the opportunity of visiting two unusual institutions for children in the city of São Paulo. One, for boys only, is the *Educandário Dom Duarte,* a charming institution located in the country, and another, the large coeducational *Reformatorio Modelo,* within the city. The former is operated by a religious order, the *Liga das Senhoras Catolicas,* but with a layman director, whereas the latter is administered by the city of São Paulo.

Dom Duarte is much smaller than the *Reformatorio,* its in-

[9] *Op. cit.,* p. 65.

mate population ranging from one to two hundred boys, from the ages of seven to eighteen. This makes for a close and even intimate relationship between the director, Dr. Hugo Fagundes, and his charges. The boys are housed in small cottages equipped with dormitories, dining-room, kitchen and living-room. All the cottages differ somewhat in their architecture and are well-planned. The design of the school is modern and very attractive. The site is among rolling hills and on top of the highest rise of ground stands a little chapel.

The director is regarded in São Paulo as a progressive educator and a friend of boys. Certainly my impression of him substantiates this appraisal. He is thoroughly familiar with boy psychology and there is no doubt that his wards are kindly disposed toward him. The program is traditional, involving academic schooling, trade training and farming on a modest scale. Each cottage has its own small garden and the boys take great pride in watching it grow. The grounds are well-kept with plenty of flowers, a small duck pond, and curving walks among the many small buildings. While this school is administered by a religious order, the entire personnel is composed of laymen. It does tend, though, to be weighted a little toward the religious. This, of course, does no harm since the wholesome relationships existing between the boys and the staff tend to offset any repression.

The chief asset of *Dom Duarte*, in the opinion of this writer, is the genuine interest in the child that quite obviously exists. In paying this tribute to the management, however, it must be frankly stated that a trifle more exuberance might not only be tolerated but stimulated. The boys seem to possess the attitude that they are "being helped" to be good. There is no spontaneity such as I found, for example, in the *Ciudad del Niño* in Santiago, Chile.

The *Reformatorio Modelo* is a vast institution housing about one thousand boys and girls in innumerable cottages. My stay there was cut short due to pressure of other commitments so I am not a fair judge of the work being accomplished. There is no religious connection so it is on its own professionally. I met its director who outlined the purpose of the school with its various units. The management is well aware of the individual approach with its analysis of each child. The personnel seemed quite enthusiastic and obviously was trained. There is much testing and of this the management is quite proud. Yet one acquires the feeling that it is overdone. In an institution of this size, it is extremely difficult to refrain from viewing the children as mere digits. But it is an attempt to approach individualized treatment in a mass-treatment institution. What is probably needed here is some type of de-centralization into smaller homogeneous units separated by much more space than is now maintained.

CONCLUDING REMARKS

In conclusion, it may honestly be stated that Brazil has real leadership in both adult penology and child care. The country, from Rio Grande do Sul, the most southerly state, to those in the far north, is well equipped with men of penal knowledge and considerable vision. Most of these, naturally, are concentrated in São Paulo, the Federal District of Rio de Janeiro, and the state of Minas Geraes, but from reading the stimulating articles in the various Brazilian *revistas*, many from the pens of penologists in other states, one may gain the impression that modern penological thought is gradually permeating the entire country.

The postponed third penal congress, now known as the Pan American Congress of Penal Sciences, will undoubtedly meet in Rio de Janeiro, now that the war is over. In 1944 the criminologists and penologists of the country did hold a meeting in Rio and it was largely and enthusiastically attended. It was the second such conference, and considered questions dealing with the penitentiary régime, military sentencing and conditional liberty as applied to both ordinary and military prisoners.

Two excellent *revistas* are published in Brazil dealing with penal science. The *Revista Penal e Penitenciária* is published under the auspices of the penitentiary at São Paulo and the *Arquivos Penitenciários do Brasil* is the official organ of the Inspector-General of the Penitentiaries of the Federal District of Rio de Janeiro. There is also a journal dealing with civil law, edited in São Paulo, known as *Revista Brasileira de Dereito Civil.*

As stated above, there is much penal insight and vision in Brazil, especially in some of the more progressive and economically wealthy states. The decentralization of the country's prisons is of course unique in South America and this is especially so since, contrary to our own decentralization, Brazil is governed by one uniform penal code. It might well be suggested that centralization of control of the prisons of the twenty states be consummated, but the political jealousy aroused might militate against such a measure. Perhaps the best assurance of penal progress is the example set the more backward states by the reforms being carried on in the states that have been making penal history in the country.

No one can criticize the administration of the prisons in São Paulo, Rio de Janeiro and Bello Horizonte, except perhaps in minor detail. There is intellectual understanding, tolerance and vision. But in the methods of supervising those released on condition there is much room for improvement. It is in this area that Brazil should give thoughtful consideration. More effective supervision in probation is also necessary. If this is done Brazil should be placed in the foremost rank of countries carrying on progressive penal procedure.

X

Inter-American Coöperation in Penology

It was demonstrated throughout the preceding chapters that in a few instances there were early contacts between penologists of Latin America and the United States. We know, for example, that Pas Soldán, the notable prison administrator from Peru, was commissioned by President Castilla to go to the United States in order to acquaint himself with both prison construction and administration. We have also noted that Señor Enrique Cortes of Colombia attended the first National Prison Congress in Cincinnati in 1870. Doubtless there were others but thus far they have not been brought to light. It would prove to be an interesting bit of research to learn to what degree others, notably architects, for example, were personally familiar with North American prisons when they designed their various national *Panópticos* during the nineteenth century.

While there is an exchange of literature on penal treatment and allied fields at this time, notably through the journals and professional publications, it is obvious that we in the United States are not equipped with sufficient knowledge of Spanish and Portuguese to learn much of Latin American practices. The Latin students, on the other hand, are quite familiar with English so they are able to learn of our methods and philosophies. Yet there is little evidence that they have thus far had the inclination or, perhaps, the influence with their governments to copy many of our techniques.

It was pointed out, not only in the *Introduction*, but in most of the preceding chapters, that European thought has dominated the Latin American leaders in penology as well as in social case work.

Part of this is probably due to the fact, little recognized by *Norteamericanos,* that prior to the beginnings of air travel, it has been much easier for nationals of most countries to visit European countries than the United States. Most of the cultural exchange has been between South America and France, England and Spain, although there is considerable Italian and Belgian influence demonstrated.

Aside from this fact, it is also true that the various Latin countries, due to their historic isolation, have not been too familiar with what each other was doing in the field of penology. Only within recent years has there been any joint action among them worthy of the name. Those interested in the crime problem throughout the area, including administrators and lawyers especially, have within the past decade inaugurated periodic meetings in which they may exchange views and discuss mutual problems. Thus far two such meetings have been held and a third was scheduled for 1944 but it was thought expedient to postpone it until the war was over.

The first conference was held in Buenos Aires in 1938; the second in Santiago in 1941. They were known as Latin American Congresses of Criminology. At the Santiago Congress there was considerable discussion regarding the matter of including all the American countries for the proposed third meeting which was scheduled to be held at Rio de Janeiro in 1944. Those who sponsored this idea were of the opinion that crime and its treatment had international, rather than local, implications and that the North American countries should all share their attitudes and opinions on these perplexing questions. It was, therefore, unanimously decided to change the name of the organization to Pan American Congress of Penal Sciences. It is possible that, within the near future, this group may issue an invitation to convene.

Subjects discussed at the two Congresses held thus far have been of the same nature as those reviewed at our own meetings of the American Prison Association or at the International Penitentiary Congresses, the last one of which was held at Berlin in

1935. There is a wide array of subjects worthy of discussion for all countries. These include prison classification, social work in penal institutions, conditional release, prison labor and the payment of wages, the short-time sentence, prison education, problems of juvenile delinquents, and many others.

Whether these Congresses accomplish anything tangible or not, they do compare favorably with our own, which meets annually. There is at least a sincere desire on the part of the delegates to discuss frankly their common problems in the hope that the interplay of ideas may redound to the best interest of the sciences of criminology and penology.

Aside from these concerted meetings, several of the countries in South America hold their own conferences on crime at periodic intervals. In 1944, for example, there was one such conference in Rio de Janeiro. This meeting was mentioned in the discussion of Brazil's penology. Its deliberations included penitentiary management and the subject of conditional release as well as problems concerning military criminals.

It was pointed out earlier that in June 1944 the first Pan American Congress of Criminalistics at Santiago, Chile. Our own Federal Bureau of Investigation was represented. Police policies, methods of coördinating police techniques, schools for police, types of coöperative activities between medical departments and the police, were some of the topics discussed.

North Americans have been charged not only with ignorance of Latin mores but also with indifference toward learning something about them. Articles and editorials in magazines published in the United States which find their way to Latin American countries are either misunderstood or attacked outright by many scholars and other intellectuals. Nevertheless, there is much to criticize in every country of Latin America just as there is in the United States. Objective evidence of reaction and resistance to change may easily be adduced by authorities in specific fields and it is the duty of those thus equipped to point out such evidence regardless of where it may be manifested. The purpose of this book is to describe and evaluate in the light of modern penology the prison systems and administrations in South America. This task has been done in both a critical and sympathetic manner. I shall welcome both favorable and unfavorable reaction from those in South America who may read this account.

Much of the same kind of criticism as well as praise set down in this book may be applied not only generally, but in detail, to our own many systems of penal treatment. Theoretical penology is far in advance of practice not only in South America but throughout the civilized world. This fact may be demonstrated in the brave deliberations by prison wardens and professors of penal law who have attended the several International Penitentiary Congresses. These have met at five-year intervals since 1872, interrupted by the two world wars. As stated above, the last was held in Berlin in 1935. The delegates to these conferences were men of good will who were sincerely attempting to learn how they could improve their prison systems at home. Yet few tangible results can be demonstrated in the actual operation of prisons or in the prevailing attitudes toward prisoners.

The countries of South America have sent delegates to these Congresses. How effective they were when they returned home cannot be ascertained but certainly they could not be ignorant of the resolutions adopted.

However, there is considerable lag in most all of the countries I visited. For example, the philosophy of probation has not been accepted although there is nothing new about its mechanics. Trained supervision of those granted a suspended sentence is almost unknown or, at best, very superficial. While many of our own judges have much to learn regarding the true import of the probation technique, those in South America suspend sentence without any thought of capable supervision. In this field alone there is wide room for improvement. One could continue by citing many other fields of penal philosophy which have long since passed the experimental stage where improvements could be made if there were the will to accept them. Even as these words are written there is controversy among penal lawyers in Santiago regarding the practice of conditional release from prison—the "parole" of our country. Of course there are some uninformed persons in the United States, as well as a few reactionaries, who frown upon parole. Yet it is almost universally accepted that no person should be released from prison except upon parole. But the arguments projected by the opponents of conditional release in Chile as recently as 1945 have long since been annihilated. One writer, advancing objections to conditional release, enumerates the following: it is not scientific; even if it were scientific it would not be practicable due to the lack of mechanical facilities in Chile's prisons; it nullifies the value or meaning of punishment; and finally, since the protection of society is more important than the protection of criminals, such conditional release should not be adopted or expanded.[1]

It is doubtful if anyone with a knowledge of penology in the United States would advance such arguments against parole today. Although the mechanics of this form of conditional release may be debatable, the philosophy of parole is acceptable to all truly informed persons.

Many of the concepts of penology which are acceptable in our country are viewed with suspicion in some Latin American country. We, on the other hand, question the validity of some concepts which find general acceptance throughout all Latin countries. An example of the former is our insistence that every child sent to a reform school should have his own individual room. In no country did I find this idea acceptable. An example of the latter is the existence of the *Patronato,* semi-official agency attempting to supervise discharged prisoners. We insist on trained parole officers employed by the state. Of course we do not realize our objectives but penologists look upon such machinery as the objective.

[1] Pedro Ortíz Muñoz, "Opiniones Sobre Libertad Condicional de las Penados," *Revista de Ciencias Penales,* January–March, 1945, VIII, 21–24. His arguments are answered in the following issue. (*Ibid.,* pp. 103–12), by Israel Drapkin.

The emphasis throughout Latin America on the biological causes of criminality is at complete variance with our emphasis on the socio-economic factors. This is perhaps the most conspicuous difference between the students of North and South America, or even between Anglo-Saxons and Latins throughout the world. An exchange of penologists and penal administrators, together with a mutual interest in the writings of students of the United States and Latin countries will undoubtedly close the gap in time.

Since my visit to South America at least one penal administrator has visited the United States. Captain Victorio Caneppa, former Director-General of Prisons of Rio de Janeiro has spent several months here studying our penal systems. Dr. Israel Drapkin of Santiago, Chile, was in our country in 1942 and at present is in Great Britain where he is making a study of penal procedure. It is this sort of exchange that is necessary if we are to understand the philosophies of penology subscribed to and followed throughout the world.

As I pointed out earlier it is possible that students of the crime problem in our own country have not given as much attention to the biological compulsions as they might have done with real profit. The South American writers, on the other hand, have almost slavishly followed the Italian Constitutional School dominated by Nicola Pende. Here, again, an exchange of students would, therefore, be quite helpful.

One favorable comment that may be reiterated regarding the work of prison administrators and penal lawyers is that their professional journals (*revistas*) are high-grade as well as numerous. The articles appearing in these publications deal with crime, penal codes, methods of penal treatment and, in general, with subjects of interest to both the criminologist and penologist. We in the United States are none too well acquainted with these excellent *revistas*, not so much because they are unavailable as because we do not know the languages.

A recent inquiry from one of the leaders in the field of penal law, suggesting that some method of exchanging journals be developed, poses the question as to how this can be done with profit. Exchanging scientific publications is one thing; reading the material is another. One or two of the leading *revistas* carry abstracts of their articles in English. It might be recommended to the editors of our own journals that an abstract be appended in Spanish although, much as we may not like to admit it, the penologists of Latin America are better prepared to read our journals—and they do—than we are to read theirs. It is we who should ask for abstracts in our language.

Recently a list of the journals published in the countries of Latin America was compiled by Señor Hector I. Navarrete A., and appears in *La Crónica Médica*, a Lima, Peru journal, for February 1943. The list of these publications, with additions since that time, is as follows:

ARGENTINA

Revista de Psiquiatría y Criminología; Director, Dr. Osvaldo Loudet; Buenos Aires,—bi-monthly

Anales de la Sociedad Argentina de Criminología; Director, Dr. Osvaldo Loudet; Buenos Aires,—annually

Revista Penal y Penitenciaría; Official organ of the Director-General of Prisons; Editor, Dr. Eduardo A. Ortiz; Buenos Aires,—quarterly

Revista de Identificación y Ciencias Penales; published by Del Museo de Vucetich de la Facultad de Derecho y Ciencias Sociales; La Plata

Revista de Medicina Legal y Jurisprudencia Médica; Editor, Dr. Raimundo Bosch; Rosario,—quarterly

Infancia y Juventud; official publication of Del Patronato Nacional de Menores del Ministerio de Justicia e Instrucción Pública; Editor, Dr. Arturo Cabrera Dominguez; Buenos Aires,—quarterly

BRAZIL

Revista Brasileira de Direito Civil; Director, Rodrigues de Meréje; São Paulo

Revista Penal e Penitenciaría; Organo del Servicio de Biotipología Criminal de la Penitenciaría del Estado de São Paulo; Editor, Dr. Pedro Augusto Da Silva,—bi-monthly

Arquivos da Medicina Legal e Identificacao; Editor, Dr. Leonidio Ribeiro; Rio de Janeiro

Arquivos da Policia e Identificacao; Del Servicio de Identificación del Gabinete de Investigaciones de São Paulo; Editor, Dr. Ricardo Gumbleton Daunt; São Paulo

Arquivos da Policia Civil de São Paulo; Editors, Alfredo Issaly and Durval de Vilalva; São Paulo,—bi-monthly

Arquivos da Sociedade de Medicina Legal e Criminologia; Editors, Arnaldo Amado Ferreyra, Hilario Veiga de Carvalho and José Cretelli y Taliverty; São Paulo,—annually

Arquivos da Instituto de Criminologia; Organo Del Estado de Rio de Janeiro, Niteroi

Arquivos Penitenciários do Brasil; Organo da Inspetoria Geral Penitenciária e do Conselho Penitenciário do Distrito Federal; Director, Dr. Lemos Britto; Rio de Janeiro,—quarterly

CHILE

Revista de Ciencias Penales; Del Instituto de Ciencias Penales; Editor, Dr. Abraham Drapkin; Santiago,—quarterly

Revista de Criminologia y de Policia Cientifica; Editor, Dr. Victor Valdez M.; Santiago,—monthly

COLOMBIA

Ediciones de Biologia Criminal y Filosofia Penal; Editor, Dr. Francisco Bruno; Bogotá

Revista Medicina Legal de Colombia; Official publication of the Central Office of Legal Medicine; Editor, Dr. Guillermo Uribe Cualla; Bogotá

Revista Colombiana de Biologia Criminal; Instituto de Antropología y Pedagogía Penitenciaría; Sociedad Colombiana de Biología Criminal; Editor, Dr. Francisco Bruno; Bogotá,—bi-monthly

CUBA

Revista Penal de la Habana; Director, Dr. José Augustín Martínez; La Habana,—quarterly

Policia Secreta Nacional; Director, Capitán José M. Bousquet M.M., La Habana,—monthly

Revista de Técnica Policial y Penitenciaría; Organo Oficial del Gabinete Nacional de Identificación; Director, Dr. Israel Castellanos G.; La Habana,—bi-monthly

Revista de Medicina Forense y Criminalística; Director, Dr. Israel Castellanos G.; La Habana,—bi-monthly

ECUADOR

Archivos de Criminología, Neuro-Psiquiatría y Disciplinas Conexas; Organo del Instituto de Criminología; Director, Dr. José J. Espinoza; Quito

EL SALVADOR

Boletín Oficial de la Policía; Organo de la Dirección General de la Policía; Director, Dr. Pedro A. Flores; San Salvador,—monthly

MEXICO

Criminalia; Director, Dr. José Angel Ceniceros; Mexico City,—monthly

Revista de Derecho Penal; Director, Lic. Antonio Roche, Jr.; San Luis Potosi,—bi-monthly

PERU

La Cronica Médica; Editor, Dr. Carlos A. Bambarén, founded in 1884; Lima,—monthly

Boletín de Identificación y Policía Técnica; Official publication of the Director-General of Investigation; Editor, M. Mier y Terán, Chief, Office Napoleón Gil; Lima,—bi-monthly

Revista Penal y de Tutela (a new journal published by the Department of Prisons)

Revista Policial del Perú; Official Organ of the Civil Guards and Police of Peru; Editor, Coronel Fernando Rincón Jaramillo; Lima,—monthly

URUGUAY

Boletín de Criminología y Ciencias Afines; Editor, Dr. José María Estapé; Montevideo

Boletín de Policía Técnica; Organo de la Jefatura de Policía de Montevideo; Director, Ernesto Alonso; Montevideo,—monthly

Index of Subjects

Academic casuistry and penal codes, 23-24
Accesorias, meaning of, 9
Accessory Authority in Chile, 181
Administration of prisons, *see* Penal administration
After-care, of adults and *Patronato*, 117; of children, 41; *see also* Parole
Agricultural colony, in Brazil, 241; in Ecuador, 113; in Panama, 60, 64
Alcoholics, treatment of, in Valparaíso jail, 177
American, meaning of term, 1-2
Amonestación Previa in Chile, meaning of, 181
Anexo Psiquiátrico Central in Buenos Aires prison, 204
Anthropologists in prison clinics, 20, 31
Apristas, imprisoned in 1944, 137-39
Architecture of prisons, 8, 26, 80; *see also* National Penitentiary
Argentina, children's institutions in, 206-11; first clinic established in, 195, 203-4; indemnity in, 201; jail reform in, 196; National Penitentiary in, 26, 198-204; parole in, 204-5; penal code of, 7, 204; pioneers in penology in, 194-97; prison labor in, 201; probation, 205; systems of jails and prisons in, 198; the country of, 191-94
Art in prisons, 30, 199, 231
Auburn system, influence of the, 8, 89
Audiencia, 6; in Bogotá, 92; in Ecuador, 108
Aymará, Indian dialect, 3, 152

Bands in prisons, 30, 84, 231
Bangú prison reservation, near Rio de Janeiro, 238-40
Banishment as a penalty, limits to, 75, 170
Begging, prevalence of, 69, 104
Belgian influence in social work, 45; *see also* Schools of social work
Bello Horizonte, Brazil, and near-by prison, 240-42
Biological emphasis on crime causation, 16-23, 83, 254; possible reason for the, 21-22
Biotipologia, meaning of, 229
Bipartite classification of crimes, 9
Bogotá, description of, 67-72
Bolivia, National Penitentiary in, 26, 154-56; parole in, 158; penal code of, 7, 157-61; political prisoners in, 156; prison labor in, 155; prisons chaotic in, 153; proposed reform in, 153; sex problem in prisons of, 155; the country, 151-52; treatment of women and children in, 156
Born criminal concept, 17-23, 31
Brazil, colonial prisons of, 219; decentralization of prisons in, 222, 248; House of Correction of Rio de Janeiro, 26, 233-38; institutions for children of, 245-47; parole in, 233-35; penal code of, 7, 222-23; penal colonies in, 220, 233; poor housing in, 216-17; prison labor in, 230, 237; prison visiting in, 34, 236; prisons of, 225-31, 233-44; probation in, 225; social work in, 218; the country of, 214-18
Brutality, in Chile's early prison at Santiago, 171; in Coiba penal colony, 53-55; little, in prisons in general, 47; of prison guards, 28; toward political prisoners, 112, 137-39, 154, 156; under Spanish rule, 6, 72, 108, 129, 157, 168

Cali, institutions in, 99-100; jail in, 99; the city of, 96-98
Canal Zone, penitentiary in the, 48-49, 63-64
Capital punishment, extent of, 9; in Brazil, 9, 223; in Bolivia, 156; in Chile, 169
Cárcel de Sumariados of Bogotá, deplorable conditions in the, 78
Cárceles, *see* Jails
Cárcel Modelo, in Bogotá, 79; in Panama City, 52, 59-60, 64
Car watching, a minor racket, 15

Casa do Pequeño Jornaleiro, Rio de Janeiro, 245
Catholic Church, and care of children, 40, 144-46; and care of women, 43, 99, 146, 182, 239; and social work, 46; trend away from, 42
Causes of crime, *see* Crime causation
Centro-Ecuatoriano-Norteamericano, 113
Chicha, drinking of, 13; as a cause of crime, 13
Children of prisoners, home for in Bogotá, 95
Children's institutions, and the Catholic Church, 40-42; in Argentina, 206-11; in Bolivia, 156; in Brazil, 245-47; in Chile, 183-85; in Colombia, 91-95; in Ecuador, 118-20; in Panama, 58; in Peru, 144-47
Chile, children's institutions of, 183-85; classification clinic of, 173-75; jails in, 177-78; National Penitentiary of, 26, 170-76; offenses in, 169; parole in, 180, 253; penal code of, 7, 169; pioneer in social work, 45; *presidios* of, 170, 176; prison labor in, 172, 176; probation in, 36, 181; proposed code of, 167, 187; punishments in, 169-70; social work in, 45, 185-87; the country of, 162-66; under Spanish rule, 168
Cholo, meaning of term, 13
Church-controlled institutions, *see* Catholic Church
Ciudad del Niño of Santiago, 42, 183-85, 246
Classification clinics, a general statement regarding, 31-33; and social workers, 43, 173, 187; and the *revistas*, 33; emphasis of, 20, 31; failure of, 32; in Argentina, 201-4; in Brazil, 228-30; in Chile, 173-75; in Colombia, 73, 83; in Ecuador, 114; in Peru, 132-33; origin of, 203-4; personnel of, 31; procedure in, 21; sterility of, 31-32, 114
Classification of crimes, 9; in Chile, 169; in Colombia, 75; in Ecuador, 109; in Panama, 61; in Peru, 134; of punishments, 9; *see also under* Punishments
Clinics, *see* Classification clinics
Coati penal colony, Bolivia, 153
Codes for Minors, in Argentina, 207; in Chile, 181; in Colombia, 91-92; in Ecuador, 119; in Panama, 58, 65; in Peru, 141
Codes, penal, *see* Penal codes
Coiba penal colony, 50-55, 64
Coll-Gómez penal code, projected in Argentina, 204
Colombia, Codes for Minors in, 91-95; court system in, 77; jails in, 77-80; National Penitentiary of, 26, 80-88; new prison construction in, 26, 88-91; offenses in, 75; parole in, 76; *Patronato* in, 94; penal code of, 7, 75; poverty in, 68-69; prison labor in, 85-86; prison reform in, 72-73, 81; prison visiting in, 33, 86-88; prisons of, 74; probation in, 75; punishments in, 75; sex visiting in, 33, 86-88; social work in, 95-96; the country of, 66-72; treatment of children in, 91-95
Colonial rule, 6, 72, 129, 157, 168
Colonia Reeducacional de Mulheres, of Rio de Janeiro, 239
Colonias-Hogares, 42, 207-11
Colonies for families of prisoners, 34, 241, 243
Commutation easily obtained, 10
Condena condicional, *see* Probation
Conditional release, *see* Parole
Conferences of criminology, 250
Congregate influence in South America, 9
Conjugal visiting, in Colombia, 33, 86-88; in Brazil, 34, 236
Constitutional School of criminal causation, 19-22
Construction of new prisons, *see* Prison construction
Continental influence in penology, 36, 250; in social work, 45-46
Contract labor, in Argentina, 201; in Bolivia, 155; in Colombia, 85
Contravenciones, meaning of, 9
Coöperation between the Americas, importance of, 1, 2, 249-51
Corporal punishment, absence of, 49
Corticos of São Paulo, 216
Court procedure, lag in, 24-25, 39, 59, 79
Courts, systems of, in Colombia, 77; in Ecuador, 118
Crime, biological emphasis on, 16-23; not

a serious problem in South America, 10-16; restitution for, 29, 173, 201
Crime causation, biological aspects of, 16-23; economic phases of, 17; psychiatric approach to, 23, 43; social conditions and, 17
Crime conferences, 250
Crimes, classification of, *see* Offenses
Criminal classes, 47
Criminal nato, *see* Born criminal concept
Criminal statistics, *see* Statistics of crime
Criminologists, Italian, 19; Spanish, 20
Criticism, of prison clinics, 21, 31-33, 114, 174; of penal codes, 23-24
Cruelty in prisons, *see* Brutality
Cultural interrelations, *see* Inter-American coöperation
Cuzco, cultural interest of, 124; its jail, 130, 139-40

Dactyloscopy and Argentina, 195
Death penalty, *see* Capital punishment
Decentralization of prisons in Brazil, 221, 248
Degradation of Indian classes, 10-11, 16, 69, 104, 152; in the jails, 37, 77-79, 176-78
Delay in court trials, 25, 39, 59, 79
Delinquency of children, 40-42; *see also* Children's institutions *and* Treatment of children
Delitos, meaning of, 9
Dependent children, 40-42, 69, 143, 146
Deplorable conditions in jails, 37, 77-79, 176-78
Deportación, meaning of, 170
Destierro, meaning of, 170
Detention, of adults awaiting trial, 38, 59, 79; of children awaiting disposition, in Bogotá, 92; in Panama, 58
Diagnostic clinics, *see* Classification clinics
Directors of prisons, *see* Wardens of prisons
Discipline in prisons, a general statement of, 48; and *Tribunales de Conducto*, in Buenos Aires, 202, in Chile, 180
Divisa agricultural colony in Panama, 60, 64
Dois Rios penal colony, Rio de Janeiro, 233
Dormitories, in children's institutions, 145, 184, 208; in jails, 38
Ducking as a punishment, in Bolivia, 154; in Ecuador, 110

Eastern Penitentiary of Pennsylvania, at Philadelphia, influence of the, 8; in Bolivia, 154; in Chile, 171; in Colombia, 81; in Ecuador, 109; in Peru, 131, 135
Economic causes of crime not stressed, 17, 21
Economic despotism, 21-22
Ecuador, children's institutions in, 119-20; classification procedure in, 114-15; Code for Minors in, 119; courts of, 121; has no penal philosophy, 106; National Penitentiary of, 26, 109-14; offenses in, 109; parole in, 116-17; penal code of, 7, 109; penal colonies in, 113; penal reform in, 108; political unrest in, 107, 121; poverty of, 121; prison labor in, 109; social work in, 120; the country of, 102-6
Educandário Dom Duarte, of São Paulo, 245-46
Education of the masses, *see* Illiteracy in South America
El Asserío, for girls in Bogotá, 94
El Buen Pastor, its work, 99, 156, 182
El Frontón penal colony, in Peru, 135, 137
El Hogar del Niños, of Bogotá, 94
El Instituto de Vigilancia y Protección del Niño, of Panama, 56, 58; and probation, 63
European influence, in penal codes, 8; in penology, 36, 250; in social work, 45
Evolution of penal codes, 7; *see also under* Penal codes
Extent of crime in South America, 12-16

Fagua Reformatory near Bogotá, 74, 93
Failure of prison clinics, 31-32
Families in prisons, 34, 241, 243
Family support by prisoners, 30
Farming-out of children, 41, 143
Favellas, of Rio de Janeiro, 217
Favored race, 14, 22

Fear of the Indian, by ruling classes, 22
Federal District of Rio de Janeiro, prisons of, 233-38
Female criminals, and homicides, 43; in Bolivia, 156; in Chile, 182; in Ecuador, 112; in Panama, 60, 65; in Peru, 146; in Rio de Janeiro, 239; treatment of, 42
Female prisons, conditions in, 43, 112; in Cuzco, Peru, 140; in Quito, 112; in Santiago, 182; in Rio de Janeiro, 239
Fernando de Noronha penal colony, 220
Fetish, of statistical charts, 33
Feudalism, remains of, 15-16, 22
Financial restitution for crime, 29, 173, 201
Finger-printing, pioneer work in, 195
Fiscal, a type of prison labor, 28; *see* State-use system
Flogging, absence of, 49
Food in jails, 38
Foster home placement, and the *Patronato*, 41, 143
Franco-Belgian system of suspended sentence, 36; *see* Probation
Franco-German system of offenses, 9, 169
Fresnes-les-Rungis, influence of in prison architecture, 8

Galápagos Islands, no longer a penal colony for Ecuador, 122
Gamboa penitentiary in Canal Zone, criticism of, 48-49, 63-64
Guards, description of, 27, 149, 173; schools for, in Buenos Aires, 200; in Peru, 132
Guilt feeling by women prisoners encouraged, 43, 239

Handicraft, in jails, 30, 53, 99, 118; in prisons, 30, 172, 176
Hobbies in prisons, 172, 176; *see* Art in prisons; *also* Sculpturing in prisons
Homes for children of prisoners, in Bogotá, 95
Homicides, extent of, 12-14; females and, 42
Hospital services, in Argentina, 201; in Brazil, 231, 235
House of Correction, Rio de Janeiro, 233-38
Housing, deplorable, 12, 216-17
Housing in Chile's *presidios*, unique, 76
Huasos, of Chile, 163, 166

Idleness in jails, 38
Ignorance, of the masses, 16, 69; in Brazil, 215; in Colombia, 215; *see also* Illiteracy in South America
Ilha Grande penal colony, Rio de Janeiro, 233
Illiteracy in prisons, 30
Illiteracy in South America, 10, 16, 69, 152, 162, 215
Imprisonment for life, 10; for long terms, 82
Indemnity, 29, 173, 201
Independence, era of, and status of penology, 7, 129, 158
Indian problem, 10-11, 16
Indians, degradation of, 10, 16, 69, 104, 151; in jails, 37
Indian-white conflict, 22
Insecurity of the ruling classes, 22
Inside cell construction of prisons, 89
Institutions for children, a general statement concerning, 40-42; in Argentina, 206-11; in Bolivia, 156; in Brazil, 245-47; in Chile, 181, 183-85; in Colombia, 91-95; in Ecuador, 119-20; in Panama, 58; in Peru, 141-46
Institute of Legal Medicine, of Quito, 116
Instituto de Ciencias Penales, of Santiago, 179
Instituto de Criminología, of Ecuador, 114-15; of Lima, 133; of Santiago prison, 173
Instituto Ernelinda Carrera, of Peru, 146
Inter-American coöperation, importance of, 1, 2, 249-51
International Penitentiary Congresses, 5, 238, 252
Italian criminologists, influence of, 19-20
Italian School of criminology, influence of, 16-23
Itamaracá prison, Brazil, 243

Jails, deplorable condition of, 37-40, 77-79, 176-78, 196; dormitories in, 38;

idleness in, 38; population of, 37; special quarters in, 39; under the Spanish, 7; work program in, 38
Jails in, Bogotá, 77-80; Cuzco, 130, 139; Panama City, 57, 59-62, 64; Quito, 118; Santiago, 177-79; São Paulo, 232; Valparaíso, 177
Juvenile courts, *see* Codes for Minors

Labor in prisons, a general statement of, 28-29; in Argentina, 201; in Bolivia, 155; in Brazil, 230, 237; in Chile, 172, 176; in Colombia, 85-86; in Ecuador, 112; in Peru, 136
La Escuela de Servicio Social del Perú, 146
Lag, between penal codes and prisons, 24; in court procedure, 24, 39, 59, 79
La Paz, Indians of, 151
La Picota prison, in Colombia, 89-91
Latin American Congresses of Criminology, 250-52
Latin American, meaning of the term, 3; problems of, 10-11
Laws of the Indies, 6, 157, 168
Libertad bajo palabra, see Parole
Libertad condicional, see Parole
Libertad vigilada, see Probation
Life imprisonment, extent of, 10
Lima, the city of, 123
Lombrosian influence, 17, 21; reasons for the, 22
Lotteries, 98

Machinery in prisons, condition of, 29; *see also* Labor in prisons
Machu Pichu, Inca ruins of, 127-28
Marionettes in children's institutions, 209
Más Afuera penal colony, Chile, 168
Medical treatment in prisons, 201, 231, 235
Mestizo, meaning of term, 13
Military pomp in prisons, 28, 200
Minas Geraes state, Brazil, and its prison, 240-42
Misery of the masses, 10-11, 68, 104, 216
Multiple-causation, theory of, 22
Murder, extent of, 12-14

National Penitentiary, of Argentina, 198-204; of Bolivia, 154-56; of Chile, 170-76; of Colombia, 80-88; of Ecuador, 109-14; of Peru, 131, 135-37
Neglect of socio-economic factors in crime causation, 21
Neglected children, prevalence of, 40, 69; *see also Patronato*
Neo-Lombrosians, 19-22
Nevez prison at Bello Horizonte, Brazil, 240-42

Offenses, in Brazil, 223; in Chile, 169; in Colombia, 75; in Ecuador, 109; in Panama, 61; in Peru, 134

Panama, agricultural colonies in, 60; city jail of capital of, 59-60, 64; offenses in, 61; parole in, 62; penal code of, 7, 61; penal colony in, 51-56, 64; penal reform in, 56-58; poverty of, 50; power of police in, 57; probation in, 62-63; provincial jails in, 57, 60-62, 64; the country, 50-51; treatment of children in, 59, of females in, 60
Pan American Congress of Criminalistics, 179, 251
Pan American Congress of Penal Sciences, 8, 250
Panopticon, 8
Panópticos, see National Penitentiaries
Parole, and the *Patronato*, 34-36, 182, 213; inadequacy of, 34-36; in Argentina, 204-5; in Bolivia, 158-59; in Brazil, 223-25; in Chile, 180, 253; in Colombia, 76; in Ecuador, 116-17; in Panama, 62; in Peru, 141
Particulares, form of prison labor, *see* Contract labor
Paternalism, symptoms of, 16, 21-22
Patronato, and child placement, 143; and children's institutions, 41; criticism of, 35, 182, 213; description of, 34-36; farming-out and, 42; in Argentina, 205; in Colombia, 94; in Ecuador, 117; in Peru, 141-43
Penal administration, a preliminary statement, 25, 27; in Argentina, 198-204; in Bolivia, 155; in Brazil, 225-31, 233-44; in Chile, 170-76; in Colombia, 81-88; in Ecuador, 109-11; in Peru, 135-37
Penal codes, and *revistas*, 33; criticism

Penal codes (*Continued*)
of, 24; evolution of, 7; in Argentina, 7, 204; in Bolivia, 157-61; in Brazil, 222-23; in Chile, 168-70, 187-89; in Colombia, 75; in Ecuador, 108; in Panama, 61; in Peru, 129, 134; slavish devotion to, 23-24
Penal colonies, in Bolivia, 153; in Brazil, 220, 233; in Chile, 168; in Ecuador, 113; in Panama, 51-55, 64; in Peru, 137
Penal law a fetish, 25
Pennsylvania system of prison discipline, *see* Eastern Penitentiary; *also* Separate system
Pensionados in jails, 39, 79, 178
Pentonville prison, influence of, 8
Período de prueba, see Probation
Personnel, *see under* Guards, *also* Wardens of prisons
Peru, care of children in, 141-46, of women, 146; classification clinic adopted in, 132; early prisons in, 130; labor program in, 136; National Penitentiary of, 26, 131, 135-37; offenses in, 134; parole in, 141; *Patronato* active in, 141-43; penal code of, 7, 129, 134; penal colony in, 137; periods of prison administration in, 129; political prisoners in, 137-39; prison construction in, 147-50; prison labor in, 136; prison reform in, 132; prison statistics in, 141; prison system in, 130, 135; probation in, 134; social work in, 146-47; the country of, 123-28
Petty stealing, extent of, 12-15, 156
Philadelphia system, *see* Eastern penitentiary; *also* Separate system
Police and jails, in Panama, 57, 64
Political imprisonment, a general statement regarding, 48; in Bolivia, 154, 156; in Ecuador, 112; in Peru, 137-39
Polivalente, type of social work school, 187
Pomp in prison administration, 28, 200
Post Carcelario y Post Asilados, of Ecuador, 117
Poverty of the masses, 10-11; in Bolivia, 151; in Brazil, 216, 217; in Colombia, 68; in Ecuador, 104; in Panama, 51; in Peru, 146
Preparatory release in Colombia, 76
Presidios, in Chile, 170, 176
Preventive custody, 117, 154, 181
Principales, meaning of, 9
Prison aid societies, *see Patronato*
Prison architecture, 8, 26; *see also under* National Penitentiary
Prison clinics, *see* Classification clinics
Prison colonies for families, 34, 241, 243
Prison construction, development of, 26; in Argentina, 196-98, 212; in Bolivia, 153; in Brazil, 226, 233-44; in Chile, 176; in Colombia, 88-91; in Panama, 60-61; in Peru, 147-50
Prison guards, 27, 111
Prison labor, *see* Labor in prisons
Prison of Minas Geraes, 240; of São Paulo, 226-32
Prison schools, 30, 83-84
Prison visiting, 33-34; in Brazil, 34, 236; in Colombia, 33, 82, 86-88
Prison wardens, *see* Wardens of prisons
Prisoners, hobbies of, 30, 155, 172; labor for, *see* Labor in prisons
Prisons, administration of, 25; *see also* Penal administration; and social work, 43, 173, 187; art in, 30, 199; bands in, 30, 84; cruelty in, 47; illiteracy in, 30; military pomp in, 28, 200
Privacy, lack of, in children's institutions, 41
Probation, a general statement regarding, 36-37, 252; for adults, 62, for children, 63; in Argentina, 205; in Brazil, 225; in Chile, 181; in Colombia, 75; in Ecuador, 117; in Panama, 62; in Peru, 141
Problems of South America, 10-11
Professional crime, dearth of, 12
Progressive stages system, influence of, 8; in Argentina, 197; in Brazil, 221
Psychiatric approach to criminal causation, 23, 43
Punishments, in Brazil, 223; in Chile, 169; in Colombia, 75; in Ecuador, 109; in Panama, 61; in Peru, 134
Punishments, under the Spanish, 6, 9; in Bolivia, 157; in Chile, 168; in Ecuador, 108; in Peru, 130
Puppetry in children's institutions, 209

Quarantine period in Rio de Janeiro prison, 235
Quechua, Indian dialect, 3
Quibo, 50; *see* Coiba
Quito, city of, 103-6; jail in, 118; social service in, 120

Racketeering, none in South America, 12
Rateros, petty thieves, 14-15
Reasons for biological emphasis on crime causation, 21-22
Reformatories for females and the Church, *see* Catholic Church; *also El Buen Pastor*
Reformatorio Modelo, São Paulo, 246
Regimentation in children's institutions, 41
Released prisoners, *see Patronato*
Relegación, meaning of, 75, 170
Restitution for crime, 29, 173, 201
Revistas, and clinics, 33; and penal codes, 23; emphasis of, on biology, 20; high-grade, 254; listed, 255-57
Revolution, in Bolivia, 161; in Ecuador, 107
Rio de Janeiro prisons, 233-38
Ritual in parole granting, in Rio de Janeiro, 224

Sanitarios, 90
Santa María, agricultural colony of Panama, 60; penal colony of Chile, 168
Santé, French prison, influence of, 8
Santiago, the city of, 164; the jail in, 177-78
São Paulo, Brazil, city jail of, 232; state prison of, 226-32
School for guards, in Argentina, 200; in Peru, 132
Schools in prisons, 30, 83, 99
Schools of social work in South America, development of, 45-47; in Argentina, 211; in Brazil, 218-19; in Chile, 185; in Colombia, 95-96; in Ecuador, 120; in Peru, 146-47; standards of, 47, 185; types of, 46, 187
Sculpturing in prisons, 30, 231
Self-government in prison at Rio de Janeiro, 237
Separate system, influence of, 8, 9; in Brazil, 230; in Chile, 171; in Peru, 136
Servicio de los Brethren, of Quito, 106
Sex visiting for prisoners, 33-34; in Bolivia, 155; in Brazil, 236; in Colombia, 86-88
Silent system, influence of, 8
Social settlement in Quito, 106
Social work, and prison treatment, 43-47, 173, 187; and released prisoners in Santiago, 180
Social work in South America, *see* Schools of social work
Sociedad Especial de Patronato de Menores, of Peru, 142-47
Socio-economic causes of crime not stressed, 17, 21
South American, penal codes, 23-25; problems, 10-11
Spanish criminologists, influence of, 20
Spanish rule, brutality of, 6, 72, 108, 129, 157, 168
Special quarters in jails, 39, 79, 178
Special vigilance, in Bolivia, 154; in Chile, 181; in Ecuador, 117
State-use system of prison labor, 29; in Buenos Aires, 201; in Chile, 172; in Colombia, 85
Statistical charts, fetish of, 33
Statistics of crime, inadequate, 13; in Peru, 140
Stealing, *see* Petty stealing
Sterility of prison clinics, 31, 174
Striped uniforms worn, in Buenos Aires prison, 200; in Gamboa, Canal Zone prison, 48; in Peru, 136
Supervision of released prisoners, desultory, 76, 117, 180; *see also Patronato*
Support of families of prisoners, 30
Surveillance of police as after-care treatment, in Ecuador, 117
Suspended sentence, *see* Probation
Swimming pool in Quito's penitentiary, 110
System of courts, in Colombia, 77; in Ecuador, 118

Telephone-pole type of prison construction, at La Picota near Bogotá; in Brazil, 241; in Peru, 148
Terms used to denote Latins, 3
Testing done in the clinics, 21

Theft, *see* Petty stealing
Third Order of Saint Francis of Assisi, in Peru, 146
Toilets, in jails, 38, 177; in prisons, 90, 155
Transportation, a serious problem, 11
Treatment, of children, 40, 49; of females, 42
Tribunal de Conducto, in Buenos Aires prison, 202; in Chile, 180
Tripartite classification of crimes, Chile, 9, 169

United States penitentiary at Gamboa, Canal Zone, 48-49; 63-64

Valparaíso, city of, 165; jail in, 177
Vaqueros, 210
Vilas, of São Paulo, 216
Visiting in prison, 33-34; in Brazil, 34, 236; in Colombia, 33, 82

Wages paid to prisoners, 29; in Argentina, 201; in Bolivia, 155; in Brazil, 230, 237; in Chile, 173; in Colombia, 85; in Ecuador, 112; in Peru, 136
Wardens of prisons, calibre of, 27, 82, 173, 203, 233, 241
Weaknesses, of clinics, 21, 31, 114, 174; of penal codes, 24
Wine drinking, a prison problem in Chile, 173
Women criminals, *see* Female criminals
Work in jails, 38

Index of Persons

Aisencitat, Jacob, 19
Alfaro, Eloy, 112
Alkimin, José María de, 241
Altmann Smythe, Julio, 128, 149, 203
Alzamora, Lizardo, 132
Arenasa, Carlos de, 207
Arroyo del Río, Carlos, 107
Augusto da Silva, Pedro, 228
Avendaño, Leonidas, 133
Aviles Robalino, Alfonso, 114
Azevedo, Noé, 245

Balbín, Valentín, 199
Ballve, Antonio, 203
Bambarén, Carlos A., 133
Behringer, Clara González de, 57, 58, 63
Bentham, Jeremy, 8, 81
Berman, Louis, 18
Bernier, Jenny, 185
Britto, Lemos, 220, 221, 224, 226, 238
Bruno, Francisco, 72, 73, 74, 76, 78, 83, 94, 100
Bueno Figuereo, Hernando, 91
Bunge, Ernesto, 199
Bustamante Rivero, José Luis, 27, 138

Cabada Dancourt, Gonzalo, 136
Caleiros Sandoval, Arnaldo, 229
Calón, Eugenio, 20
Campos, Francisco, 223, 234
Caneppa, Victorio, 233, 234, 236, 237, 238, 239, 254
Cantor, Nathaniel, 16, 17
Carhalho, José Augusto de, 229
Carpena, Frustoso, 52
Carrera Sister Ernelinda, 131, 146
Carulla, María A., 95
Castilla, Ramón, 129, 131, 249
Castro Movilla, Jorge, 83
Coll, Jorge Eduardo, 200, 204, 207
Collela, Rosolino, 20
Collet e Silva Filho, Tomaz de A., 229
Cooper, Helen, 236, 237
Cornejo, Angel Gustavo, 129, 133
Cornejo, Francisco, 57, 58
Cortes, Enrique, 72, 249
Costa e Silva, A. J., 223
Cousiño MacIver, Luis, 179
Crawford, Rex, 227
Croft-Cooke, Rupert, 200
Crofton, Sir Walter, 8, 221
Cruchaga, Elvira Matte de, 186
Cruz Cueva, José, 114

Davenport, Charles B., 18
Delgado, Honorio F., 133
Demetz, Frédéric Auguste, 241
Di Tullio, Benigno, 19
Doria, Alessandro, 95
Dos Santos, Alvara Pedro, 229
Drapkin, Israel, 173, 174, 175, 178, 179, 187, 230, 253, 254
Dugdale, Richard, 18

Endara, Julio, 114
Enochs, Elisabeth Shirley, 46, 47
Enríquez, Alberto, 108
Escallón, Rafael, 73
Escobar, Gabriel, 126
Espinosa, José Justiniano, 114

Fagundes, Hugo, 246
Faundes, Manuel, 57
Fávero, Flamíno, 228
Fernández, Helvio, 204
Ferri, Enrico, 17, 233
Flanagan, Father Edward J., 42, 183
Frias, Jorge H., 205
Fry, Margery, 25

Gajardo Villarroel, Oscar, 175, 183
Galdino, Siqueira, 222
Galton, Francis, 195
Gamallo, Gavino, 139
García Moreno, Gabriel, 109
Giana, Felipe M., 207
Gill, Howard B., 56, 57, 60, 61
Goddard, Henry H., 18
Goméz, Eusebio, 132, 200, 204
González, A. R., 167, 187, 188
Goodman, Philip, 217
Goring, Charles, 19
Gunther, John, 138

Hardy, Rufus, 49
Haviland, John, 8
Haya de la Torre, Victor, Raúl, 3, 138, 139
Herschal, Sir William, 195
Hooton, Earnest A., 18
Horta Barbosa, Luiz Hildebrando, 234, 239
Hoskins, R. G., 18
Howard, John, 9
Hungría, Nelson, 223

Ingenieros, José, 174, 194, 195, 203, 204
Izquierdo Phillips, Rebeca, 186

Janet, Pierre, 83
Jebb, Sir Joshua, 8
Jiménez de Asúa, Luis, 24, 132
Justiniani, Camilo A., 57

Lagarrigue, Juan, 183
Lama, Thomas, 131
Lamastus, Robert C., 52
La Torre, Roberto, 139
León y León, Bernardino, 129, 130, 132, 133
Llontop, Augusto, 129, 132
Lombroso, Cesare, 17, 20
López-Rey y Arrojo, Manuel, 153, 156, 157, 158, 159
Loudet, Osvaldo, 174, 204
Lucino, Gabriel de, 240
Lyra, Roberto, 223, 238, 241

Machado Alcántara, 222
Mannheim, Hermann, 4
Means, Philip Ainsworth, 11
Medicis, Julius de, 35
Medina, Miguel, 130, 131
Meréje, Rodrigues de, 227
Michel, Rudolf, 19
Mitchell, Ruth Comfort, 23
Monachesi, Elio, 16, 17, 20
Montero, Dorado, 20
Montoya, Hernan, 73
Morais, José Amancio de, 229
Morselli, Arturo, 20

Navarrete, Hector I., 255
Naylor, Kurtis F., 106
Newman, Horatio H., 18
Nogueira, Acácio, 228

O'Connor, Juan José, 26, 194, 195, 196, 197, 203, 211
Olavarría Avila, Julio, 175
Ortíz, Eduardo, 197, 198, 201, 203, 212
Ortíz Muñoz, Pedro, 253
Ottolenghi, Salvatore, 19

Páez, Federico, 114, 117
Park, Mercedes Gallagher de, 142, 143, 144, 146
Parmelee, Maurice, 17
Pascal, Vincent, 209
Paulino, Brother Vicente, 145
Paz Anchorena, José María, 197, 201
Paz Soldán, Mariano Felipe, 8, 129, 130, 131, 249
Pedreira, Bulhoẽs, 222
Pende, Nicola, 19, 229, 254
Perdigão, Espedito, 240, 241
Perkins, Rollin M., 195
Pinzón Ferro, Jorge, 73, 74, 78, 82, 83, 86, 87, 91, 93
Pirovano, José, 212
Porras, Balisario, 52, 64
Prado, Manuel, 138
Prescott, William H., 123

Queiroz, Narcelio de, 223
Quiros, Bernaldo de, 20
Quiros, José Ignacio, 57

Renault, Abgar, 223
Ribeiro, Leonidio, 229
Ríos, Juan Antonio, 42, 168, 183
Ríos, Marta Ide de, 42, 183
Rocco, Salvador, 229
Romoli, Kathleen, 13
Rubiana, Tuzio, 73

Sáenz, Carlos, 81
Saldaña, Quintiliano, 20
Sales, Campos, 221
Salgar, Eustorjio, 81
Salmón, Julio, 159
Sanctis, Giustino de, 95
San Martín, Ernesto, 136, 147
Santa Cruz, Andrés, 129, 130, 158
Saporito, Filippo, 20

Sastro, Manuel J., 114
Schlapp, M. G., 18
Seminario Helguero, Gabriel, 130, 147, 148, 149
Serrano Canadas, Gonzalo, 114
Sheldon, William H., 18
Sifontes, Jesús María, 53, 54
Siricura, Pietro, 199
Smith, E. H., 18
Stevenson, Burton Egbert, 23
Stokes, William S., 160

Tallack, William, 171
Teeters, Negley K., 4
Telles, João Carlos da Silva, 228, 229
Timasheff, N. S., 36, 37, 225, 245
Turbay, Gabriel, 72

Urguidi, Melchor, 159
Uzcátegui, Emilio, 107

Vargas, Getulio, 245
Velasco Ibarra, José María, 107
Videla, Carlos, 204
Vieira Braga, Antonio, 223
Vieira de Araújo, João, 222
Vieira, Deocleciano A., 229
Villarán, Aurelio, 131
Violich, Francis, 12, 216, 217
Vucetich, Juan, 194, 195

Ward, F. B., 171
Whitaker, Artur de Aguiar, 229
Wilder, Thornton, 124
Wines, Enoch C., 5, 6, 8, 72, 131, 219, 220, 221, 222

Zurita, Guillermo, 24, 58, 132

www.ingramcontent.com/pod-product-compliance
Lightning Source LLC
LaVergne TN
LVHW011820200926
848484LV00005B/1256
* 9 7 8 1 5 1 2 8 0 7 6 3 9 *